# DOING BUSINESS IN THE UNITED STATES

# DOING BUSINESS
# IN THE
# UNITED STATES

BY

FRANK G. OPTON

and

HERBERT FEILER

KLUWER LAW AND TAXATION PUBLISHERS

DEVENTER/THE NETHERLANDS

ANTWERP — BOSTON — LONDON — FRANKFURT

*Distribution in USA and Canada*
Kluwer Law and Taxation
190 Old Derby Street
Hingham MA 02043 U.S.A.

**Library of Congress Cataloging in Publication Data**
Opton, Frank G. (Frank Gerd), 1906–
    Doing business in the United States.

    Bibliography: p.
    Includes index.
    1. Business enterprises—United States.    2. Commercial law—United States.
3. Law—United States.    I. Feiler, Herbert.    II. Title.
KF1355.068   1984            346.73′07            84–820
ISBN  90–6544–170–0

D/1984/2664/14

ISBN 90 6544 1700

© 1984, Kluwer, Deventer, The Netherlands

First published by Kluwer, Deventer/The Netherlands

We dedicate this book to
our partner and friend

LLOYD B. GOTTLIEB

with affection

# PREFACE

This book is addressed primarily to businesspersons outside the United States and their professional advisers. It is not intended as an academic treatise. It aims to furnish an overview of the various topics discussed, with full appreciation of the unfamiliarity of most foreign individuals with the nature of American legal practices and institutions. Much more could be said on each subject, but space constraints have imposed the requirement of selectivity. The selection of topics is based on the authors' extensive experience with the problems and needs of overseas businesspeople. This experience also led the authors to devote what may appear to be disproportionate space to certain topics, such as, for instance, distribution agreements (Chapter 10), letters of credit (Chapter 14), and the treatment of reserves in accounting (Chapter 26). The reader will not find in these pages a 'do it yourself' guide. Any businessperson or company seriously contemplating doing business with the United States or establishing commercial operations in this country is advised to seek competent professional assistance.

We thank our law partners for indulging our use of time and staff and offering helpful suggestions. Special thanks are due to three of them: Peter Landau for letting us have the benefit of his expertise in the field of securities law (Chapter 18), Eugene Parker, our tax counsel, for reviewing Chapter 8, and Paul M. Godlin, one of our litigators, for reviewing Chapters 23 and 24. We are much indebted to the eminent specialists who wrote for us Chapters 16, 19 and 26: Mr. Henry Salfeld, Daniel H. Kane, Esq., Gerald Levy, Esq., Lewis A. Helphand, CPA, and Roy M. Hoffman, CPA. Mr. Helphand also gave us valuable counsel with respect to Chapter 8. We are grateful to Messrs. Bruce Roberts, Vice-President, and Joseph F. Cook, Assistant Vice-President, of Morgan Guaranty Trust Company, for a very helpful critique of Chapter 14, on banking and finance, and we thank David H. T. Kane, Esq., for expert advice regarding Chapter 20, on trademarks, copyrights and unfair competition. Thanks go to Lawrence Kotik, legal intern, for useful services in reviewing the manuscript and offering helpful suggestions. We are grateful to our copy editor, Dorothy Opton Scott, for the conscientious correction of our manuscript. For their patient labors in preparing the manuscript, we express our appreciation to Anne L. Coale, Tina M. Lane and Melinda J. Lew. Finally, we cannot fail to record our gratitude to Miss Anita de Visser LL.M., the publisher's editor, for the application of her skill and learning, and her forbearance.

Notwithstanding all this help, all responsibility for any error or omission rests with the authors.

New York, N.Y.                                                    Frank G. Opton
January 31, 1984                                               Herbert Feiler

# TABLE OF CONTENTS

CHAPTER 1

# THE AMERICAN SCENE

Time was when America (the popular name for the United States of America) was regarded as an exotic country where buffalo herds roam the countryside, cowboys predominate and everybody is rich. That time is long gone. Persons from all continents have visited the U.S., as students or as travelers. Business connections have been established. The land is no longer exotic. Many of its habits and mannerisms have been adopted. Blue jeans and Coca Cola, symbols of the U.S. life style, are popular all over the world. In many respects, the pupils and imitators have surpassed the former preceptors. People abroad no longer aspire to a degree from the Harvard School of Business or similar institutions in the U.S. The U.S. automobile industry has lost its image as a paragon of industrial efficiency.

And, yet, there are many facets of U.S. business that escape the foreign observer, and are worth knowing if one wants to do business in the U.S. While some of these aspects may be familiar, others will surprise the reader. This book touches upon most of the facets that are of importance to foreign businesspeople and their professional advisers. This is not a treatise or an exhaustive coverage of the subjects which are dealt with. The intent is to acquaint the reader with the problems involved, and to encourage him or her to seek local assistance if a problem is encountered in the course of doing business in the U.S., or, better still, to seek counsel before such activity is commenced. To be successful in doing business in the U.S., it is important to understand the behavioral characteristics of the Americans that one is likely to encounter. It is, therefore, worthwhile to point to some general landmarks on the U.S. scene that should not be overlooked.

## 1. LAW

Law dominates U.S. life. Lawyers and legal advice are indispensable to the businessperson. In many other countries, an experienced businessperson feels free to write an agreement without legal assistance. In the U.S. there is one lawyer for approximately 450 persons, as compared to one lawyer for 10,000 persons in Japan, and one for 1,000 persons in Western Europe. Lawyers in the U.S. do not enjoy the esteem with which they are regarded in other parts of the world; they are regarded as a necessary evil. The reason that no seasoned businessperson in the U.S. would do without a lawyer is the plethora of U.S. legal principles, laws and regulations, and the peculiarities of the tax laws which make taxation often dependent on the form in which a transaction is cast. The dependence of the businessperson on legal advice is, of course, no unmixed blessing, especially as it increases the cost of doing business. However, it has been found that the lack of legal assistance is frequently even more expensive.

One of the great achievements of U.S. law is that it has educated us to respect and recognize new values, owing to the flexibility of the U.S. Constitution. Chapter 4 deals with that aspect as it affects doing business. It must be borne in mind that the law is in constant flux. If one starts a new business, or is faced with a new problem, no court decision, no statute and no treatise (including this one) can be relied upon. New inquiry is required.

## 2. AMERICAN LAW IS A MISNOMER

The reference to American law is inaccurate, for two reasons.

(a) The United States of America occupies only 38% of the North American continent and only 22.2% of the Western Hemisphere. The law of the United States of Brazil or of Chile, or of the United States of Mexico, is also American law. And yet, if one speaks and writes about America, the popular conception is that America means the United States of America. Indeed, even the phrase, *United States (U.S.)* is generally understood to mean the United States of America. This popular, although misleading, usage is perpetuated in the present book.

(b) As the name indicates, the United States of America consists of fifty states. In addition, there is the District of Columbia (Washington, D.C.), the Commonwealth of Puerto Rico, and three territories (Guam, the Virgin Islands and Micronesia).[1] Each of these has separate laws; each of these constitutes a different jurisdiction. We thus have fifty-five different bodies of law in fifty-five different jurisdictions. Most of the laws in which a

---

1. Micronesia is the collective name of the Pacific Islands east of the Philippines and north of the Equator, principally, the Mariana, Marshall, Caroline and Gilbert Islands. Guam has lately been used as a tax haven.

foreigner doing business in the U.S. is interested are state laws. Thus, a corporation is organized in accordance with the laws of the state of New York, or the state of California, or the state of Illinois, or wherever the corporation is domiciled. Similarly, each of these fifty-five jurisdictions has its own law on the sale of goods, taxation, etc. The tax laws differ; but in most instances the commercial laws in the different jurisdictions (with some subtle differences) are very similar. The situation becomes more complicated if one operates in several states, and is thus confronted with overlapping and sometimes conflicting laws.

To complicate the situation further, there is also a body of Federal law that applies uniformly through the entire U.S. An example of this is the law with respect to the sale of corporate stock, which is regulated by the Securities Act of 1933, the Securities Exchange Act of 1934, and related Federal statutes. Thus, if one organizes a corporation in the state of New York, one must do this in the manner prescribed by the law of New York. If one engages in the sale of the shares of that corporation, one may be obligated to observe not only the laws of New York, but also Federal law and possibly the laws of other states as well. More about this in Chapter 18.

Each state jurisdiction has its own court system. Parallel thereto is the Federal court system. Frequently, but not always, a party can choose which court system to use. This is discussed in Chapter 23.

## 3. PRECEDENTS AND STATUTES

Foreigners, especially foreign lawyers, often believe that American law is a law of precedents, and that there are no statutes (written laws), as in other countries. It is true that the basis of U.S. law is the common law that the American colonists imported from England more than 200 years ago. However, since the adoption of the common law, countless statutes have been enacted and regulations have been promulgated for the administration of these statutes. While judicial decisions are still very important for the interpretation of the statutes and are voluminous, the law itself is primarily statutory.

The fundamental statute is the Constitution of the U.S. Its unique distinction is that it reaches into all corners of daily life, including that of commercial life. Also, any law enacted by the Congress of the U.S. or by any state legislature, that violates the Federal Constitution, is invalid. An administrative action is likewise invalid if it contravenes the Federal Constitution. Whether the Constitution is violated in a particular instance is often a hotly debated issue, and leads to lawsuits. It astonishes many foreigners to find that virtually any lower court judge may rule that a given Federal or state statute or governmental action violates the Constitution and, therefore, is to be regarded as a nullity.

## 4. LAWYERS

Increasingly, business organizations in the U.S. employ 'in-house counsel'. Large corporations often have a large law department which is headed by the corporation's *general counsel*. Even corporations with such 'in-house' law departments generally retain outside counsel for special and non-routine transactions.

Lawyers in the U.S. do not receive the same preparatory training as do lawyers in many foreign countries. After attending a law school for three years, and then passing a bar examination in the state where he or she wishes to practice, the young lawyer is admitted to practice law. There is no distinction between courtroom lawyers (barristers) and other lawyers (solicitors). All of these people are called *attorneys-at-law*. Sometimes, one finds the additional appellation, *counselor-at-law*, but this additional title has no significance. Many lawyers specialize in particular fields such as patent law, criminal law, or real estate law. There is a movement afoot to certify such specialization, but this is not the general rule. A notary or notary public in the U.S. does not have to be a lawyer or a person trained in the law. The principal function of a notary is to certify the authenticity of signatures and to administer the oath to one making an affidavit. A newspaper vendor in the lobby of an office building may be, and often is, a notary. This is often a surprise to a foreign businessperson.

The law protects the confidentiality of all communication between lawyer and client. It is illegal for a lawyer to betray the confidence of the client, and such betrayal is also a breach of professional ethics. It is, therefore, safe for a person to discuss with a lawyer even questionable or illegal transactions. However, a lawyer may not conspire with the client to violate the law. The Securities and Exchange Commission (see Chapter 18) holds lawyers to a very high standard of conduct in the observance of the laws on securities trading.

Good faith reliance on the advice of a lawyer is an important factor, and often a defense, for somebody who is charged with violating the law. Cases of this kind often arise in the fields of taxation and securities trading. That is why some businesspeople insist on having a lawyer certify to them that a given transaction is legal.

Beyond that, it is customary in important transactions to require each lawyer to certify that the client's participation in the transaction complies with the law and that the client's statements are true. This is a somewhat archaic custom, especially when each lawyer requires such certification from his adversary, although he does not rely on it. More defensible is the practice of public accountants to require a lawyer's certification about significant transactions as a pre-condition for issuing a financial statement for the client.

## 5. VERBOSITY

An American contract is generally much lengthier than the form of contract to which the foreigner is accustomed, and that a businessperson can generally write without professional assistance. It is a fact of commercial life that lawyers in the U.S. have accustomed businesspeople to a verbose style. Even simple documents, such as an assignment of rights or a power of attorney, are generally couched in 'legalese' language to which one must get accustomed. Americans try to anticipate and provide solutions for a wide range of future contingencies, and try not to leave the solution to the future and the application of general principles. In that sense, Americans are less pragmatic and less flexible than one might expect. An extreme example of legalese is the phrase 'tender offer', encountered in connection with the regulation of traffic in corporate shares (see Chapter 18). According to the dictionary, tender offer simply means 'offer offer'.

## 6. CANCELLATION OF CONTRACTS

This is only a short word of warning to foreigners doing business in America.

A British machine tool exporter once came back to New York from a successful sales trip to the U.S. Midwest. He phoned a customer in Milwaukee to verify a small detail, and was flabbergasted when the customer told him that he had changed his mind. He wished to cancel the order. The Britisher was uncomprehending. Had the customer not committed himself? The customer did not deny that he had.

It is not unusual for a U.S. purchaser to thus cancel a contract; and, as a rule, the seller accepts such cancellation. The buyer is surprised if the seller, rather than acquiescing, insists on performance. There are similar situations where the seller cancels.

The law is clear. If there is a binding contract, one need not accept the cancellation. The warning to the foreign party is that he should always obtain a written and binding commitment that enables him to insist on performance.

## 7. SECRECY

Americans dislike secrecy. Most of them believe they have a 'right to know' everything. This led to the Freedom of Information Act which entitles everyone to obtain copies of government records. Only a few official records are excluded. Trade secrets are protected (see Chapter 20), but beyond that, there are few restraints against curiosity about one's profits, salary, age or bank accounts which a foreigner might prefer to keep confidential. The information that a businessperson furnishes in response to inquiries by the government is supposed to be confidential; but the curious will often find ways to obtain this information. Not everybody doing business in the U.S. will be deprived of the confidential aspects of his business activity, but everybody should be prepared for it.

Public disclosure is not only tolerated, it is often required. While the statutes which were prompted by the tide of consumerism (see Section 12) are primarily designed to protect the unsophisticated 'little man', disclosure is widely required by the securities laws that apply to corporations whose shares are publicly traded (see Chapter 18).

In many instances, the government requires reports which tend to discourage attempts to maintain secrecy.

## 8. POLITICAL CLIMATE

A foreigner doing business in the U.S. should not overlook the political climate in which business operates. The most important generality that can be stated about the political climate is that it changes frequently. It is, therefore, advisable to be acquainted with it. President Reagan came into office in 1981 because he promised (among other things) to liberate business from burdensome regulations and restrictions. Such liberalization requires the enactment of new laws, or the repeal of old laws. This cannot be achieved without the cooperation of Congress, which is the law-making body. Other restrictions are of an administrative nature, and solely subject to the executive branch of the government, headed by the president. Most import/export restrictions are in that category. All government departments and agencies, other than certain independent agencies, are subject to the direction of the president.

For decades, prior to the two World Wars, the U.S., like many developing countries, enacted laws that encouraged foreigners to invest in the U.S. Much of that legislation persists, as, for instance, death tax exemption of nonresidents in respect of U.S. bank accounts and life insurance proceeds. Another aspect of the same policy is that many states and municipalities offer tax and other financial incentives for establishing a plant or business. For instance, a foreign steel manufacturer established a steel mill in South Carolina because the local authorities agreed to substantial concessions. Sometimes, the local or state authority will build a plant and lease it at nominal cost. For similar reasons, nonresidents have not been taxed on capital gains made in the U.S. (see Chapter 8). However, lately, Americans have become very nervous because many foreigners have invested money in U.S. farmland and other real property. As a result of such anxiety, the tax law has been changed, and capital gains of foreigners resulting from real estate transactions are now taxed (see Chapter 7). This legislation reveals two trends that bear watching: (a) a trend to restrict real estate acquisitions by foreigners, and (b) a trend to discourage investment by foreigners altogether. Canada has enacted legislation to that effect (primarily directed against the U.S.). and it would not be surprising if the U.S. followed that example.

The political climate for the export business is good and can be expected to remain so. Some details are discussed in Chapter 22.

The import business is less fortunate. For years, domestic manufacturers have complained about imports from abroad and have asked for import restrictions. Businesspeople interested in selling foreign-made steel, textiles, shoes or automobiles in the U.S. have experienced the pressure for government intervention (see Chapter 22). The trend will probably continue.

The labor unions have supported the import restrictions because of their interest in reducing existing unemployment. Labor, therefore, opposes the sale of Japanese automobiles; but the sale of German Volkswagens has not thus far encountered the same opposition from Labor. The reason is that Volkswagens are manufactured in substantial volume in the U.S.

Although the political influence of organized Labor seems to be diminishing, it is an important factor in the political climate. Protection of the American labor force is the principal reason for the growing campaign against so-called illegal aliens, which means foreigners who come to the U.S. without a valid immigration visa. These aliens are popular with employers because they work for low wages. The changing trend in the administration of the immigration law is worth watching by foreign businesspeople who operate a branch or subsidiary in the U.S. and wish to staff it with employees from the home office (see Chapter 5).

## 9. FREE ENTERPRISE

Enthusiasm for the ideals of Free Enterprise has caused the present government of the U.S. to sponsor what is known as *deregulation*. Almost everybody agrees that government regulations have become too extensive and too expensive. However, the practical execution of the deregulation program is very controversial. From a business viewpoint, it is not an unmixed blessing. For instance, the steel industry is heavily dependent on a protective tariff and on regulations which hinder foreign imports. The air transport industry prospered under regulations which made market entry by others difficult. Now there are numerous new airlines which threaten the financial health of the old established lines. At least one of the latter is in bankruptcy; others are on the brink of collapse. The communications industry is adversely affected by deregulation. Deregulation has caused disarray in the banking industry, as will be noted in Chapter 8.

American businesspeople like to state that they live in a free enterprise system where everybody is given the opportunity to build a business in accordance with individual ability and initiative and without interference, so that the public will have the advantage of a competitive economy. Foreigners must be cautioned not to take such statements literally. It is true that the U.S. system is freer than many other systems. However, foreigners must be aware that tariffs and non-tariff barriers hinder the import business. U.S. agricultural products receive governmental price supports, and food surplus storage by the government interferes with the free marketing of food products. Trade union activities and labor agreements sometimes restrict the use of labor-saving devices and increase the cost of production. Pension plans tend to tie employees and workers to their jobs, and hinder the mobility of the work force. The antitrust laws, while promoting competition, also at times hinder it and forbid unbridled free enterprise. Numerous administrative rules restrict a businessperson's freedom of action. A person who plans to do business in the U.S. will do well to investigate whether and to what extent private initiative is likely to be curbed.

It is true, nevertheless, that business in the U.S. enjoys more freedom and elbow room that in most other areas of the world.

## 10. CAPITALISM

Most Americans are capitalistic, in the sense that they strive for the accumulation of some assets beyond their day-to-day needs. Most of them, even if they are poor, esteem middle class values. Napoleon said that every French soldier bears a marshal's baton in his knapsack–meaning that every soldier aims to become a field marshal or, at least, an officer. Many American workers aim for themselves or their children to become businesspeople or members of the learned professions. Most of them want to become home-owners. The man who polishes shoes or sells newspapers considers himself a businessperson. The average American worker is not class conscious. He or she does not consider himself or herself as a member of the proletariat. Many doctors, lawyers and successful businesspeople are children of the working class, and are proud of it. Labor unions are capitalistically oriented. They pay their leaders high salaries and often want them to stay at the best hotels. The typical American worker is not a socialist. Each is as individualistic as all other Americans. When a Japanese company opened a plant in California and tried to introduce uniform jackets for the workers in accordance with Japanese custom, the American workers rebelled and the attempt had to be abandoned. Labor unions assert the economic interests of their members, but they are not wedded to a political party. The position is the opposite of that which one observes in England, the cradle of trade unionism. In the U.S. labor unions typically support political candidates of the Democratic party; but some labor leaders have been, and are, strong supporters of the Republican party.

There are many contradictions in the politics of Labor. The workers want a share of the entrepreneurial profits, but they also want the security of the welfare state. Economists and social scientists have written interesting books on this subject. What is of interest to a foreigner doing business in the U.S. is that capitalism in the U.S. is rather stable.

The foregoing should not be regarded as an attempt to gloss over the disruptive, and sometimes criminal, behavior of labor unions and union leaders. Nor should these remarks be construed as overlooking the difficulties that entrepreneurs face when they sit across a bargaining table with labor union representatives. These union representatives are sometimes as unreason-able and unfriendly as some businesspeople with whom the entrepreneur negotiates.

## 11. MARKET RESEARCH

The demands of American consumers differ markedly from those of overseas consumers. Foreign manufacturers sometimes make the mistake of assuming that their product will sell well in the U.S. because it is in demand at home. Thus, a Dutch exporter of foodstuffs failed in the U.S. because the exporter did not realize that eye appeal and packaging are very important to the American consumer. A French manufacturer of watches did not take into account that if the U.S. consumer buys an imported watch, he or she almost invariably expect it to be of Swiss origin. A German exporter of cutlery was unsuccessful because his market research and knowledge of competing manufacturers was inade-quate. Said the magazine, *Time*, in a recent survey (December 1981):

'The (foreign) investments that did not work were aimed directly at the

American consumer. Foreign businesspeople are unaccustomed to the ethnic diversity in the U.S., where blacks, Hispanics and Chinese are as ubiquitous as the Irish and the Italians. Overseas investors are often unprepared for the competitiveness of the American market, in which promotion and image are crucial. European companies have acquired 21 major retailers since 1973, but only two of these foreign firms have earned large U.S. profits: Belgium's Delhaize Le Lion group, which owns Food Town grocery stores and Britain's Cavenham, which bought the Grand Union supermarket chain.'

The competing supermarket chain, known as A & P, was purchased by the German Tengelman concern; but Tengelman lost heavily, possibly because of non-American management.

## 12. CONSUMERISM

The word *consumerism* refers to the doctrine which grants special protection to the consumer. The term *consumer* means the ordinary retail purchaser who buys goods for his or her own use, such as a washing machine, a typewriter, food, a pen, and the like. The consumer has often been victimised by shrewd traders. He or she does not have the same bargaining power or sophistication as a businessperson (*Vollkaufmann* in Germany, *Commerçant* in France). The underlying principle in the law of consumerism is that the consumer is assumed to be uninformed about his or her rights and obligations, and that all details must be disclosed to him or her in simple, non-technical language. The fine print in written contracts is viewed with great suspicion. There are many Federal laws on the subject that supersede all state laws to the contrary. While the consumer can often initiate action against an offender, the chief enforcement agency of the Federal Government is the Federal Trade Commission, which is referred to in greater detail in Chapter 18.

The doctrine of consumerism permeates the entire body of U.S. commercial law. This is evident in the law on product liability (see Chapter 10). A typical piece of legislation is the Consumer Protection Act. The *truth in lending* provision of the statute requires every financier to clearly disclose the cost of financing. The law assumes that most instalment buyers do not understand the cost of credit. Failure to do so exposes the lender to a civil action by the aggrieved party. Another statute in this category is the Fair Credit Reporting Act, which requires a credit-reporting agency to do more than currently report information supplied to it by creditors. It must adopt and follow reasonable procedures to assure maximum possible accuracy.

Mention must also be made of the Consumer Products Safety Act, which is a Federal statute enacted in 1972. This law was enacted because many millions of Americans are injured each year in and around their homes by products which turn out to be hazardous. The law created a commission to establish and enforce safety standards. Dangerous products can be banned, if the producer does not take remedial action. A foreign manufacturer cannot avoid the ban by pointing out that the product complies with the safety regulations of his home country. When a product presents, in the opinion of the commission, an 'imminent and unreasonable risk of death, serious illness or severe personal injury', the commission may proceed in a Federal Court against the manufacturer, distributor and retailer.

Ordinarily, a foreigner doing business in the U.S. will not be concerned with the consumer protection legislation unless he manufactures, distributes or engages in a retail business here. However, it may become important for him if he finances exports to the U.S. A foreigner who exports merchandise to a distributor in the U.S. should also be aware of the problems that face the distributor in the U.S. when he makes retail sales.

## 13. EXTRATERRITORIALISM

The U.S. has a tendency to export its economic policy and its legal order. This is frequently resented abroad. It not only concerns people doing business in the U.S., but it disturbs people doing business with the U.S.; and even people abroad who have no intention of being involved with the U.S. A good illustration of this aspect of the American scene is the recent international dispute about supply contracts for the Russian pipeline from Siberia to Western Europe. The U.S. Government forbade supplies of goods and technology to Soviet Russia, and it claimed that this ban must apply to European corporations that are owned or licensed by U.S. companies. A wholly owned French subsidiary had contracted for machinery that had been manufactured in France with licensed U.S. technology, and which was ready for shipment. The U.S. Government tried to stop shipment, but the French Government ordered the French company to disregard the U.S. boycott. Shipment was made. Similarly, John Brown in Scotland had contracted for the sale to Russia of equipment that had been manufactured with licensed U.S. technology. The British Government ordered John Brown to make shipment and to disregard the U.S. directive. The British Government acted in accordance with a statute known as the Protection of Trade Interest Act of 1980. The object of that statute was to strengthen British firms against attempts by other countries (meaning, without saying it, the U.S.) to enforce economic policies outside their own territory.

After the Second World War, the U.S. dominated the world markets, and it seemed then reasonable that America should regulate foreign trade. This did not last long. In 1965, the U.S. Treasury Department attempted to stop the export of French-made trucks to China by a French subidiary of the U.S. Fruehauf concern. The French Government would not tolerate this interference with its China trade, and succeeded in defeating the American effort.

The extraterritorial application of the U.S. antitrust laws has caused much controversy. It was the cause of the abovementioned British statute, when the U.S. Government sought to apply its antitrust law against Imperial Chemical Industries Ltd., which had been ordered by a U.S. court to produce certain documents thought to be important. The British Government considered the American court order to be an improper intrusion upon British sovereignty. Similar resentment has been caused by a grand jury investigation of the role of two British airlines in the collapse of Laker Airways, also a British company. The investigation was triggered by a treble damages antitrust suit that Laker's liquidator commenced in a U.S. court. A further illustration of the problem of the extraterritorial reach of the antitrust laws is the case of a U.S. bank that refused to produce the records of one of its branches in Germany. The American authorities wanted these German records in connection with the investigation of an alleged criminal violation of the antitrust laws by an American citizen. The bank asserted that compliance would violate German law. The court ruled that this refusal was justified. Another example of the controversial U.S. approach is the Export Administration Act. The regulations implementing this Act contain complex re-export provisions that purport to be binding on all persons in a foreign country, regardless of their nationality.

The problem of extraterritorial reach is also encountered in the application of securities laws (see Chapter 18). Switzerland's highest court denied a request from the Securities and Exchange Commission for the identity of investors involved in insider trading (see Chapter 18, Section 9) in connection with the take-over of Sante Fe International Corporation by Kuwait Petroleum Corporation. In Switzerland, insider trading is not a crime.

A number of attempts have been made to export U.S. environmental laws, especially the National Environmental Policy Act. A telling illustration is a case that was instituted by the Sierra Club, renowned protagonist of environmental protection. The case involved the building of a part of the Pan American Highway in Panama and Colombia. The court ruled that U.S. law was applicable even though the environment sought to be protected lay in foreign countries. In a similar case, the Supreme Court allowed the state of Florida to enforce a criminal statute involving regulations on sponge diving, despite the fact that the conduct complained of occurred beyond Florida'a territorial waters.

After IBM sued Hitachi Ltd., accusing it of stealing trade secrets, Hitachi filed its own suit in Japan. Hitachi contended that if any wrong was committed, it was done in Japan, and that the courts in Japan and not those in the U.S. should hear the case.

Former U.S. Senator William Fulbright, in his book, *The Arrogance of Power*, ascribes America's tendency to impose its laws beyond its territorial limits to a belief in its superior wisdom. This is an oversimplification. The U.S. has a legitimate interest in preventing acts abroad which have an adverse effect on persons in the U.S., or on U.S. markets.[2] However, it is clear that this view is uncomfortable for many foreign businesspeople.


## 14. PUBLIC POLICY

It is important to understand the concept of public policy because courts sometimes examine whether a given statute (foreign or domestic), or a given agreement, is compatible with the public policy of the U.S., or of the state

2. This is the so-called 'effect doctrine' that was first enunciated about forty years ago in *U.S. v. Aluminum Co. of America*, 148 F. 2d 415 (1945). There are indications that the U.S. Government and the courts are now more sensitive to foreign resentments.

where the court sits. If it is held to be not compatible with public policy, it is declared invalid.

Public policy is a legal phrase. It denotes the policy of the law. The phrase is comparable to the French *ordre public*. It embraces the principles that underlie and are expressed in the Constitution. But the concept of public policy is broader. A law or an agreement may violate public policy without being unconstitutional. For instance, a profit sharing agreement between a prostitute and her procurer (popularly known as a pimp) violates public policy, but it is not unconstitutional. Public policy reflects the basic principles of justice and morality in communal living on which most Americans agree. The public policy of the law is not the same as the policy of the government. For instance, the government may decide, as a matter of foreign policy, to impose a boycott against a foreign country. The boycott measures may or may not reflect the public policy of the law. On the other hand, when former President Jimmy Carter made the protection of human rights a touchstone of foreign policy, the public policy of the law was made the basis of governmental policy. The idea of personal freedom, freedom of expression, and freedom of assembly are well known as expressing the policy of U.S. law.

A few examples will further illustrate the scope of this aspect of U.S. law. A clause in an employment contract that forbids the employee to engage in any competitive activity after termination of employment is generally held invalid as violating public policy. Similarly, a clause in a sales contract and common in many contracts that stipulates exclusive jurisdiction of the courts of Baltimore, or Berlin, or Birmingham, or any other locality, is often refused enforcement in the U.S. because it is declared to be against public policy to oust an otherwise competent U.S. court from its jurisdiction (see Chapter 23, Section 3). A New York court held invalid a corporate bylaw that required unanimous consent for any decision by the shareholders. The public policy here involved was that an American corporation must be democratically governed. The requirement of unanimity gives too much power to the minority. Public policy also forbids contractual penalties, which are common in many foreign countries. This may be circumvented, to some extent, by the stipulation for liquidated damages, as discussed in Chapter 9.

Another device by which this impact of public policy can be avoided is to require a performance bond (see Chapter 15, Section 2), which is generally available from an insurance company.

Foreign tax claims may not be enforced in U.S. courts because public policy forbids it. Foreign expropriation decrees that call for expropriation of property without adequate compensation are held to be against public policy. This means that such foreign decrees are not given effect in the U.S., although it is recognized that foreign governments may effectively expropriate property within their own borders.* A typical example is the case of expropriation by the Cuban Government. The expropriated owner may have a claim against a customer in the U.S. If he brings an action against the customer, he is likely to win because the U.S. court will disregard the expropriation decree. For the same reason, if the Cuban Government should sue the customer, it is likely to lose.

* This is the "act of state" doctrine.

A related problem arises in connection with foreign currency regulations. This subject is very complex and is not within the scope of this discussion.

In 1970, the Internal Revenue Service withdrew the tax exemption generally accorded to educational institutions from those institutions that practice race discrimination, on the ground that such discrimination violates public policy. Subsequently, the Reagan Administration reversed that position, asserting that the Internal Revenue Service had no right to enforce public policy. The Supreme Court disagreed.

It is against the public policy of the U.S. to bribe domestic and foreign officials, which is sometimes done to promote business. For that reason the Supreme Court disallowed income tax deductibility for such payments, because allowance of the deduction would 'frustrate the sharply defined policy of the law that was violated'. However, the Internal Revenue Service will disallow deductibility only if the payment abroad is illegal there.

Public policy does not forbid a tax deduction for lawyer's fees paid in connection with the defense of a crime. While crimes violate public policy, the legal defense of those charged with crimes, even if unsuccessful, does not.

Public policy may vary in different states. Thus, in New York it is against public policy for a corporation to indemnify a director beyond the statutory limit. The public policy of Delaware and other states is to the contrary.

## 15. GOVERNMENT HELP

The U.S. Government can be very helpful to those entering the American market. The U.S. Department of Commerce, and especially its Office of International Trade, publishes a number of helpful books and periodicals. The Department of Commerce in Washington, D.C., has sixty-eight field offices throughout the country. Here are some of the addresses. Others are freely available from the Department at:

> Department of Commerce
> Commerce Building
> 14th Street between Constitution Avenue
>   and E. Street
> Washington, D.C. 20230

*Atlanta*, Georgia 30309 – 1365 Peachtree Street N.E.
*Boston*, Massachusetts 02116 – 441 Stuart Street.
*Chicago*, Illinois 60603 – 55 East Monroe Street.
*Los Angeles*, California 90049 – 11777 San Vincent Blvd.
*New York*, New York 14202 – 111 West Huron Street.
*Philadelphia*, Penn. 19106 – 600 Arch Street.
*San Francisco*, California 36013 – 450 Golden Gate Avenue.

CHAPTER 2

# METHODS OF DOING BUSINESS

## 1. INTRODUCTION

This chapter surveys the various forms in which aliens who reside abroad transact business in the U.S. There is no single right method. The method that one chooses depends on the particular business and personal circumstances of each case, and also on the predilections of the person who makes the decision.

## 2. DIRECT CONTACT WITH THE U.S.

The majority of foreigners transacting business in the U.S. do so by direct contact, either through correspondence or through occasional personal visits. They learn quickly that the social habits and business customs in the U.S. are in many respects different from those to which they are accustomed. When they make contracts, they often fail to acquaint themselves with U.S. legal principles.

Although the general principles of business law are very similar all over the world, the foreigner, even a Britisher, must not assume that the law in the U.S. is exactly the same as at home; or that certain words or clauses have the identical meaning or effect as in his own country. Many foreigners have learned too late that they did not have the rights and claims which they thought they obtained when making a contract with an American party. Some of the more frequent peculiarities of U.S. contract law are dealt with in Chapter 9.

The business visitor from abroad who enters into transactions in the U.S. should familiarize himself with the applicable tax laws, in order to make sure that he does not incur avoidable tax liabilities. The visitor's tax liability is not necessarily limited to what he earned during his sojourn. He or she may have contracted for business that leads to taxation on personal future profits or on those of the corporation for whom the visitor acted.

15

## 3. DOING BUSINESS THROUGH AGENTS

A nonresident alien (individual or corporation) who has or seeks a regular business in the U.S. will often employ a U.S. agent as his permanent representative. When doing so, the alien should understand the nature and the consequences of an agency relationship in the U.S. This is discussed in Chapter 13.

One aspect of this method of transacting business in the U.S. merits particular attention because it is so often overlooked. A nonresident alien, by transacting business through a local agent, may be considered as *carrying on a business* in the U.S., and in the particular state where the agent resides. If the nonresident alien is thus considered as carrying on business in the U.S., there are certain tax consequences for the alien (see Chapter 8), and the alien may become subject to the jurisdiction of the U.S. courts. If the alien is considered as carrying on business in the state in which the agent resides, he or she may also be subject to taxation in that particular state and subject to its jurisdiction. To be subject to a U.S. court's jurisdiction means, in this connection, that the alien may be sued in such court by any party (not only by Americans), regardless of whether such lawsuit concerns the alien's business in the U.S. This, at least, is the general rule.

Soliciting a purchase order in the U.S. is not considered doing business in the U.S. Therefore, if the agent merely calls on potential customers, solicits the potential customers' orders, and then transmits them to the foreign principal for acceptance or rejection, the latter is not regarded as doing business in the U.S. On the other hand, if the agent has the authority to accept orders, for instance, on the basis of a published price list, the foreign principal is considered as doing business in the U.S. Cautious foreign principals, therefore, will often stipulate that no order shall be considered as accepted unless the acceptance is confirmed by the home office. If the foreign entrepreneur wants to avoid the appearance of carrying on business in the U.S., it should not allow its name to appear on the office door of the agent, on the directory of the building where the office of the agent is located, or in the telephone directory. Caution is indicated in the use of the agent's business stationery, as well as that of the foreign party itself.

Some agents are manufacturers' representatives, often called 'manufacturers' reps'. A manufacturers' rep represents several manufacturers in different lines of commerce. Generally, he does not represent competing manufacturers; and it is customary for a manufacturers' rep to list on his business stationery various firms which he represents. Such use of the agent's stationery is harmless for the foreign entrepreneur, so long as the agent has no exclusive right.

Exclusivity also has a disadvantage in connection with the assessment of customs duties on imported merchandise, as is noted in Chapter 22.

Sometimes the realities of business life make it hard, if not impossible, to observe all the rules and to be as careful as here suggested. But it is obvious that every foreign businessperson or corporation should think twice before assuming the consequences resulting from the employment of an agent in the U.S. Of course, it is often necessary, and even worthwhile, to bear these consequences. But nobody should carry on business in the U.S. or any state thereof without being aware of them.

## 4. DOING BUSINESS THROUGH A DISTRIBUTOR

The risk of being taxed in the U.S. is small or non-existent if the foreigner works through a U.S. distributor. A distributor is an independent individual or a company that buys and sells for its own account. Independence is an important characteristic. Independence is sometimes lost when there is an *exclusive* arrangement with the distributor. The arrangement should be such that the foreigner is not doing business in the U.S. This requires that the foreigner not proclaim himself to be carrying on business in the U.S. In practical terms, as in the case of an agent, this means that the foreign party's name should not appear on the office door, on the building directory where the office of the distributor is located, or in the telephone directory. Again, caution is indicated in the use of the business stationery of the distributor, as well as of the foreign party itself. Distribution contracts are discussed at greater length in Chapter 10, Section 10.

## 5. DOING BUSINESS THROUGH A BRANCH OFFICE

Some foreign businesses do not like to work through a U.S. agent. They want their own office in the U.S., subject to their direction and staffed by one or more of their employees. Another desired advantage of such a branch office is that it will bring the name of the principal concern more forcefully to the attention of the interested public.

Obviously, the maintenance of a branch office in the U.S. is carrying on business and it has the consequences mentioned in the preceding discussion of working through agents. By acquiring jurisdiction over the branch, a court in the U.S. also acquires jurisdiction over the headquarters organization. Thus, if X corporation in Tokyo opens a branch in Chicago, a claimant in any part of the world can commence a lawsuit against X corporation in the Chicago courts.

A businessperson who has reached the stage where he is prepared to open a branch office in the U.S. must ask himself whether it would not be advisable to organize a separate business organization in the U.S. (see Section 6, below). By doing this, he may avoid liability of his home organization for acts and debts of the U.S. organization; this is particularly desirable where the U.S. business is in the charge of persons not closely connected with the home organization. If the person in charge of the U.S. business is paid on a percentage-of-earnings basis, it may be more convenient to have a separate business organization for that reason. Often, separate U.S. organizations are established to obtain a greater measure of independence in relation to the homeland.

Another consideration is taxes. Whether or not it is more advantageous to have a branch office or a separate U.S. organization depends on the circumstances of each case. The principal factors to be considered in this connection are discussed in Chapter 8.

Of course, one should never lose sight of the commercial requirements of the business, which may outweigh all tax and other legal considerations. That is something to be addressed in each individual case.

If a foreign corporation opens a branch in the U.S., it is advisable to register in the state or states in which such branches are opened, as explained in the next chapter.

## 6. SEPARATE BUSINESS ORGANIZATION

Commercial expediency or tax reasons will often prompt a foreigner to establish a separate business organization in the U.S.

The two conventional types of business organizations are the partnership and the corporation. Each of them is dealt with in separate chapters. It will there be noted that there are two types of partnership, but generally speaking only one type of business corporation.

In a few states, including New York, the law also provides for the organization of a so-called joint stock company. This is, in reality, an outmoded kind of partnership. Another type of organization, the so-called Massachusetts Business Trust, is likewise of little practical importance, except perhaps where it is desired to organize an investment trust. The outstanding characteristic of the Business Trust is that it is operated by one or more trustees for the benefit of investors. For tax purposes, such Business Trusts are treated as corporations.

While Business Trusts are, as a rule, not practicable, the use of an ordinary trust may occasionally be a sound vehicle for carrying on business in the U.S. A foreigner may transfer funds to a trust with instructions that the trustee shall invest them in a business as a partner or as a shareholder. The trustee may be the sole shareholder of a corporation. Such an arrangement may be desirable because the real investor does not wish to publicize his interest in the business. Moreover, depending on the terms of the trust instrument, the invested funds will be treated as those of a U.S. resident and citizen, provided the trustee qualifies as such.

The advantage of a properly appointed trustee over a so-called strawman is that the real investor has better protection in case of death. Also, the trust funds will be clearly separated for income tax as well as inheritance tax purposes.

As a rule, however, the foreign businessperson desirous of having his own business organization in the U.S. will prefer a partnership or corporation. If the U.S. corporation is a wholly owned subsidiary of the foreign enterprise (and if the foreign enterprise wants to avoid the risk of being regarded as carrying on business in the U.S.), care should be taken not to operate it as a branch of the home organization. This risk arises where the foreign management issues orders, instead of suggestions, to the U.S. subsidiary, and where the U.S. subsidiary makes no decision without permission or direction from abroad.

## *7. DOING BUSINESS AS PARTNER OF A U.S. ENTERPRISE*

A foreigner who becomes a partner in a U.S. enterprise is considered as doing business in the U.S., even if he or she never sets foot on American soil. This follows from the general principles of partnership law, which are dealt with in Chapter 12.

CHAPTER 3

# QUALIFICATION

## 1. INTRODUCTION

In order to start a business or trade in the U.S., it is generally not required to seek anybody's permission. One just opens one's establishment and commences to do business, as a steel fabricator or a dress shop, or whatever.

## 2. LICENSE

Exceptions are made by the laws of the various states where such exceptions appear to be in the public interest. In a few instances, this is done in order to restrict the number of businesses of certain types. Banks and retail liquor stores are, for instance, in this category. In many states, today, it is practically impossible to obtain a license to open a new bank. It is different with respect to branches of foreign banks (see Chapter 14, Section 12).

Generally, the sole reason for requiring a trade license is to protect the public from abuse by unqualified persons. Barbers and plumbers, for instance, are often required to be licensed for reasons of health and safety. An employment agency needs a license in many states in order to prevent exploitation. Travel agencies are often subject to licensing because of the large funds they handle. In all such cases, a qualified person will generally find no difficulty in procuring a license.

Many states require that a real estate broker, an insurance broker and a consulting engineer be licensed; and such license can be obtained only by passing an examination which establishes that the individual is familiar with the field in which he or she wishes to engage. However, hardly any qualified person finds it hard to pass these tests. It is almost like passing the test for an automobile driver's license.

## 3. *REGISTRATION*

In the exceptional cases where a license is required to engage in business, there is generally some sort of registration in connection with the license. In all other instances, it is not necessary to register a business with any governmental office, so long as the owner of the business does the business under his or her own name. However, if one chooses to do business under an assumed or fanciful name, then one must register that name. Such registration is a very simple and inexpensive formality. Examples of assumed names are: 'Amsterdam Antique Company' and 'The Golden Rule Store'. Any name is allowed which does not cause confusion with the business name of others.

In the case of a partnership, it is necessary to register the names and addresses of the partners and the name under which the partnership is conducted. Publication of further details is required in the case of a limited partnership (see Chapter 12).

Corporations must be registered. In fact, they do not come into existence before they are registered, as is noted in the discussion on corporations in Chapter 11.

Unlike many foreign countries, there is no official register of American business organizations. There is no *Handels-register* or *Registre de Commerce* or any public record comparable thereto. Those who want to know how much a particular company is worth, how it is organized, and who the owners or directors or officers are, often inquire at credit bureaus. Dun and Bradstreet is the best known of these. Sometimes, banks are asked for information. Neither the reports from credit bureaus nor bank reports are necessarily reliable. The Securities and Exchange Commission keeps records of the public corporations which are under its jurisdiction. These records generally consist of official reports from the corporations. They are accessible and generally reliable, as are the records of the stock exchanges with respect to corporations whose shares are traded on such exchanges. None of the records, however, have the protective value of an official register, which exists in other countries. If one intends to purchase a controlling interest in a corporation, or make an important transaction with the corporation, one will often require the furnishing of a certificate from the Secretary of State of the state(s) where the corporation is organized and is registered as doing business, to the effect that the corporation is 'in good standing' as of the date of the certificate. Such certificates, in order to be timely, will, if requested, be furnished by telegram.

## 4. *ALIENS*

Aliens who reside permanently in the U.S. can engage in business in the same manner as citizens. Some states require that at least one member of the board of directors of a domestic corporation be a citizen. Otherwise, corporations generally may be owned and managed by aliens (see Chapter 11). There are few limitations on the investment of foreign capital (see Chapter 6, Section 2).

## 5. ALIEN VISITORS

In order to qualify as a permanent resident, an alien must have come to the U.S. as an immigrant with an immigrant visa. Most foreigners come as visitors. What is relevant in this connection is discussed in Chapter 5.

## 6. FOREIGN CORPORATIONS

A corporation which is organized in a foreign country may, without obtaining any governmental permission, open a branch office in the U.S. from which it will conduct business.

The laws of all states have special provisions for foreign corporations. Each state regards as foreign any corporation that is organized in another state. For instance, in New York or Illinois or California, a Pennsylvania corporation is as much a foreign corporation as a corporation which has been organized under the laws of Spain or Japan. A foreign corporation is generally required to register in the state in which it is engaged in business. For instance, a California or a French corporation that opens an office in New York is required to register in New York. The reason for this is that the host state wishes to levy a tax on the foreign corporation. Registration facilitates taxation. Failure to register leads to sanctions (see Chapter 11), primarily to a denial of access to the courts of the host state. In the above example, if the California corporation fails to register in New York, it may not sue in the New York courts a customer who defaults in making a required payment. However, a foreign corporation which is not engaged in business in the U.S. need not, and is not expected to, register. As stated above, soliciting orders is not considered doing business. Thus, if a foreign corporation occasionally sends a salesman to the U.S. and obtains an order from an American customer, the foreign corporation need not register to be permitted to sue the American customer, who may have breached the contract.

CHAPTER 4

# CONSTITUTIONAL LAW

## 1. INTRODUCTION

The U.S. Constitution touches so many aspects of life in the U.S. that many Americans who are not lawyers are nonetheless greatly interested in questions of constitutional law. The cry, 'that is unconstitutional', is often heard in the land. Although the Constitution is more than 200 years old, courts are still engaged in interpreting it. Each state also has a constitution, but the state constitutions are generally of lesser importance and as a rule mirror the Federal Constitution. This book is concerned with only two aspects of constitutional law. One is the position of aliens, the other is U.S. commerce.

## 2. THE CONSTITUTIONAL RIGHTS OF ALIENS

It comes as a surprise to many aliens that they can invoke the same rights of constitutional protection as U.S. citizens. This is illustrated by an old case involving a law of the state of Arizona. The law stipulated that any employer of more than five workers must employ a minimum of 80% who are voters, meaning citizens. An Austrian citizen who was employed as a waiter was, therefore, discharged. When he sued, the Supreme Court reinstated him and declared the law unconstitutional. Lawfully admitted aliens must be accorded the same rights as citizens, the Court declared. The Constitution also forbids laws which place on a foreign corporation a greater burden than on a domestic corporation. A Kentucky corporation (and this applies also to a British or a Brazilian, or any foreign corporation) sued a debtor in Wisconsin for the repossession of an automobile. The Wisconsin court ordered an examination of the plaintiff's records. Under Wisconsin law, this examination ordinarily would have taken place at the plaintiff's headquarters in Kentucky, where the records were located. But because the plaintiff was a foreign corporation, Wisconsin law required that the records be brought to Wisconsin. This was unconstitutional discrimination against a foreign corporation, the Supreme Court ruled. The importance of this principle for foreign corporations doing business in the U.S. is clear.

## 3. INTERSTATE AND FOREIGN COMMERCE

In the field of commerce, the various states exercise exclusive jurisdiction if the commerce takes place entirely within the boundaries of the state (intrastate commerce). The Federal antitrust laws, for instance, are not applicable if one complains about a monopoly within a state, although there may be a violation of state law. The U.S. Constitution assigns jurisdiction of interstate commerce and of foreign commerce to the Federal Government. The concept of interstate and foreign commerce is ever-expanding, and it is not the same as when the Constitution was adopted. This is illustrated by a landmark decision of the Supreme Court. The National Labor Relations Board, an agency of the Federal Government, had proceeded against a steel producer in Pittsburgh, Pennsylvania on the ground that some of its workers had been ill-treated. The steelmaker argued that the Federal Government had no right to interfere because the plant was a purely local (intrastate) operation. Not so, said the Supreme Court, pointing out that the ore came from other states, and that the finished steel was shipped to many states and foreign countries. The Pittsburgh plant was held to be a mere way station in interstate and foreign commerce. In 1945 the Supreme Court ruled that it was unconstitutional for the State of Ohio to levy a property tax on imported raw materials retained in their original package pending manufacture. Another illustration is a recent lower court ruling which invalidated as improper interference with foreign and interstate commerce an Idaho statute that deprived undomesticated foreign corporations (see Chapter 11, Section 2) of the benefit of the Statute of Limitations.

Another aspect of the constitutional impact on doing business in the U.S. is illustrated by the experience of the French tire manufacturer, Michelin. Some tires were imported and stored in a warehouse in Georgia. The warehouse was used as a distribution center for shipments to other parts of the country. The state of Georgia levied a property tax on the Michelin inventory. Michelin contended that this was an unconstitutional interference with foreign commerce by the state of Georgia. Michelin lost the case. In a comparable case, where the circumstances were different, the Xerox corporation stored machinery, intended for eventual export to South America, in a Texas warehouse. The Supreme Court ruled that it was unconstitutional for the local authorities to levy a property tax on the stored machinery, as the tax interfered with foreign commerce.

## 4. MISCELLANEOUS ILLUSTRATIONS

Some states levy a so-called unitary income tax against the local subsidiaries of foreign corporations. The constitutional problem that is here involved is alluded to in Chapter 8, Section 25. It must be noted that any lower court judge may refuse enforcement of a law that he determines to be unconstitutional. An example of this occurred not long ago in Alaska. A law in that state prohibited the sale of state-owned timber, unless the buyer cut the timber in an Alaskan mill. An Alaska judge ruled that the law violated the Constitution and could not be enforced because it interfered with foreign and interstate commerce.

The involvement of the U.S. Constitution in American business is limitless. In 1980, Congress enacted the Multi-Employer Pension Plan Amendment Act. This imposed on some employers a new financial liability. Employers in California and in Illinois refused to pay, and challenged the constitutionality of the Act.

In 1969, the Supreme Court ruled unconstitutional a Wisconsin statute that permitted the attachment of wages without a prior hearing. In 1972, for similar reasons, the Supreme Court outlawed Florida and Pennsylvania statutes that authorized self-help by creditors against defaulting debtors. The rationale of those decisions was that the state law violated the constitutional requirement of due process of law.

Other decisions have upheld state laws that permit self-help, on the ground that it does not involve state action. The constitutional command of due process of law is addressed to governmental authority, not to individual citizens.

CHAPTER 5

# IMMIGRATION LAWS AFFECTING BUSINESS

## 1. INTRODUCTION

In order to enter the U.S., an alien needs a visa. The visa is issued by a U.S. consul abroad. The consul is bound by the immigration law and the interpretive directions of the Department of State in Washington, D.C. Within that framework, the U.S. consul is allowed a good deal of discretion. It may happen that one consul refuses the issuance of a visa, whilst the consul in another locality grants it in an identical situation.

## 2. EXCLUDED ALIENS

Certain aliens are declared by law to be ineligible for admission to the U.S. The list of ineligible aliens is very long, but the average foreigner doing business in the U.S. need not be concerned therewith. The list bans primarily criminals, drug addicts, anarchists and sick persons. The long statutory list explains the searching inquiry at the U.S. consulate, which often annoys foreign visa applicants.

The list also excludes from admission a person who has made an employment arrangement in the U.S. without first obtaining a labor certification. This is dealt with later in this chapter. If the consul denies a visa, the applicant may lodge an administrative appeal to the Visa Division of the Department of State. But the alien has no right to appeal to the courts.

## 3. IMMIGRANT VISA

There are two broad categories of visas, the immigrant visa and the nonimmigrant visa. An immigrant visa is one that entitles an alien to

29

permanent residence in the U.S., and the right to become a resident alien. Most resident aliens in the U.S. apply in due course (generally after five years) for naturalization. However, naturalization is not compulsory. If the immigrant wishes to preserve allegiance to the home country, he or she may remain a permanent resident alien as long as desired. The immigrant visa does not bar the alien from returning permanently to the homeland.

A declaration of intention to become a citizen, frequently called 'first papers', is no longer required for naturalization. However, since in some states certain occupations or professions are closed to an alien who does not have first papers, the law still allows aliens to file a declaration of intention to become naturalized. The declaration is not a binding commitment, and leaves the alien free to do as he or she pleases.

Immigrant visas are hard to obtain because there are numerical limitations. The law gives certain people – generally family members – a preference. The preferred visa applicants frequently use up the numerical limitation. There are, altogether, six preferences which are established in sequential order. Four of them are for members of the family of a resident of the U.S., who may be an alien. The third and sixth preferences are for persons possessing special skills.

## 4. VISITOR'S VISA

All nonimmigrant visas are for a temporary visit. Nonimmigrants, after entry, become nonresident aliens. The most frequently sought nonimmigrant visa is commonly referred to as the 'visitor's visa'. There is a great variety of such visa, depending on the purpose of the visit. Each has a special designation and is subject to special regulations. In the context of this book, only business visitors' visas are of interest.

## 5. TREATY TRADERS

Of particular importance to international trade are the treaty traders' visas. They are based on the treaties of commerce and navigation that the U.S. has with many foreign nations, including most Western nations, Japan, China and some other Eastern and South American nations. Under these treaties, nationals of the treaty countries, and their spouses and children, are entitled to enter the U.S. for the purpose of promoting trade between their home countries and the U.S. In the case of a corporation, the home country is not the country where it was organized, but that in which the controlling shareholder or shareholders live. For instance, if a Liechtenstein corporation is controlled by a citizen of Holland, it is the trade between the U.S. and Holland that counts, even though Liechtenstein has no treaty with the U.S. The requirement that the U.S. business promote trade with the home country does not mean that it must be exclusively devoted to such trade. The U.S. business may also engage in domestic business or export to other countries, but at least 50% of the business must be with the home country of the person who seeks a treaty trader's visa.

There are two types of treaty traders: the treaty investor (visa designation:

E–2) and the ordinary treaty trader (visa designation: E–1). The treaty investor is a person who comes to the U.S. because he has made, or will make, a substantial investment in a business that promotes trade between the U.S. and his home country. The U.S. enterprise in which the visa applicant wishes to invest must actually be in existence, or in active process of formation. It is not enough that the visa applicant makes a small investment in order to earn a living for himself and members of his family. If that is the case, the investor would be presumed to be entering the labor market without the required labor certification to which reference is made below. The business that the investor plans to engage in must be substantial. The law does not say what *substantial* means. This is left to the discretionary judgment of the U.S. consul. At the present time, a minimum investment of $40,000 is required, but that alone does not make the business substantial. If the business creates employment opportunities for U.S. workers, the chances of obtaining an investor's visa are heightened.

As a practical matter, a person who is interested in obtaining a treaty investor's visa will find it useful to become a partner or a shareholder in a U.S. enterprise that either exists or is being organized for the purpose of promoting trade with the home country. As a rule, the foreign investor will prefer to come to the U.S. as a visitor, in order to investigate the situation before returning home and applying for a treaty investor's visa.

The ordinary treaty trader's visa (E–1) is frequently used to staff the American enterprise of a foreign company. The advantage of a treaty trader's visa is its unlimited duration. It is a temporary visa, but the temporary visit may last for a lifetime. The holder of the visa remains a nonresident alien, but may be taxed like a resident (see Chapter 8). The treaty trader's visa for employees often will be applied for by the foreign company that seeks to staff its U.S. enterprise. From the viewpoint of the foreign employer, this has the advantage that the employee generally will lose the U.S. visa if he leaves the employ of the foreign company. Thus a treaty trader's visa often leads to involuntary servitude.

## 6. OTHER TEMPORARY VISITORS

Most alien nonimmigrant business visitors, who do not qualify as treaty traders, will obtain visas as 'temporary visitors for business' (Designation: B–1). The foreigner who seeks such a visa at a U.S. consulate abroad will have to show that he or she maintains a home in the foreign country, and that his or her principal place of business and principal source of income are abroad. The visa will be issued for a limited period, but generally will allow several visits. The alien visitor is not allowed to take employment in the U.S., unless the visitor has previously obtained labor certification, to which reference will be made below.

A foreigner who enters the country on a visitor's visa may not engage in any other activity than the one for which the visa was granted. A visitor who received the visa for the purpose of touring the country or visiting friends (temporary visitor for pleasure, Designation: B–2) has no right to engage in business. A person who comes with a student's visa (Designation F) must confine himself to the pursuit of study.

The sole penalty for disregarding the nature and the scope of the visitor's visa is deportation. Contracts made in violation of the visa restriction are not invalid. A party who makes a contract with an alien who is illegally in this country is not excused from performing the contract. Aliens who violate a visa restriction and are deported, or ordered to leave the country, jeopardize any future admission to the U.S. Similarly affected are those aliens who obtain a visa under false pretenses or commit crimes.

It is not considered a business activity if a visitor from abroad merely looks after his investments in America. If a visitor becomes a member of the board of directors of an American corporation, he is not violating the rule against taking employment. The director of an American corporation is not regarded as an employee (see Chapter 11).

## 7. LABOR CERTIFICATION

All aliens who have made arrangements for employment in the U.S. require Labor Certification, regardless of whether they obtain an immigrant visa or a treaty trader's visa or an ordinary visitor's visa. Labor Certification is obtained from the Department of Labor, and, as a rule, the prospective U.S. employee applies for such certification. If certification is denied, the prospective employee can institute a law suit against the Secretary of Labor. There are quite a few such cases in which the applicants were successful. Aliens who will be employed in the U.S. in managerial or executive positions, and who have been with the home organizations abroad for at least one year, are entitled to a special visa (Designation: L) and can obtain such certification automatically. If the prospective employee is expected to work in a minor capacity, Labor Certification can only be obtained if it is demonstrated that there are not sufficient U.S. workers who are able, willing, qualified and available in the locality of the prospective employer. The Department of Labor has issued regulations that are not easy to comply with and that are sometimes unreasonable. Among other things, the regulations require proof of an unsuccessful recruiting effort for U.S. workers on the part of the prospective American employer. Knowledge of the language of the home country is not regarded as a special qualification. The U.S. subsidiary of a Japanese company desired to employ a Japanese citizen whose sole special qualification was familiarity with the Japanese language, which would facilitate communication. The application for Labor Certification was denied.

The application for Labor Certification is handled by one of the ten regional offices of the Department of Labor nearest to the prospective employer's location. Some regional offices are more efficient than others. However, experience indicates that it take a long time – six months or longer – until certification is issued.

The law provides for an immigration preference for aliens who are professionals or who, because of their exceptional ability in the sciences or the arts, will substantially benefit U.S. cultural interests. U.S. enterprises sometimes encourage qualified aliens to apply for an immigrant visa under this so-called third preference. It must be pointed out that even such highly qualified persons require Labor Certification if they are to be employed by U.S. enterprises.

Another special class that has no difficulty in obtaining Labor Certification is that of temporary visitors who come to the U.S. to perform services requiring unique skills (visa designation: H–1 or H–2). This is important for foreign companies that have sold machinery to customers in the U.S. and, in the contract of sale, have agreed to install the machines at the plants of the U.S. customers.

## 8. TAX PLANNING

As explained in Chapter 8, resident aliens are more comprehensively taxed than nonresident aliens. Therefore, aliens who contemplate immigration and thus become resident aliens, might find some pre-immigration tax planning useful. There are opportunities to do so. The value of these opportunities depends on the tax laws of the country from where the alien emigrates. The following remarks are based on U.S. law.

One of the more important opportunities is the acceleration of income prior to immigration. This may include the distribution of income from controlled corporations and from foreign trusts. The alien might also dispose of appreciated property and repurchase it after immigrating, in order to obtain a stepped-up cost basis for future capital gains. On the other hand, an immigrant may be able to avoid capital gains tax on the disposition of real property in the U.S. if, after immigrating, he exchanges the property, tax-free, for like kind property.

If transfer of an asset to a non-U.S. organization is contemplated, it should be done prior to immigration, as such transfers are taxed in the U.S. A restructuring of a non-U.S. corporation may be indicated, especially if it is a personal holding company.

If the prospective immigrant contemplates gifts, he might make them before immigration. Not only would this avoid U.S. gift taxes, but it would also reduce the taxable estate for estate (death) tax purposes. On the other hand, the size of the U.S. tax bite may not be important because of the substantial tax exemption under the so-called unified tax credit, and the marital deduction.

CHAPTER 6

# INVESTMENTS AND ACQUISITIONS IN THE U.S.

## 1. INTRODUCTION

Foreign investments have increased enormously during the past decade. High interest rates seem to have contributed to this development. However, the chief attraction of U.S. investments seems to be the relative stability of the American political system.

Generally, a foreign investor wishes to protect his American investment against political hazards in the home country. Sometimes, the foreign investor uses an intermediate country such as Liechtenstein, the Cayman Islands, Bermuda, or Panama, in order to make an investment in the U.S. In such a case, the political hazards in the intermediate country are also of importance. Sometimes the Netherlands Antilles or the British Virgin Islands is chosen as the intermediate country because of assumed tax advantages. These tax advantages have become questionable (see Chapter 8, Section 25). The political hazards also include the possibility that a foreign investment in the U.S. may be blocked, frozen, or expropriated in the U.S., if the foreign investor resides in a country that becomes an enemy of the U.S., or if political hazards arise, such as the hostage crisis in 1979, which resulted in the freezing of Iranian assets in the U.S. This is not the place to discuss the legal justification for such measures, nor the possible safeguards for foreign investors. There are precautionary measures that can be taken, the safest of which is the organization of one or more trusts. It is noteworthy that Switzerland and the Netherlands, which profess to abjure trusts, have made express provisions for protective trusts in emergency situations.

Trusts are often a suitable investment vehicle. Most countries whose legal systems do not have the English heritage, profess not to recognize trusts. This need not prevent anybody from establishing a trust in the U.S., in any country of the British Commonwealth, or in Panama or Liechtenstein, where trusts are regulated by law.

In a U.S. trust, the trustee is the nominal owner of the trust property. The income, and ultimately the property itself, goes to the designated beneficiary(ies). Distributions of income are taxable to the beneficiary(ies). Undistributed income is taxable to the trust. The trust is a separate taxpayer.

The volume of foreign investments has caused some fear of possible political pressures. A thus motivated attempt to gain access to government data about portfolio investments of certain Arab states has been rebuffed by the U.S. Government and by the Supreme Court.

Foreign investors are being deterred from making investments in a state which applies the so called unitary tax system (see Chapter 8, Section 26).

## 2. LIMITS ON ANONYMITY

Section 7 of Chapter 1 alludes to the lack of secrecy and the trend toward public disclosure. This gains importance in the field of foreign investment because the investment of foreigners often represents 'black' money, which the owners wish to conceal from their own government. That desire is frustrated by many disclosure and reporting requirements of which the alien doing business in the U.S. should be aware. In many instances, this difficulty can be overcome by making the American investment in the name of a bank, or a holding company, or through an American trust or some other third party.

The following is a summary of the most important disclosure requirements. Applicants for a visa to enter the U.S. (see Chapter 5) will be asked to fill out a form that requires disclosure of their assets, and they may be questioned further. *The Agricultural Foreign Investment Disclosure Act of 1978* requires aliens – no matter where they reside – to report to the Secretary of Agriculture any investment in the U.S., specifically land used for agriculture, forestry or timber production. The *International Investment Survey Act of 1976* provides for monitoring of foreign direct investments. Reports must be filed with the Secretary of Commerce with respect to every business enterprise that includes 200 or more acres of U.S. real property, in which foreign persons have a direct or indirect interest of 10% or more. An exemption is provided if the combined total assets, annual net sales and gross operating revenues, and annual net income (after U.S. income taxes) do not exceed $5 million. The law expressly provides for confidentiality. Section 13(d) of the *Securities Exchange Act of 1934* requires that any person who becomes the beneficial owner of more than 5% of the registered capital stock of any corporation must notify the Securities and Exchange Commission (SEC), the corporation, and each securities exchange where the stock is traded. If a company plans to acquire a certain amount of stock or assets of a U.S. company, through merger or otherwise, and the sales or assets of one or both of the parties are of a certain magnitude, the *Federal Trade Commission* and the *Antitrust Division of the Department of Justice* must be notified in advance (*Antitrust Improvements Act of 1976*). The *Internal Revenue Code* contains a number of provisions designed to insure the payment of taxes on income paid to aliens. Most tax treaties provide for an exchange of information between the Internal Revenue Service and the tax authorities of the treaty partner. If an alien acquires an interest in U.S. real property, reporting is required, as discussed in Chapter 7.

## 3. LIMITATIONS ON FOREIGN INVESTMENTS

In a few fields, the U.S. discourages or prohibits investments by aliens. In some of these cases, the limitation applies only to individuals, and not to corporations that may own or control an American corporation.

Restrictions exist in the aviation and aeronautics field, in the communications industry (radio, television, telegraph and telephone) and in the maritime industry. However, investment in the shipbuilding field is barred to aliens only in time of war or national emergency.

The extraction industry (coal, oil, gas and other minerals) is subject to certain restrictions, but aliens are generally not barred from participation as shareholders or partners of a U.S. enterprise that is engaged in such activities. Leasing of government owned land is restricted.

Foreign investment in the defense industry is limited. This applies not only to manufacturers of tanks, airplanes, weapons, and the like, but also to manufacturers of component parts for such military products. The Federal Department of Defense requires that plants and personnel obtain security clearance before a contract or a subcontract for defense work is obtained. Alien individuals, with the exception of British and Canadian citizens, are ineligible for such clearance. A person who has not obtained such clearance cannot become an officer or even a director of a corporation that is engaged in manufacturing or dealing in articles used for, or in connection with, the national defense. In addition, a foreign owned or controlled facility requires security clearance by the Department of Defense regardless of the nationality of the foreign individuals involved. It appears advisable that the chief executive officer of a foreign owned or controlled facility be a U.S. citizen.

Similarly, aliens, or corporations owned by aliens, are barred from obtaining a license to build atomic power plants. Power-generating establishments require a Federal license, which is not available to aliens. However, it is available to an American corporation, even if the corporation is owned or controlled by aliens. Given the scarcity of generator production in the U.S., this is not unimportant.

Foreigners also encounter certain limitations in the banking industry and in the insurance field. This is discussed in Chapters 14 and 16.

The *Buy American Act*, in spite of its formidable name, is no bar to foreign investments. The Act applies only to the product involved, not to the ownership of the seller. If over 50% (in value) of a product is produced in the U.S., there is no limitation. The Federal Government must observe the Buy American Act; other purchasers are not required, but sometimes choose, to do so.

## 4. SECURITIES AND MONEY

The most common investment in U.S. business occurs when an alien buys securities (shares or bonds) or makes a dollar deposit with a bank in the U.S.

Many foreigners do this through their home bank. Such banks sometimes have a branch office in the U.S., where the securities are kept in physical custody. The shares are recorded in the name of the bank, and dividends are paid to the bank. The U.S. records do not disclose ownership by the foreign individual. When the foreign individual dies, the bank does not report it to the U.S. tax authorities, and the U.S. death taxes on the security portfolio of an alien nonresident are avoided. Money in the bank is not subject to U.S. death taxes. Interest on bank deposits is also exempt from income taxes. But the money must be in a bank account; money kept for aliens with a stockbroker is not exempt from death taxes. The distinction between banks and brokers is not always understood by foreigners (see Chapter 14).

Some foreigners prefer to make their security investments through stock-brokerage houses, many of which maintain offices in the principal cities abroad. Such investors should be conversant with the peculiar jargon of the securities market. *Blue chips* are the shares of leading corporations that have a long history of dividend payments. They are considered particularly safe and their price is usually high, particularly in relation to their earnings. The *price/earnings ratio* often is considered significant. Most corporations distribute as dividends only a fraction of their earnings. Sometimes, a stockholder receives *Rights* from a corporation. These are rights to purchase additional shares, usually at a price below the market price. *Rights* can be sold. Usually, shares are purchased in *round lots*, which means 100 shares or multiples thereof. The purchase or sale of fewer than 100 shares involves an *odd lot*. The purchase price of an *odd lot* is 1/8 point or 0.125 cents higher per share than the generally quoted price, and the proceeds of a sale of an *odd lot* is 1/8 point less. *Selling short* occurs when a seller sells shares that he does not own but expects to buy later at a lower price. Since sold shares must be promptly delivered, a *short sale* requires the seller and his broker to borrow shares. In the bond market it is important to realize that interest on bonds is usually paid twice a year and, therefore, a purchase and sale involves mostly *accrued interest*, which the purchaser must pay and the seller receives in addition to the price. Shares, and some bonds, are registered in the name of the owner. Some bonds, called *coupon bonds* are payable to the bearer. *Bearer bonds*, which are common in many countries, are now practically outlawed in the U.S. Investors sometimes speculate in *Puts and Calls*. A *Put* is a contract by which a person agrees to sell a certain stock at a certain time for a certain price. For instance, one has purchased a certain stock at $30. He *puts* it at $40 to somebody who wishes to buy a *Call* at that price. The buyer of a *Call* has the right to purchase a certain stock at a certain time for a certain price. Some U.S. stockbrokers specialize in *Puts and Calls*. Then there is the *Option* market, in which options for the purchase and sale of securities are traded. Most foreigners stay away from *Puts* and *Calls*, and from the *Option* market.

## 5. AMERICAN BRANCH OR SUBSIDIARY

An alien entrepreneur may wish to invest in the U.S. by opening a branch office in the U.S., or by organizing a corporation. If the alien entrepreneur is a corporation, the new corporation will be a subsidiary. This is touched upon in Chapter 2. Some of the pertinent tax aspects are dealt with in Chapter 8.

## 6. PARTNERSHIP AND JOINT VENTURE

Some aliens become partners in a U.S. enterprise, or invest money in an American joint venture. This is discussed in Chapter 12. The tax consequences are noted in Chapter 8.

## 7. ESTABLISHING A NEW BUSINESS

The Federal Government, as well as the state governments, welcomes the establishment of a new business. Indeed, some state governments and local municipal governments make special efforts to attract new business ventures, which are expected to create new products and new employment opportunities.

In Chapter 1 (Section 15), reference was made to the Federal Department of Commerce in Washington, D.C., and its sixty-eight field offices, where the foreign investor can obtain helpful information. The Economic Development Administration, a part of the Federal Department of Commerce, may make long-term loans of up to 65% of the cost of new equipment, land, and buildings, if funds are not otherwise available (Public Works and Economic Development Act of 1965). Another Federal helper is the Small Business Administration. The meaning of the term *small business*, in this context, will surprise many foreigners. A manufacturing company is considered small if it has fewer than 1,500 employees and its annual revenues do not exceed $8 million. The Small Business Administration is a source of loans, which may be needed to start a new business. Finally, the facilities of the Federal Export-Import Bank should be mentioned, and the Foreign Credit Insurance Association.

The assistance rendered by state and municipal governments takes various forms. This was alluded to in Section 8 of Chapter 1. Many states have special Industrial Development Offices, which can be located through the Federal Department of Commerce. Some foreign investors prefer to work through a U.S. Senator or other political leader(s). Puerto Rico offers particularly alluring incentives to new investors.

## 8. INDUSTRIAL REVENUE BONDS

Mention must also be made of the so-called Industrial Revenue Bonds, which are available in most states. A local government agency will establish a fund to be used for the building of a new factory, warehouse or office building, or the purchase of the necessary land. The money for the fund is raised by the sale of bonds. The interest income from the bonds is exempt from Federal and state income tax, and is, therefore, relatively low. The fund leases the property to the investor at a price that enables it to pay the bond interest. As the bond interest is low, the rental charge is low. Ultimately, of course, the bonds must be retired at the expense of the investor, at which time the investor usually can acquire the property at a nominal price. The Industrial Revenue Bonds thus help the investor with his cash flow problems in the early period, which under the law may last twenty-five years.

## 9. PURCHASING AN EXISTING BUSINESS

The U.S. business that a foreign enterprise seeks to acquire is generally incorporated. The foreign investor must ask whether it is preferable to purchase the shares, or a majority of the shares, of the American corporation or whether it is advisable to buy the assets or certain assets of the American corporation. In colloquial language, the acquisition is either a stock deal or an asset deal. The same question is raised in the case of a purely domestic acquisition. The purchaser will generally prefer an asset deal because it does not involve the assumption of liabilities, such as unknown future tax claims against the acquired corporation. There are other tax advantages in an asset deal, all of which should be explored. An important factor is the book value of the inventory. If the book value is low and the purchaser pays more, the purchaser will want an asset deal because it enables him to 'step up' the cost basis of the inventory and thus lower future taxable profits. Sometimes, in a domestic acquisition, the shareholders will accept as payment, shares of the acquiring corporation. Such a swap has tax advantages for the selling shareholder, and may be acceptable to the purchaser if the shares of the seller are traded and easily saleable on a national stock exchange. A swap is rarely acceptable if the shares, in order to be marketable, first must be registered with the Securities and Exchange Commission, or if their sale is otherwise restricted. If the acquiring corporation is a foreign entity, it is not likely that such a swap is acceptable either to a majority of the U.S. shareholders or to the foreign acquirer. A swap of shares, therefore, is hardly ever contemplated. The foreign purchaser of a domestic business will generally pay cash for the shares, if a stock deal is involved.

In an asset deal, the foreign investor will generally be interested in acquiring the name and the goodwill of the acquired business, even if he does not acquire the U.S. shares. This offers no difficulty because the existing U.S. corporation can be made to change its name; and it can be stipulated in the contract for the sale of the assets that the foreign investor shall have the right to use the name of the U.S. corporation. The foreign investor will also make sure that the acquisition contract prevents the U.S. company and its officers from competing with the acquired business.

The allocation of part of the purchase price to the non-competition agreement, as well as the allocation to goodwill, presents a conflict situation of which the purchaser must be aware. The price of the non-competition agreement represents ordinary income to the seller, and may be amortized (tax deducted) over its term by the purchaser. The seller ordinarily prefers to keep the figure low. Goodwill cannot be amortized by the purchaser, but it constitutes capital gain for the seller. The purchaser generally likes to keep this figure low. The price allocated to inventory and fixed assets determines future depreciation as well as the computation of the purchaser's future profits and capital gains. In most instances, it is desirable to fix the allocation of the total price to the various items in the purchase contract.

Before an investor approaches the shareholder(s) of the *target company*, he will generally negotiate with the management and the board of directors of the target company, in order to obtain their consent and their backing. The foreign investor will then make an offer to the shareholders, which is called a tender offer. Section 13 of the Securities and Exchange Act of 1934, often referred to as the Williams Act (named after Senator Williams who sponsored the legislation), requires the prospective purchaser to state the terms of the offer in great detail and to disclose if special arrangements have been made with the present management. More about tender offers in Chapter 18.

Section 11 of Chapter 1 has alluded to the pitfalls that some foreign investors have encountered after acquiring control of a U.S. enterprise. These remarks should be regarded as a note of caution rather than as a deterrent. No adverse reports are known about the department stores (Gimbels and Saks Fifth Avenue) that were acquired by a British tobacco firm, or about various banks that were acquired by Arab investors.

CHAPTER 7

# REAL PROPERTY INVESTMENTS

## 1. INTRODUCTION

One of the last official acts of former President Carter was his signing, in December 1980, of the Foreign Investment in Real Property Tax Act, which became Sec. 897 and 6039C of the Internal Revenue Code. The Act was revolutionary in that (a) it imposed a capital gains tax on the disposition of a real property interest by aliens who theretofore were not treated as being engaged in U.S. business, and (b) it imposed reporting requirements, which interfere with such desires for anonymity as may exist.

It makes no difference whether or not the real property is income-producing. A real property interest within the meaning of the new law is more than naked ownership of real property. It can be indirect ownership through a corporation, a partnership or a trust. There are two exceptions: (a) the Act applies only to a substantial investment, which is defined as an investment having a value of $50,000 or more; and (b) the Act does not apply where the alien is a mere creditor or lender. The statute speaks of an interest in real estate other than an interest *solely as a creditor*. The statute does not say what this means, nor do the applicable treasury regulations. One may, therefore, assume that a lender who has secured his interest by obtaining a mortgage on the property is not subject to the Act. However, it can also be argued that a mortgagee's interest is not solely that of a creditor. It has been suggested that a participating debt falls within the exception. A participating debt exists where the creditor, in addition to receiving normal interest payments, is entitled to participate in future appreciation or in a future rental increase or in the profit of a future sale. Such participation may well be regarded as equivalent to an equity investment and not a mere debt, in which case the investor's interest would not be regarded as solely that of a creditor.

The new legislation was a reaction to the great number of foreign investors who had acquired land and buildings of all sorts in all parts of the U.S., in cities as well as in rural areas. Some Americans feared that their country soon would

43

be predominantly in alien hands, a fear that is belied by the statistics. It was also felt that foreigners should be subjected to the same capital gains tax as citizens and residents.

One of the attractions of U.S. real estate investment is the comparative ease of financing. Loans are available for extended periods, sometimes as long as thirty or forty years. Often loans are made for as much as 70% or 80% of the value of the underlying property. In many cases, such loans can be obtained without personal liability of the borrower, so that if default occurs, the lender can only look to the property.

## 2. THE PURCHASE OF REAL PROPERTY

The technique of purchasing real property in the U.S. is more complicated than in most other countries. The chief reason for this is that there is no official record that can be relied upon as proof of ownership (title). In consequence, a purchaser cannot be sure that the seller is in a position to convey to him a *good title*. The purchaser must arrange for a *title search*, which is usually done after the contract of sale has been signed. The title report will reveal whether the property is encumbered by any mortgages or other liens. This information is not readily available. A careful purchaser will also buy *title insurance*, which compels the insurance company to remedy (or compensate for) any title defect that is not revealed by the title report. Both title search and title insurance are generally available from a title company for a fee. The practicality of this is illustrated by the following example: An entrepreneur made a contract for the purchase of a factory. A subsequent title search revealed that a former owner of one of the parcels of land on which the factory was located had sold the parcel some 100 years earlier without the required written consent of his wife. Consequently, the title to the factory was defective and the purchaser refused to complete the transaction until title was cleared. This involved a court action against the unknown heirs of the non-consenting deceased wife. The *closing* (as the final step is generally called) of the transaction was delayed for many months, to the chagrin of the seller. In California and other western states, it is customary to put the property in escrow until title is cleared. An escrow is held by a neutral third party depository.

Even when the purchaser does not search the title of the seller, there is generally a time lapse between the date of the purchase agreement and the closing of title or the closing of the escrow. During the interim period, the investor has occasion to inspect the property and the financial accounts pertaining thereto. The interim period also will be used to complete the financing arrangements, if any are made. It should be noted that U.S. financing institutions invariably insist on a title search, and generally title insurance as well. Payment to the seller will be made only if the purchaser (and the financing institution) is satisfied with the title of the seller.

## 3. *ADDITIONAL SERVICES AND EXPENSES*

Foreign investors are often inadequately informed about the cost and the kind of assistance needed in connection with a real estate investment. The first contact is usually with a broker, who finds the property and brings buyer and seller together. His commission is customarily paid by the seller. He cannot be expected to guarantee the title of the seller or the quality of the property.

The investor is generally well advised to obtain an independent appraisal of the property, as well as an engineering and land survey. The investor must understand that the broker, while an important source of information, is primarily motivated by the desire to make a sale. So is the foreign correspondent of the broker, who may share the broker's commissions and who may be the party with whom the foreign investor is in direct contact. The investor will probably need the services of an independent lawyer, who will guide him through the entire transaction. The lawyer's services may be limited to strictly legal matters, such as the applicable real estate law, title questions and tax law; or the lawyer may be used as a general adviser in selecting a suitable investment vehicle, obtaining financing, and the selection of necessary other aides, such as a public accountant and a property manager. The accountant should be requested to analyze the financial condition of any prospective investment. He will also be needed to monitor the financial operations, if the investment is made, and to prepare tax returns. It is desirable to employ an accountant who understands the accounting technique and the tax requirements of the investor's homeland.

Most properties need repairs from time to time, and they always need maintenance. To attend to this is the task of the property manager. A property manager is also needed where leases are involved, to collect rental payments. Sometimes the lawyer or the accountant, or even the broker, will act as property manager. Any of them must be compensated for this work. Before deciding on a particular investment, the foreign investor should obtain (usually through the broker) a projected financial statement, which reflects annual income and expenses of the property. In case of rental property, provision should be made for an expense reserve for possible vacancies. Insurance costs should not be omitted.

If the investment consists of unimproved land, the investor may hold the property either in the expectation of value appreciation, or for purposes of development. In the latter case, the foreign investor will probably deal with a local developer. This involves a sophisticated knowledge of the rules and practice of land use, and it may be a very profitable venture. This book does not explore the many technical aspects of land use, which are governed by Federal, state and municipal law.

## 4. *FINANCING*

Foreigners are sometimes astonished about the extent of real estate financing. It is not unusual to borrow 60–80% of the purchase price. In a recent substantial transaction, the seller received only 15% of the purchase price in cash. The seller was required to finance 85% of the purchase price. He did this by taking back a mortgage on the property. A mortgage that the seller retains on the property is called a purchase money mortgage. In times when interest rates run high, it is often difficult to find a buyer and, in desperation, the seller will take back a purchase money mortgage, possibly at an interest rate that is below the high current rate. The disadvantage of mortgage financing is, of course, that the purchaser is burdened with high interest costs. On the other hand, he enjoys tax advantages. The interest payments are income tax-deductible. More important still, as owner of a commercial building, the purchaser can claim depreciation on the basis of the full value of the real property, even if he has only paid a small fraction of the value. Depreciation is also an income tax-deductible item. The value of land is not depreciable, nor is the value of a private residence that is not rented out.

## 5. TAXATION

The decision of the investor will also hinge on the tax implications of the proposed transaction, both at home and in the U.S. In all instances, the ownership of U.S. real property involves a local real property tax. In addition, there is the Federal capital gains tax referred to earlier in this chapter. The tax consequences depend largely on the vehicle which is used for the investment.

Some investors shy away from any investment vehicle. They prefer direct personal ownership. The U.S. income tax consequences are discussed in Chapter 8. It should be borne in mind that as a result of the 1980 act (mentioned earlier in this Chapter) aliens owning a real estate interest will be taxed as being engaged in business in the U.S.

If several foreign individuals are involved, it is desirable, but not necessary, to designate one person who can act for all and in whose name the ownership (title) is recorded in the U.S.

## 6. INVESTMENT VEHICLES

The involvement of several investors will often lead to the formation of a partnership, which can be organized in the home country or in the U.S. (see Chapter 12). In that case it is also practical, but not necessary, to give one partner the power to act for all and to record the title in his or her name. Participation in the development of U.S. real property is often obtainable by the acquisition of a limited partnership interest. This is a convenient way of participating in a U.S. real estate venture that has tax attractions. Real estate partnerships frequently offer tax sheltered income as well as the prospect of long term capital gains. These are mentioned here because a partnership interest is generally available for relatively little capital. Many investment bankers and stock brokers offer shares in publicly syndicated partnerships. More about this subject in the Chapter 12 discussion of syndication.

The investment may also be made through a trust. This is discussed in Chapter 6, Section 1.

## 7. STATE LAWS

A foreign investor contemplating the acquisition of U.S. real estate should investigate the law of the state in which the investment is contemplated. A few states prohibit land ownership by aliens; other states restrict it. The prohibition or restriction generally also applies to indirect ownership through a partnership, a trust or a corporation. In most instances, the state obstacle is not very serious, but the prudent investor should not disregard or overlook it.

CHAPTER 8

# TAXATION

## 1. INTRODUCTION

The system of taxation in the U.S. is in constant flux. Anyone planning a specific transaction must investigate the applicable tax rules, and may then find that the transaction should be abandoned in favor of an alternative. This chapter is limited to a survey of the principal rules and concepts that are of importance to a foreigner who in some way may be subject to taxation in the

49

U.S. The estate (inheritance) and gift tax will only be considered where it is germane to a foreigner's business in the U.S. Excise and sales taxes will be disregarded altogether, because they are of minor importance and rarely influence a decision with respect to doing business in or with the U.S. There is no value added tax (VAT) in the U.S. This chapter concentrates on the Federal income tax (which is lower than that of many other countries). The Federal Government levies no property tax, as such. This is often a surprise to foreigners.

The taxes levied by the several states are, likewise, of subordinate importance. Some states have income taxes, some have property taxes, and some have both. The difference in the taxing methods of the states sometimes will influence the choice of location of a business. Ordinarily, however, business reasons and personal convenience are stronger factors in determining the location of a business than are state tax reasons. Moreover, the state tax rates are, as a rule, comparatively low. They apply to an alien individual only if he resides in the state or, in the case of a foreign corporation, if the corporation is engaged in business in the state.

All commercial activity involves tax problems. They surface in almost all chapters of this book. There is a distinction between tax avoidance, which is legal, and tax evasion, which is not. There are fewer tax law violators in the U.S. than in other countries. The reason is not greater morality but greater fear. The fear is justified because violations are more severely prosecuted than elsewhere. Tax fraud is generally punished by a jail sentence.

## 2. TAXABLE INCOME

Unlike other tax systems, the U.S. taxes its citizens and residents on all income from all parts of the world. However, if a citizen resides permanently in a foreign country, income earned in that country up to $85,000 ($90,000 in 1985 and $95,000 thereafter) is tax exempt. The exemption is subject to special rules.

Income taxation is initially based on self assessment. Each taxpayer must file a tax report after the end of each year (calendar or fiscal). The report is called a return.

Ordinarily, each person or corporation is a separate taxpayer. The amount of a taxpayer's income is computed either as of the time it is actually received (the cash basis) or as of the time when the right to receive it accrues (the accrual basis). Most individuals and businesses that render services are on the cash basis. Where inventory is involved, the taxpayer is on the accrual basis.

Not all revenue is subject to taxation as income. A capital repayment, e.g. the repayment of a debt, is not ordinarily taxable income. Nor is the payment of damages as compensation for the loss of a capital asset. Receipt of an inheritance is not taxable income, but income from a trust is. The redemption of a bond ordinarily would be a capital repayment, and not taxable income. This is not always the case, however, and redemption is, therefore, subject to special rules. Property received in a corporate reorganization, or upon liquidation of a corporation or an unincorporated business, is also subject to special rules.

## 3. EXEMPT INCOME

Some income is exempt from taxation. The foremost example is interest payments on municipal bonds.

Corporate reorganizations, in which property is moved from one taxpayer to another, are often tax-free by reason of specific statutory rules. The rules concerning tax-free reorganizations are complex. Foreigners doing business in the U.S. encounter these rules, for example, in connection with new acquisitions or the liquidation of a subsidiary. If a transfer to a foreign taxpayer is involved, tax exemption requires the approval of the Commissioner of Internal Revenue. A major purpose is to prevent tax-free removal of appreciated stock or assets from the U.S. tax jurisdiction.

## 4. CAPITAL GAINS

U.S. tax law distinguishes between ordinary income and capital gains. The latter are taxed at a lower rate than ordinary income, if the capital item has been owned for a long term (at present, more than one year). The lower rate is achieved by making 60% of the long-term gain nontaxable. Taxpayers and their advisers, therefore, constantly try to find ways of converting ordinary income into long-term capital gains. The attraction of capital gains transactions is sometimes marred by the recapture provisions of the law. If capital assets are disposed of, and the disposing taxpayer or a previous owner of the asset had the benefit of a depreciation or amortization deduction, a portion of these benefits will be subject to recapture by the tax collector, and taxed at ordinary income tax rates.

## 5. FOREIGN CURRENCY INCOME

For income tax purposes, foreign currency income must be expressed in U.S. dollars. This may lead to losses or gains that ordinarily are not thought of. It is an accounting problem and, therefore, discussed in Chapter 26.

## 6. DEDUCTIONS

In order to compute taxable income, gross income is reduced by a number of deductions. The deductible items are enumerated in the statute, but many of them are often the subject of dispute with the tax authorities. Business expenses are deductible, but they must be ordinary, necessary and reasonable. Travel expenses from London to New York may be necessary, but the extra cost of an expensive Concorde flight may not be reasonable. Payments for the benefit of employees, as discussed in Chapter 13, are generally deductible. Bribes to foreign persons may be allowable business expense deductions if they are not illegal. There may be a regular annual bad debt allowance, even if there are no bad debts in a particular year. The cost of a burglar alarm system for a warehouse may be a necessary business expense, but such an installation in a home is not. Interest payments are generally deductible from gross income. Dividend payments are not deductible, because they constitute a distribution of profits. Depreciation and depletion are very important deductions because they do not represent actual cash outlays. The allowance for depreciation and depletion, and the applicable rates, are provided for in the Internal Revenue Code. See also the discussion in Section 4, Chapter 26.

## 7. INVESTMENT TAX CREDIT

The difference between a tax deduction and a tax credit is not always understood. A deduction reduces taxable income. A credit reduces the tax.

The Internal Revenue Code provides for a number of tax credits. The most important is the investment tax credit. It is granted to the purchaser of capital goods. This may be costly industrial equipment or merely a typewriter. The credit is generally 10% of the purchase price. It amounts to a contribution by the Federal Government of 10% of the cost of capital assets, but it is taken, not in cash, but as a credit against income taxes.

The tax credit is of significant interest in the leasing of capital goods. If the user of the capital goods cannot utilize the credit because of insufficient taxable income, he can, in effect, transfer the benefit of the credit to another party who can use it. This is done by having the other party purchase the capital goods and lease them to the user. The user then pays a rental fee, which should be somewhat lower than would ordinarily be the case, since the owner of the capital goods has the benefit of the credit. Any credit that cannot be used may be carried back for three years and forward for fifteen years.

Investment credit is also important to homeowners. The cost of certain energy-saving improvements also qualifies for a tax credit.

## 8. FOREIGN TAX CREDIT

Taxable income may include foreign source income that has already been taxed abroad. Most international tax treaties aim to avoid such double taxation (see Section 24). The Internal Revenue Code offers an independent remedy against double taxation. This is the foreign tax credit. It can be applied against the U.S. income tax. The credit for foreign taxes extends to third tier foreign subsidiaries if their income is included in the U.S. parent's gross taxable income.

The foreign tax credit provisions of the Internal Revenue Code, and the regulations thereunder, are extensive and complicated.

## 9. THIN CAPITALIZATION

This refers to the capitalization of corporations. An investor often will prefer to make part of his investment in the form of a loan. A loan is preferable to an equity investment, because the equity investment is frozen and a loan can be easily repaid. A corporation is considered *thinly capitalized* when the investment in the equity of the corporation is too small in comparison to loans made to fund the corporation. In such cases, repayments of principal and payments of interest are treated as dividends, which cannot be deducted from the taxable income of the paying corporation. Foreign investors who decide on the establishment of a subsidiary in the U.S. are well advised to consider a proper ratio between equity investment and loans. The U.S. Treasury is currently engaged in the promulgation of regulations covering this complex subject, which has wide ramifications, and the assistance of a competent tax adviser is highly desirable in this area. If, as sometimes happens, no interest is paid to the foreign lender, the question of deductibility does not arise. If the foreign investor induces a third party to make a loan to the corporation, care must be taken that interest is actually paid. If no interest is paid to such friendly third party, the ultimate repayment of the loan may be treated as equivalent to a dividend, which is subject to U.S. withholding tax (see Section 22).

If several stockholders make loans in proportion to their stock ownership, it is difficult to avoid the inference that the loans are not equity in disguise.

## 10. INCOME DEEMED RECEIVED ALTHOUGH NOT ACTUALLY RECEIVED

When, at the end of a year, the U.S. taxpayer lists the income for the year, he is sometimes required to include sums that he has not actually received. A foreign enterprise sometimes overcharges its U.S. subsidiary; or, conversely, it makes sales at an unreasonably low price. This is done in order to manipulate the taxable profits. The Internal Revenue Code provides that in such a case the tax authorities may reallocate the profits between related parties, and the U.S. enterprise may thus find itself taxable on income that it has not actually received, but that, in the view of the tax authorities, it ought to have received. The reallocation of profits may carry with it a corresponding reallocation of business deductions.

In a DISC (see Section 24), a part of the income is taxed as a *deemed* dividend to its shareholder.

Imputed interest is another type of fictitious taxable income. If one makes a sale on credit without stipulating a normal interest rate for the deferred payment, the law will treat a part of each deferred payment as an interest payment. Interest may also be imputed in the case of an interest-free loan. The interest that a borrower would normally pay is generally taxed as income to the lender. This does not necessarily apply to short-term loans (six months) or to family loans.

Personal Holding Company income must also be mentioned here. The Internal Revenue Code distinguishes between a domestic Personal Holding Company and a Foreign Personal Holding Company. A Personal Holding Company has two principal characteristics: (*a*) it is owned by not more than five individuals, bearing in mind that members of a family and close associates count as one, and (*b*) a substantial part of its income, as defined in the statute, is passive income, such as dividends and rent. In both instances, undistributed corporate income is taxed. In a domestic Personal Holding Company, the corporation must pay a penalty tax, but the tax is limited to certain types of income (so-called Personal Holding Company income). Since the Foreign Personal Holding Company is outside the U.S. jurisdiction, it cannot be taxed in the U.S.; but all undistributed income, from all sources, that is allocable to U.S. shareholders (citizens, alien residents, and resident foreign corporations), is included in the taxable income of the U.S. shareholders. It is no excuse that the holding company may not have distributed the income because foreign blocking regulations forbade distribution. A confusing aspect is that in appropriate cases a foreign corporation may be regarded as a domestic Personal Holding Company.

In order to avoid arguments with the tax authorities and possible tax penalties, a taxpayer may include in his taxable income sums not actually received from a Personal Holding Company, as a so-called consent dividend.

The principle of tax liability for undistributed income is also applied in the case of a Controlled Foreign Corporation, except where the law permits the taxpayer to defer taxability until the foreign income of the corporation is repatriated. Here, too, the U.S. taxpayer may pay income tax on a consent dividend, which generally avoids source country withholding taxes.


## 11. PARTNERSHIPS

Investments in the U.S. are increasingly made in the form of a partnership participation. Chapter 12 deals with partnerships. For tax purposes, a partnership is merely a conduit for the partners. It is not a taxpayer, but it is required to file an information tax return. One of the partners is responsible to the Internal Revenue Service for the filing of the partnership return and dealing with any examination (audit) of the return. The partners must pay income tax on their *pro rata* share of the partnership profits, regardless of whether they are distributed to them. Since the partnership is a conduit, any long-term capital gains of the partnership are taxed to the partners at the lower capital gains tax rates. If the partnership year ends with a loss, each partner is entitled to claim the allocable part of the loss on his income tax return.

An unincorporated organization will be taxed as a corporation if it possesses three of the following four characteristics, which are considered corporate characteristics: (*a*) continuity of life, (*b*) centralized management, (*c*) limited liability and (*d*) free transferability of interests. These guidelines spring from the general principle that U.S. tax law looks to the substance rather than the form or label of a transaction.

If a nonresident alien acquires a so-called working interest in a partnership, joint venture, or syndicate that is engaged in oil or gas drilling operations in the U.S., such nonresident alien is considered, for tax purposes, as being engaged in trade or business in the U.S. As a result, he is taxed in the U.S. like any resident, but only with respect to income derived from sources within the U.S. This includes capital gains. Therefore, the fact that a nonresident alien has acquired a working interest in oil or gas drilling operations may subject more of his income to taxation, and at higher rates, than would otherwise be the case. (If the nonresident has acquired the partnership interest via a trust, he is not regarded as engaged in business in the U.S.)

However, this disadvantage may be offset by possible tax deductions that are allowed to a taxpayer who, with respect to his U.S. income, is taxed like a resident. Such taxpayer is allowed to deduct from his gross income his business expenses and losses connected with the U.S. income. Specifically, if he is engaged in oil or gas drilling operations, he may deduct his proportionate share of the intangible drilling costs of the operation; he can also claim the ordinary depreciation of his share of the capital investment, such as pipes and equipment, as well as deductions for other normal expenses incurred in connection with his business activity in the U.S. Furthermore, if income is received from the oil or gas operation, he can deduct therefrom the statutory depletion allowance, which at the present can be as high as 22% of gross income.

The advantage of the foregoing is that these deductions (other than the depletion allowance) can be taken against ordinary investment U.S. source income of the nonresident alien.

## 12. TRUSTS

Trusts are also conduits, but only with respect to income that is distributed or distributable to the trust beneficiaries. Trusts must pay taxes on income that is not required to be distributed. The trust is not used often by foreigners doing business in the U.S., possibly because its potential for investment is not well known abroad. However, there may be circumstances that make a trust a suitable and attractive investment vehicle for a nonresident alien (see also Chapter 6, Section 1).

## 13. RESIDENT ALIENS

An alien who resides in the U.S. is treated like a resident U.S. citizen. His entire income, from all parts of the world, is subject to tax. The fact that some or all of that income may also be taxed in his homeland, or in some other country, does not prevent full tax liability in the U.S., except where treaties avoid or minimize such double taxation. In one respect, alien residents are worse off than U.S. citizens. The law allows citizens to reduce the amount of their income tax by the amount of foreign income taxes levied in the same year. Alien residents may claim such tax credit only if their homeland allows similar privileges to U.S. citizens. An alien resident who cannot claim a foreign tax credit may still deduct the amount of the foreign tax from his gross income, thereby reducing his taxable income. This is often overlooked.

When is an alien a resident of the U.S.? If the alien has immigrated to this country and makes his permanent home here, the question offers no problem. However, there are immigrants who maintain no residence in the U.S., and there are residents who came as visitors and never immigrate. Such people often misunderstand their tax status. B immigrated from Switzerland in 1940. In 1941 he returned to his homeland after procuring a re-entry permit, to which an immigrant is entitled when he goes abroad for a temporary visit. He never came back to the U.S. It was held that for tax purposes B was a resident of the U.S. during the entire year 1941. His application for a re-entry permit precluded him from claiming that he was a resident of Switzerland for part of the time. The case illustrates a principle that applies (in the absence of an emergency) to all aliens who avail themselves of an immigrant visa without actually intending to reside in the U.S. Incidentally, it does not follow that payment of the tax, as a resident, would secure Mr. B's re-entry; the immigration authorities could still turn him back on the ground that his visit to Switzerland was, in reality, not *temporary*. Nevertheless, an immigrant desirous of maintaining his status while away from the country should continue his income tax payments as a resident, as this will be powerful proof of his intention to remain a resident of the U.S. In a borderline case, the authorities will probe the intent of a party, and draw inferences from the party's conduct.

The visa classification through which an alien gains entry to this country is not controlling with respect to residence status under the tax law. A person who comes to the U.S. with a visitor's visa may be a resident for tax purposes, if he is not a mere transient who wishes to accomplish a definite purpose within a limited time. Under the tax law, the length and nature of the visit determines the residence status of an alien. The ordinary business visitor is not a resident. However, if he comes with a treaty merchant's visa, which entitles him to stay indefinitely in order to promote trade with his homeland, he will probably be treated as a resident, even if he maintains a domicile in his homeland. For this reason, a foreign businessperson who must make frequent visits to the U.S., must consider the consequences carefully before availing himself of the convenience of a treaty merchant's visa, even if it is available.

The line between the concept of residence and of domicile is blurred. It is said that a person may have several residences, but only one domicile. Domicile is the place where one intends to stay for an indefinite period of time. A resident, even if not domiciled here, must pay U.S. income taxes. But gift taxes and estate (death) taxes are levied only against a domiciliary.

## 14. NONRESIDENT ALIEN INDIVIDUALS NOT DOING BUSINESS IN THE U.S.

Alien individuals, who are not engaged in business in the U.S. and are not residents, are only taxed on certain income derived from sources within the U.S., or which is effectively connected with a U.S. business. With minor exceptions, such aliens pay income tax only on fixed or determinable annual or periodic income (dividends, interest, rent, salaries, annuities, royalties, license fees and the like) and on gains from the sale of a patent. The tax is a flat rate of 30%, which the U.S. payor must withhold at the source. Tax treaties have abolished or lowered this tax in many instances.

An important exception provides that interest on bank deposits is tax-free, including interest on a certificate of deposit.

If a nonresident alien sells property in the U.S., he is not regarded as being engaged in business here, provided he is not a dealer in property. Except for the sale of real property (see Chapter 7), such an alien is not liable for capital gains taxes, which is particularly important in connection with the sale of U.S. stocks and bonds. If such an alien is the beneficiary of a U.S. trust, care should be taken on the occasion of the termination of the trust, when the alien may be entitled to receive the proceeds of the securities portfolio of the trust. If the U.S. trustee sells the securities, capital gains tax must be paid. If the securities are distributed to the alien or his U.S. agent and the alien then makes the sale, no capital gains tax is due.

Some securities portfolios contain shares of non-U.S. corporations, such as those of International Nickel Corporation, a Canadian corporation. Their dividends are not from sources within the U.S. and, hence, are not subject to U.S. withholding tax. Some dividends of U.S. corporations constitute, at least in part, repayment of capital. Such part is not subject to tax. No deductions, credits, or other offsets are allowed against the flat rate withholding tax.

Férenc Molnar, the famous playwright, who was, at the time, a nonresident alien, sold his rights to a play to a U.S. publisher for a lump sum. He contended that his profit therefrom was not taxable, inasmuch as it was a capital gain. However, it was held that the payment to Molnar was, in reality, a license fee, in the nature of fixed periodic income, and hence taxable. The British humorist, Wodehouse, had a similar distressing experience.

## 15. NONRESIDENT ALIEN INDIVIDUALS DOING BUSINESS IN THE U.S.

Nonresident aliens engaged in business in the U.S. are taxed, at the variable rates applicable to citizens and residents, on all business income from U.S. sources, and on such income from foreign sources as is *effectively connected* with the nonresident's U.S. business. They are also taxed, at the flat rate of 30% (or lower rate, if provided by a tax treaty), on U.S. source investment income (i.e. fixed or determinable periodic income, see above) that is effectively connected with the nonresident's U.S. business. There are detailed rules as to when foreign income is considered effectively connected with the nonresident's domestic business.

## 16. FOREIGN CORPORATIONS

Foreign corporations are treated in much the same fashion as foreign individuals. If they are not engaged in business in the U.S., only their fixed, periodic income, such as dividends, interest, etc., and income effectively connected with the U.S., is taxed. The tax rate is also the same flat percentage, namely 30% of the gross income, unless lowered or abolished by a tax treaty (see Section 24 below).

If the foreign corporation is engaged in business in the U.S., it is considered to be a resident foreign corporation, although it may not have an office or place of *residence* in the U.S. In such case, the foreign corporation is taxed like a nonresident alien doing business in the U.S., as described in the preceding section of this chapter. To determine net income, there may be deducted from gross income all proper expenses allocable to the business from which the gross income is derived. Also 85% of the dividends that such resident foreign corporation may receive from U.S. corporations is tax-exempt. However, no tax credit is allowed for taxes that the corporation may pay in its home country or any other foreign country. The tax rate is graduated, just as in the case of domestic U.S. corporations, except that the minimum tax is higher, that is, never less than 30%.

Shipping corporations and foreign insurance companies are subject to special rules.

The tax burden on some foreign corporations has been lessened by the tax treaties between the U.S. and many countries referred to below (see Section 24 below).

Foreign corporations are not eligible for inclusion in an affiliated group, which may file a consolidated tax return. A Controlled Foreign Corporation is a foreign corporation of which U.S. shareholders own at least 50% of the voting power. U.S. shareholders are taxed on their proportionate shares of certain of its income, whether distributed or not (see Section 9 above).

## 17. WHAT CONSTITUTES BEING ENGAGED IN BUSINESS

This is a tricky concept. 'Doing Business' has no precise legal definition and is, therefore, a flexible term. Negatively, it can be stated that the collection of investment income, the mere ownership of property, or an isolated purchase or sale does not constitute being engaged in business in the U.S. But when is a purchase or sale isolated? Will a second purchase or sale change the tax status of the foreign party? Even one purchase or sale cannot be regarded as isolated if it marks the beginning of a regular activity. A safe guideline is that, to be engaged in business for tax purposes, the activity of the alien or foreign corporation must be substantial, continuous and regular in nature. Maintaining an office in the U.S. is not necessary. If an alien or foreign corporation acts through a U.S. agent, the agent's activity constitutes doing business by the foreign principal. The situation is different if the so-called agent is an independent distributor not subject to the direction of the foreign principal. A tailor from Hong Kong or London who visits the U.S. periodically and sees his customers or prospective customers in hotel rooms is engaged in business in the U.S.

Ownership of shares of a U.S. corporation does not constitute doing business in the U.S. The situation may be different if the foreign owner controls the day-to-day operation of the corporation.

Naturally, if an alien opens an establishment in New York, he is engaged in business in the U.S. A branch office or a factory would be such an establishment.

The alien is, of course, also engaged in business in the U.S. if he buys merchandise in New York and sells it in San Francisco. Or if he sells merchandise in the U.S. which he has brought with him for that purpose. The performance of personal services in the U.S. for which an alien receives a commission or other compensation also constitutes doing business in the U.S. An exception prevails if an alien stays in the U.S. no longer than ninety days of the year, and if his total U.S. compensation during such year is not more than $3,000. The exemption is often broader in the case of aliens who enjoy the benefit of tax treaties between their countries and the U.S.

A foreign businessperson who visits the U.S. for the purpose of soliciting orders, or simply to supervise his or his company's investment in the U.S., is considered as engaged in business in the U.S., although a person may not earn any taxable income here. The same applies to a foreign employee whose compensation for services in the U.S. is paid abroad. If a foreigner uses the occasion of a visit to America for a stock exchange speculation, any profit derived therefrom is taxable to him as a capital gain, but only if he spent at least 183 days of the tax year in the U.S. This rule applies to all capital gains of nonresident aliens that are not *effectively connected* with a U.S. domestic business.

Ordinarily, the mere buying and selling of stocks, bonds, or commodities by a nonresident alien is not considered as being engaged in business, so long as such trading is done through a U.S. broker. Aliens abroad do this all the time without exposing themselves to U.S. income tax claims. A nonresident alien may earn his livelihood by daily stock exchange or commodity exchange transactions through a broker or bank in New York – that still is not considered being engaged in business. But if he establishes his own office or employs a salaried person in the U.S. for the purpose of assisting in such transactions, he is engaged in business, even if the transactions are effectuated through a broker.

If the nonresident alien is the grantor or a beneficiary of a U.S. trust that is administered by a U.S. trustee, the alien is not regarded as engaged in business in the U.S., although his trustee is.

The ownership of a building, or other real estate from which a nonresident receives rental income, is not regarded as doing business in the U.S., even though the income stems from a U.S. source, unless a local management agent is employed. An alien who is a partner of a firm that is engaged in business in the U.S. will, himself, be treated as so engaged, although he may never visit the U.S. in person.

An interesting and controversial court decision concerns a Mexican broadcasting station. Its principal income was derived from U.S. advertisers whose advertisements were broadcast from Mexico to the U.S. The company had an office in a Texas hotel room, where it also received mail. The corporation had an agent in Texas who solicited business and collected debts in the U.S. The courts ruled that the income of the Mexican company was not taxable because it was not engaged in business in the U.S., nor was its income from U.S. sources (see Section 18 below).

The tax treaties that the U.S. has with many nations generally are more precise in defining what constitutes doing business in the U.S. The treaties, while not uniform, generally require that the alien have a permanent establishment in the U.S.

## 18. WHAT IS INCOME FROM U.S. SOURCES?

In the Mexican broadcasting decision, the court considered Mexico as the source of the advertising income because the broadcast originated there. In the case of manufacturing, the country of manufacture is always treated as the source of the income. Where the profit is derived from buying and selling, the place where ownership passes to the buyer is generally regarded as the source of the income. If a person in New York sells an article to a man in Bombay, it is generally within the choice of the parties whether, legally speaking, New York or Bombay is the place of sale. It is a question of sales contract law, which is dealt with in Chapter 10.

If a manufacturer in the U.S. sells directly to a customer in a foreign country, the tax law considers the profit as deriving partly from sources within and partly from sources without the U.S. The same rule applies under some double taxation treaties.

In these cases, the taxpayer faces the difficult problem of allocation of profits. The problem can be avoided by organizing two separate companies. Unless this is done to artificially reduce a normal profit, such an arrangement will not be questioned by the U.S. tax authorities. Whether it is commercially feasible depends on the particular circumstances of each case. It must suffice here to draw attention to the general principle involved.

Some confusion exists in the minds of international trade people with respect to the taxation of compensation paid for services. In U.S. tax law, the source of the payment for services rendered is not the payor of the money, but the place where the services were performed. In consequence, the foreign agent of a U.S. concern is not subject to U.S. taxation on the commissions he receives from the U.S. for services rendered abroad. The American principal has no right to withhold a part of such commission for taxes, although this is sometimes mistakenly done. However, if the alien receives payment for his services in the U.S., he is subject to U.S. taxes, except when his stay in any one year does not exceed ninety days and his total U.S. compensation does not exceed $3,000. These figures differ in the case of some nationals who enjoy the benefit of tax conventions.

Income from investments in the U.S., such as dividends and interest, is from sources within the U.S. This is easily understood, and yet even that rule has exceptions. If the gross income of the U.S. person or corporation paying such dividends or interest is largely derived from foreign sources (more than 80%), then such interest or dividends are not considered income from sources within the U.S. That is the reason why nonresident aliens pay no income tax on interest paid to them on bonds of the International Bank for Reconstruction and Development.

If a foreign writer sells the motion picture rights in a play to a Hollywood producer, or if a foreign investor transfers his patent to a U.S. manufacturer on a royalty basis, he should distinguish in his contract between the royalty payable for the use of his rights in the U.S. and the royalty payable for the use of his rights in foreign countries. The former is taxable income from sources within the U.S.; the latter is not. People have overlooked this distinction and sold their world rights for one fixed royalty. In such case, the Commissioner of Internal Revenue cannot readily determine the part of the royalty allocable to domestic, and the part allocable to foreign, exploitation. Under these circumstances, the law gives the Commissioner the right to treat the entire income as from sources within the U.S., and he will usually do just that. Royalty income is generally considered as coming from the source where the patent, trademark or copyright is used. Many tax treaties exempt royalties from U.S. taxation.

The framework of this book does not permit a further discussion of this problem. The foregoing will sufficiently demonstrate its practical importance.

## 19. DOMESTIC CORPORATIONS

It seems appropriate at this point to survey the tax position of the domestic American corporations, a substantial number of which are owned or controlled by foreign owners. It is not intended to present the entire body of U.S. corporate tax law. That law fills many learned volumes.

Most foreigners doing business in the U.S. do so by organizing a domestic corporation. If the foreign investor is a corporation, the domestic corporation becomes a subsidiary of the foreign parent corporation. The subsidiary should not operate as a mere branch of the foreign parent, lest the foreign parent be considered as doing business in the U.S., and be taxed accordingly.

In Chapter 1, Section 8, reference was made to tax incentives offered by states and municipalities for the establishment of new plants. The Federal tax law also offers a powerful incentive by granting a substantial credit for new investments in plants, equipment and the like – the so-called investment tax credit, described in Section 6, above.

Unlike its counterpart in other countries, a U.S. corporation is taxed on its profits without regard to any dividend distributions. Thus, the corporate profits are, in effect, taxed twice: first at the corporate source, and then in the hands of the dividend-receiving shareholders. This cannot be avoided by not paying dividends, because the unreasonable accumulation of corporate profits attracts a penalty tax. There are exceptions to this harsh principle. The liquidation of a corporation can be so structured that the corporation pays no tax while the shareholders pay (with some exceptions) only the lower rate capital gains tax on the liquidating distributions made to them. Certain corporations (formerly known as Subchapter S corporations and now called S corporations) may elect to have their profits taxed directly to the shareholders. This is subject to a number of technical rules. Nonresident aliens are not eligible for this benefit, but might obtain it through a properly structured accumulation trust. Another small business provision is of more practical interest for one starting a business in the U.S. Ordinarily, if the new venture is unsuccessful and the shares become worthless or the corporation is liquidated, the owner has a capital loss that permits a limited tax deduction. In the case of a small business corporation (capital of not more than $1 million), the failed entrepreneur can claim up to $50,000 as an ordinary operating loss, which is fully deductible from other taxable income. See also the discussion of start-up expenses in Chapter 26, Section 7.

There is a variety of special rules for special types of corporations, many of which are of little interest to an alien doing business in the U.S. In view, however, of the lively participation of foreigners in the U.S. real estate market and construction activity, it seems worthwhile to state that interest costs and taxes paid during the construction period must be capitalized. They will generally be amortized over ten years.

The Internal Revenue Code accords favored treatment to certain types of corporations that promote U.S. exports. These are dealt with in Section 23.

## 20. TAX RATES

Except for the withholding tax rates on the fixed and periodic income of nonresidents, the annual income tax rate is graduated and increases with the income. Individuals must pay at rates from 12% to 50%. Domestic and foreign resident corporations are taxed at 15% of the first $25,000 of taxable income; the second $25,000 is taxed at 18%; the third $25,000 at 30%; the fourth $25,000 at 40%; and all taxable income over $100,000 is taxed at 46%. These rates may sound paradisiacal to many citizens of other industrial countries, but the picture is a little more complicated. Taxpayers may be liable for additional taxes if they enjoy substantial so-called tax preferences, such as the benefit from lower capital gains taxes. Tax preferences are defined in detail in the Internal Revenue Code. For instance, the tax exemption for municipal bond interest is not considered a tax preference.

## 21. TAX YEAR

The income tax must be computed for each twelve-month period. Individuals are always calendar year taxpayers, except that the first year may be a short year. Corporations can choose any twelve-month period as their first fiscal tax year, and they also may, at the inception, choose a short year.

## 22. PAYMENT DATES

Individuals must file a tax return three and one-half months after the end of each tax year (April 15). The filing and payment date for nonresident aliens is June 15. Corporations must file two and one-half months after the end of each tax year – March 15 in the case of a calendar year corporation. It is possible to obtain extensions; but then, interest must be paid from the original due date to the date of payment. All taxpayers also must prepay, quarterly, the tax that they estimate will be due at the end of the year. An underestimate, as well as delay in any payment, is subject to interest and penalty.

## 23. WITHHOLDING TAX

The technique of withholding U.S. tax on payments to foreigners is so well known in most parts of the world that it requires no explanation. The wages of resident employees and certain pension payments are also subject to withholding tax. The same applies to dividends from U.S. mutual funds which invest primarily in non-U.S. securities and Eurodollar certificates of deposit (see Chapter 14, Section 13). It bears repeating that foreigners can avoid the withholding tax if their investments in the U.S. are from sources without the U.S.

## 24. EXPORT INCENTIVES

Like many other countries, the U.S. grants special concessions to the export trade. This is noted here because many foreigners who are engaged in business in the U.S. are involved in the export business. A popular vehicle is the Domestic International Sales Corporation (DISC). Generally, the DISC is the export arm of a U.S. manufacturing corporation. It is organized as a subsidiary of the manufacturer. The parent may be a foreign corporation located outside the U.S. The necessary qualifications of a DISC include the requirements that at least 95% of its gross receipts must be qualified export receipts, and at least 95% of its assets must be qualified export assets of U.S. origin. The DISC pays no tax on its income, so long as it maintains its status. 57.5% of its income, even if not distributed, is deemed to be a taxable dividend to the DISC's shareholders, generally the parent corporation. 42.5% may be loaned as a so-called producer's loan to an export manufacturer, generally, also, the parent corporation. Interest on such loan is deemed to be a dividend to the shareholder of the DISC; the shareholder must treat this as *deemed* paid, and hence, taxable income. The DISC need not be a seller. It can also act as a commission agent for export sales.

The DISC has been attacked abroad as an improper subsidy that violates U.S. commitments under GATT (see Chapter 22). The U.S. Government has promised a revision. It is uncertain what Congress will do (see Chapter 22).

The Western Hemisphere Corporation export benefit has been discontinued (Sec. 922(b), IRC). The Export Trading Company Act of 1982 is another device to spur the development of export trading companies. The law encourages joint ventures and loosens certain antitrust strictures.

*The Controlled Foreign Corporation*, mentioned in Section 15 above, may be regarded as an export incentive because its taxable income is taxed to U.S. shareholders only if repatriated.

The Export Trade Corporation is a sub-species of the Controlled Foreign Corporation. The export income of this corporation is never taxed.

## 25. TAX TREATIES

The U.S. has concluded, and continues to negotiate, tax treaties with numerous countries. The principal aim of these treaties is to avoid double taxation. The treaties are often revised. They are not uniform, and, therefore, should be examined in each case. Most treaties provide that they are for the benefit of residents of the treaty country. Some treaties stipulate that the alien must be not only a resident, but a national or a citizen, of a party country. The U.S. treaties generally limit the taxability of a nonresident individual and corporation to situations where the nonresident maintains a permanent establishment in the U.S. The concept of permanent establishment is important, and often is defined and circumscribed in the treaty. A U.S. subsidiary as such is generally not regarded as a permanent establishment. The general effect of the treaty provision is to prevent the taxation of nonresidents beyond the provisions of the treaty. As a result, a treaty often removes the statutory strictures that treat a nonresident as doing business in the U.S. This is not an unmixed blessing. The nonresident who is not doing business has no right to claim tax deductions that are available to one who is engaged in business in the U.S. The tax treaties generally reduce the flat withholding tax on dividends from 30% to 15%, and often eliminate the withholding tax on interest and royalty payments. Foreigners sometimes seek to obtain the benefit of a U.S. tax treaty by dealing through an organization that they establish in a treaty country. For that reason, the U.S. has terminated a number of its tax treaties, and is now renegotiating its treaty with the Netherlands Antilles. The subject of what is called *treaty shopping* and the abuse of so-called tax shelters are matters of constant concern to the U.S. Government. This injects a note of caution in all tax planning.

Some treaties contain special provisions for intercompany pricing. It was noted above that related companies sometimes manipulate their prices, and that a provision of the Internal Revenue Code allows the Commissioner to reallocate such profits in a realistic manner.

Another feature of many treaties is a provision for cooperation and mutual disclosure among the parties to a tax treaty. Foreign investors must realize that if they obtain a treaty tax reduction in the U.S., the event will be communicated to the tax authorities of their home country.

The tax treaties do not affect the income taxes levied by the states of the United States.

## 26. STATE TAXATION

For the reasons stated at the outset of this chapter, the minor, but not negligible, state taxation systems are not discussed here. However, two state tax problems warrant mention.

Most states tax the income of taxpayers who do business in several states on a proportionate basis, i.e. the proportion of the income allocable to the taxing state. The allocation is generally made by using a formula, the most common of which is the three factors formula. The three factors are payroll, property, and sales in the taxing state. Many states, among them California, apply this formula to the worldwide consolidated income of the local corporation, including the income of its domestic and foreign subsidiaries, provided they are an integral part of the taxpayer's operation. This is called the unitary business principle. The Supreme Court has ruled that states that use this unitary principle do not violate the constitutional prohibition against taxing interstate or foreign commerce, even though the state bases its tax on income that is not earned in the state.

At this writing, twelve states have adopted the unitary method of tax assessment. This has caused considerable irritation abroad and threats of retaliation. President Reagan has appointed a task force to examine whether it would be appropriate to resolve the problem by Federal legislation. A report, but no change, may be expected by the end of 1984.

The second problem of general interest is the property tax that some states levy on property temporarily stored in the state, but which is part of interstate or foreign commerce. The French Michelin company was unsuccessful when it complained about the Georgia property tax. The Xerox Corporation was successful when it protested against a similar tax in Texas. Each case depends on its peculiar facts.

# CHAPTER 9

# CONTRACTS

## 1. INTRODUCTION

Contract law permeates the entire field of doing business in the U.S. This chapter deals only with general contract concepts, and a few special types of contractual relationships that are not discussed in other parts of this book. The subject of sales is covered in Chapter 10.

## 2. FORMATION OF CONTRACT

As in other countries, a U.S. contract is formed by an offer and acceptance. This applies to contracts that are made by word of mouth (oral contracts) as well as to written contracts. An astonishing number of controversies arise because the rule is not properly understood.

The acceptance of the offer must be on the terms of the offer. Otherwise it is not an acceptance. A limited exception to this rule exists with respect to sales contracts, as mentioned in Chapter 10, Section 2. Generally, if an acceptance contains new or different terms, it is regarded in law as a counter offer. If it is accepted, expressly or by conduct, the terms of the counter offer will govern the contract.

Unless the terms of the offer provide otherwise, an acceptance becomes effective when it is mailed or wired, not when it is actually received by the offeror. Consequently, if seller Smith, offers merchandise to buyer, Bliss, by mail, and three days later writes another letter revoking the offer, such revocation is ineffective if before he receives the letter Bliss has placed a letter of acceptance in the mails. An offer may be accepted long before the party making the offer learns about it. Since an offer, if not revoked, is ordinarily binding for a reasonable time within which it may be accepted, caution is indicated, particularly in times of fluctuating markets and where long distance transactions are involved.

Two common precautions are (*a*) a clause in the offer that it shall not be considered accepted unless and until acceptance is received by the offeror, and (*b*) a clause limiting the time for acceptance. Another method of protection is to stipulate that acceptance shall not be binding upon the offeror until confirmed by him. In such a case, the original offer is actually no offer at all but merely the solicitation of an offer.

Contracts are not always made by formal *offer and acceptance* or *order and confirmation*. Frequently, a contract develops out of a series of communications by letter, cable or telex. In that case, it is often difficult to determine which communication constitutes the *offer* and which the *acceptance*. It may be necessary, nevertheless, to make such determination, because only thus can it be ascertained at which time and at which place the contract was made. It is the act of acceptance that effectuates the contract.

The time of the acceptance is important, because any conditions that a party may thereafter attempt to inject are of no legal effect, unless the other party agrees. Some sellers state on their invoices conditions of payment that were not agreed upon at the time of the making of the contract. Such new conditions may be disregarded.

The place where the contract was concluded is often significant in international trade, from a tax point of view (see Chapter 8). In addition, the place of the formation of the contract may determine the state law by which the contract is to be governed. A realization of this will often lead the prudent businessperson to arrange the organization of his business or his correspondence so that the *acceptance* of the contract takes place in the country whose law is most advantageous for him.

An agreement to agree in the future is not a binding contract. Nor is a so-called letter of intent, which is very popular in the U.S. Businesspeople in the U.S. often do not realize that a letter of intent is legally meaningless.


## 3. WHAT LAW GOVERNS

The law permits the parties to stipulate in the contract the law that shall govern its interpretation and performance, so long as the choice of law has some reasonable connection with the subject matter of the contract. It is advisable to include such a provision in every contract when the parties reside in different jurisdictions. In the absence of such a provision, judges or arbitrators will apply general choice of law principles, but which are not always clear. Courts and scholars often disagree on this subject. A contract clause can remove the uncertainty of interpretation.

In New York, a loan contract that requires an individual to pay more interest than is allowed by New York usury laws (see Chapter 14, Section 11) is absolutely illegal, and the lender cannot even demand the repayment of the loan. If a contract is made outside of the state of New York, the law of that other place governs and the contract may be legal, and hence enforceable even in the courts of New York.

As a general rule, the validity and the interpretation of a contract is governed by the law of the place where it was made. If at the place of making the contract, a stamp is required to make it legal, the lack of a stamp makes the contract invalid in the U.S. A Frenchman may enter into a contract in violation of the French currency control laws. If the contract is made in France, it is invalid, and U.S. courts will so hold. But if the contract is made in the U.S., it is enforceable, as the French law is generally not binding in the U.S. However, that is not true if the contract is to be performed in France. While the validity of a contract is determined by the law under which it is made, all matters relating to performance are generally governed by the law of the place of performance. If performance in France is illegal, then U.S. courts will recognize this and nonperformance in France will not be considered a breach of contract.

Similarly, if the question arises whether a seller has done all the acts required of him under a sales contract, that question will be determined by the law of the place where such performance is called for. This is one of the reasons why a foreigner who does not wish to become involved with U.S. legal requirements will make it clear in his export contract that performance on his part will be completed in his own country.

All these rules about what law governs in a given situation are subject to the general principle that U.S. courts will not enforce any contract obligation that is contrary to U.S. public policy (see Chapter 1, Section 15). For instance, the stipulation for a penalty in case of breach of contract, which is quite common in foreign countries, is against U.S. public policy. Likewise, it is against public policy for a public carrier, such as a railroad or a steamship company, to exclude liability for its negligence. Thus, a bill of lading of the Canadian Pacific Railroad provided that the railroad should not be liable for damage to the shipper's merchandise caused by the negligence of the railroad. That clause was valid at the place where the contract was made. Nevertheless, when the shipper sued the Canadian Pacific Company in a New York court for damages resulting from negligence, he won his case. The court disregarded the exemption clause in the bill of lading because it violated its public policy.

The Cuban branch of a Canadian insurance company sold a life insurance policy to a Cuban resident. When the Cuban died, the beneficiary of the policy, residing in Florida, sued the insurance company in Florida for payment of the insurance benefit in U.S. dollars. The insurance company asserted that Cuban law governed the contract, and required payment in pesos. The court applied Florida and Canadian law, both of which required payment in U.S. dollars.

Another instance in which the question of the governing law arises is the statute of limitation, sometimes referred to as prescription. The time limits for commencing a court action are not the same in all states. When a contract is silent as to what law governs, a shrewd plaintiff will avoid a jurisdiction that outlaws the claim.

## 4. STIPULATION OF FORUM

In many countries, it is not unusual to stipulate in a contract that all disputes must be submitted to a certain judicial forum, which shall have exclusive jurisdiction. Such a contract clause will not be recognized by U.S. courts unless the forum state has substantial contacts with the transaction. The rule does not apply to arbitration clauses, where the arbitration tribunal is virtually always agreed upon by the parties (see Chapter 24, Section 3).

Another exception to the rule seems to apply in the field of maritime law. In the celebrated *Zapata* case, the Supreme Court ruled that the parties were bound by their agreement to submit to the London Court of Justice all disputes arising out of their transoceanic towing contract. Neither party was British, and the London court was apparently regarded as an expert arbitrator. Also, the contract contained an exemption-from-liability clause that would be given effect in an English court but not in the American courts. This, incidentally, points up that heated disputes over choice of law and forum selection are often motivated by reasons that are not apparent. The *Zapata* decision of the Supreme Court was a departure from the theretofore universal rule that forum selection clauses oust the jurisdiction of the courts and therefore are void as violating public policy. The *Zapata* decision was a recognition of the requirements of international business. Said the Court, '. . . in an era of expanding world trade and commerce, the absolute aspects of the [ouster of jurisdiction] doctrine of the *Carbon Black* case have little place and would be a heavy hand indeed on the future development of international commercial dealings . . .'. *Zapata* has been viewed by some as applying beyond the field of maritime law, and as allowing generally private forum selection clauses if they impose no unreasonable burden, as sometimes happens in adhesion contracts (to which reference is made below).

## 5. FORM OF CONTRACT

Contracts may be made by word of mouth. Agreements between stockbrokers and their customers usually are made by telephone and are held binding by common usage. Generally, however, U.S. law is based on the assumption that oral contracts invite fraudulent claims. The law that requires that most significant contracts be in written form is known by the English common law term, the Statute of Frauds. The Statute of Frauds is rather complex and often litigated. As a practical matter, anybody doing business in the U.S. is well advised to have all meaningful contract terms incorporated in a written agreement.

## 6. GENERAL REQUIREMENTS OF A CONTRACT

There must be a complete agreement of the contracting parties with respect to all essentials. Consequently, a sales agreement that leaves open the price generally is not a binding contract (but see Chapter 10, Section 4), because an essential element has not been agreed upon. For the same reason, there is no valid contract where a person agrees to render services and to be paid therefor a percentage of profits to be agreed upon later.

An astonishing number of commercial contracts have been held invalid by U.S. courts on the ground that the agreement was indefinite. Businesspeople often are intentionally indefinite; they want to see how matters develop. The result may be that neither party is bound to anything. One doing business in the U.S. should guard against this pitfall.

The British film actor, James Mason, once made an agreement with a Hollywood film executive. They agreed to form a company that was to produce James Mason films. Each party was to own 50% of the shares of the company, and was to receive a salary. Mason was to work exclusively for the company, but he did not. The Hollywood executive was to make all necessary financial arrangements. The Hollywood executive sued Mason, but lost. The court ruled that the agreement was invalid because it lacked definiteness. It did not furnish particulars as to how the Hollywood executive was to arrange the financing.

A second requirement is that a contractual obligation must be supported by a consideration. If Jones signs a paper in which he agrees to pay Brown $1,000, such promise will be enforceable in the courts of many countries. Not so in the U.S. Brown cannot sue for the payment of the $1,000 because Jones's promise to pay is not supported by anything given by Brown to Jones. That is what consideration means. The consideration need not be money, so long as it has some value to Jones, or involves a sacrifice by Brown. For instance, if Brown agrees not to compete with Jones, that would be a consideration for Jones' promise to pay $1,000 to Brown. The consideration need not be as valuable as that which is given in exchange. Brown's promise to do something for Jones would not be a valid contract without a consideration promised or paid by Jones. But if Jones pays just $1 to Brown, that makes the contract valid. This is why American contracts recite so often a consideration of $1 – a stipulation that baffles many foreigners.

In most instances, Jones does not even pay the $1 to Brown. In almost all states, it is enough that Brown acknowledge in the written contract that he has received the $1. It does not make much sense, but it is one of those technicalities that is justified by unconvincing legalistic reasoning that is best accepted without question.

A third requirement is that, where there is no other consideration for a contract, there must be mutuality of obligation. No agreement between two parties is binding unless it binds both parties. For instance, if a seller agrees to furnish a buyer with all the oil that he may require, and the buyer does not obligate himself to purchase any oil, such agreement does not constitute a valid contract and the agreement does not bind the seller. The desired objective of such an agreement, however, often can be accomplished by an appropriate option agreement. The requirement of mutuality does not apply to so-called unilateral contracts, as where one party makes a promise conditioned upon the doing of an act by another party.

Under the statutes of many states and under the influence of modern thinking, the rules regarding consideration have been liberalized. Indeed, such doctrines as promissory estoppel have been developed to ease the requirement of consideration in special situations. Generally, however, it is not safe to make a contract without providing for mutual consideration unless the question is checked carefully.

## 7. THE PAROL EVIDENCE RULE

Under this rule, when parties put their agreement in writing, all previous oral agreements are deemed to be superseded. The plain meaning of the language used in the written agreement may not be altered by oral evidence, unless there is ambiguity or fraud or mutual mistake. However, the rule does not forbid oral testimony that is not inconsistent with the written contract and that merely supplements the writing.

## 8. WARRANTIES

Warranties are at the heart of every contract. The term warranty has many meanings. In the context of contract law it means, in essence, the guaranty that a certain state of facts exists, and that the party giving the warranty assumes liability for breach of the warranty and, thereby, breach of the contract, if the warranted state of facts does not exist. A warranty may be expressed in a contract clause, or it may be implied. For instance, in a sales contract it is implied that the article to be sold is fit for the contemplated use (see Chapter 10). In many contracts one finds that the party *warrants and represents*. A knowing misrepresentation is a fraud. In some situations the measure of damages for misrepresentation differs from that for breach of warranty.

Warranty claims are particularly important in the U.S. automobile industry. In 1969 the Federal Trade Commission found that quality control in the industry was unsatisfactory, and that the manufacturers' warranties were insufficient to protect the public. The result was the Automobile Quality Control Act, which established new standards and requires the automobile manufacturer to repair defective automobiles and automobile parts that do not conform to the governmental standards.

The subject of warranties is dealt with further in the discussion of sales in Chapter 10.

## 9. VALUE CLAUSES AND FOREIGN CURRENCY

Value clauses are often used to assure that the value of the stipulated payment will have the same purchasing power as was contemplated when the price was fixed. This is of particular importance in long-term contracts, of which loans and pension agreements are examples. The unstable world economy, inflation, and currency fluctuations make such a clause desirable. The oil-producing countries that are members of OPEC still use the U.S. dollar as a price basis. The classic stabilizer is the gold clause. Since gold has become a commodity of fluctuating market value, the gold clause has lost some attraction. Where it is used, care should be taken to stipulate which gold market shall control. The usual markets are Zurich and London, but the markets of New York and Tokyo are also used.

U.S. contracts often contain a so-called index clause. The dollar price is fixed but is made subject to increase or decrease in accordance with the consumer price index, which the U.S. Government publishes monthly. When this is done, care should be taken to select the price index that is applicable for a specified region. The drawback of the consumer price index is that its computation is based on housing costs and other items that may not have any bearing on the contract at hand. Some courts have ruled that the index clause violates state usury laws (see Section 13), which limit the amount of interest that may be charged debtors.

Some international contracts contain a value clause that is based on the Special Drawing Rights (SDR) of the International Monetary Fund. Some Eurobond issues are expressed in SDRs. SDRs may be developing into an international monetary unit. Most U.S. businesspeople are not familiar with SDRs.

The European Currency Unit (ECU), which plays a key role in the European Monetary System, is not suitable for one doing business with the U.S. The problem of developing a useful value clause has been debated among legal experts, but a satisfactory general solution has not yet been found.

In connection with contracts that call for payment in foreign currency (other than U.S. dollars), two points should be mentioned here: (*a*) when a lawsuit is instituted in the U.S., the demand for payment must always be expressed in U.S. dollars, and (*b*) published balance sheets must always be translated into U.S. dollars.

## 10. BREACH OF CONTRACT

A contract can be breached either by non-performance or by bad performance. In case of non-performance, the laws of most foreign countries make it possible for the other party to institute a court action to compel performance. Such an action for specific performance of a contract is, ordinarily, not permissible in the U.S. The general remedy is an action for payment of money damages.

An action for specific performance may be maintained only if the subject matter of the contract is so unique that money damages will not compensate for the loss caused by the breach of contract. This is generally considered the case where realty (land) is involved. The principle is narrowly applied and if specific performance is demanded, the claimant must convince the court that such performance has a unique value.

Sometimes, it is possible to insert a special clause in the contract that will provide for specific performance. Ordinarily, however, if Adams refuses to ship Murphy the steel that Adams has agreed to sell, Murphy cannot sue for specific performance. He has a claim for money damages, if he can show that Adams's breach of contract caused him such damages.

As an alternative to claiming damages, the innocent party in a breach of contract situation may prefer to rescind or terminate the contract. In that case, the party who is in default must return what he may have received under the contract. As a rule, the party terminating the agreement must also give back what he received, although that is not always required.

Where a businessperson is in a position to choose whether he will demand damages for breach of contract or whether he will rescind the contract and demand restitution, he will ordinarily make his decision from the viewpoint of commercial expediency. In international transactions, however, he must also consider what law will apply. A damages claim rests on the law of the place where the contract is to be performed. A restitution claim depends on the law where restitution is to be made. The two places may be in different countries, and upon examining the laws one may find that, as a practical matter, only one of the two remedies is available.

## 11. DAMAGES

As a businessperson can usually not enforce specific performance of a contract, he will want to know what damages he can claim if there should be a breach by the other party. He will also consider to what extent he may be held liable if he himself should be unable to perform. The question of a possible damages claim should, therefore, be considered before the contract is made. This will enable the prudent businessperson to protect himself by appropriate clauses in the contract, and perhaps provide a method of adjusting damages that differs from the general rule of law.

The general legal principle is that the payment of damages should put the other party in the same position in which he would have been had the contract been performed. This is called compensatory damages. The principle has many ramifications. We can here consider only a few significant aspects.

If Adams fails to ship to Murphy the steel that he sold him for $100 a ton, and Murphy can buy the same steel elsewhere at the same price, then Murphy has sustained no damages and Adams does not suffer for his breach of contract. But if the market price for steel has gone up, then Murphy can demand from Adams the difference between the market price and the contract price of $100. If the steel is not available elsewhere, only then may Murphy demand as damages the profits that he expected to make on the transaction, provided he can prove the amount of such profits.

Loss of resale profits are allowed as damages only if the defaulting seller at the time of the contract knew that the buyer intended to resell the merchandise. This rule is based on the general principle that nobody is liable for consequences that were not contemplated by both parties when they made the contract. If Smith agrees to sell Brown a machine that Smith knows is needed for the operation of Brown's factory, delay in delivery may make Smith liable for the loss caused by the stoppage of production. These are called consequential damages. Sellers often stipulate that they will not be liable for such damages.

If Brown's factory is a new enterprise and has never been in operation, he will not be in a position to prove what profits he lost unless there is a similarly situated business and its figures are available to Brown. U.S. law does not allow the recovery of speculative, uncertain commercial profits.

One method of protection against the difficulty of proving one's damages is to stipulate in advance that in case of a breach of contract a specified sum of money shall be paid as so-called liquidated damages. However, U.S. courts will not tolerate a penalty clause in a contract. An agreement for liquidated damages will, therefore, only be upheld if it is not in reality a penalty. The stipulated amount must be based on a reasonable estimate of what will be a just compensation in case of breach. If that estimate is reasonable at the time when the contract is made, it matters not if later events show that the estimate was exaggerated.

Obviously, a liquidated damages clause is particularly helpful in international contracts, where the difficulty of proving actual damages is increased by the distance between the parties and the markets.

Another damages problem, which is of increasing importance in international trade, is that of currency fluctuation. American courts will always render judgment for damages in terms of dollars, even if the loss was suffered in a foreign currency. They are then faced with the problem of converting the value of the foreign currency into dollars. Some courts use the rate of exchange prevailing at the date when the damages claim arose – the day on which the contract was breached. Other courts will compute the dollar damages as of the date of judgment.

The expenses of a lawsuit generally are not part of recoverable damages. A successful plaintiff will be allowed certain costs. This, however, is only a small part of the actual expense of litigation. Unfortunately, this fact encourages some people to breach their contracts. They know that many a good claim is not pressed because the claimant wants to avoid the expense of litigation.

In addition to compensatory damages, a claimant may be able to recover punitive damages in exceptional cases. This requires, generally, the showing of some particularly reprehensible and wanton conduct of the defendant. Its award depends on the discretion of the judge or jury, and on the law of the state where the action is brought.

## 12. ILLEGAL CONTRACTS

A unique type of illegality springs from the so-called antitrust laws, which are an outgrowth of the general principle that restraint of trade is illegal and freedom of competition must be maintained. Consequently, contracts that are designed to lessen competition or that have a tendency to create a monopoly are, as a rule, illegal. Chapter 17 deals with this matter in greater detail.

Other grounds that make a contract illegal are of the conventional type, familiar all over the world. Typical examples are usury, commercial bribery, and violation of ceiling price laws.

Illegal contracts are invalid. Not only are invalid contracts unenforceable, but the courts will also refuse to aid a party in recovering what was paid under an invalid contract, unless such party was innocent. For instance, if a sales contract is made in violation of the regulations regarding ceiling prices or regarding export licenses, and the buyer makes a payment under such contract with knowledge of the illegality, the buyer cannot recover such payment if the seller fails to perform.

An unlicensed real estate broker cannot enforce a commission claim if the contract is made in a state where such brokers are required to be licensed.

Green transferred money to Richards in order to hide it from claims of his partner, whom he desired to defraud. Richards then refused to give the money back to Green. When Green sued Richards, the court held that the transfer was illegal, and Green lost the case. Richards was allowed to keep the money.

A contract will not be held illegal on the ground that it violates the law of a foreign country unless the contract was made in such country. However, if performance of a contract is illegal in the country where it is to be performed, U.S. courts will excuse non-performance. This, however, does not apply where there is a choice of the place of performance. For instance, if a bond is payable either in Prague, London, or New York, the fact that payment would be illegal in Prague or London would not excuse performance in New York. That is so even if the debtor's residence is in Prague or London. Of course, the creditor will not be able to proceed against such debtor unless the debtor comes to New York or has funds there.

As is noted in Chapter 5, an alien who comes to the U.S. on a visitor's visa is prohibited by the immigration laws from taking up employment. However, if he does, his employment contract is not illegal, and the alien's violation of the immigration laws does not give the employer the right to breach the employment contract.

An illegal clause may invalidate the entire contract. To avoid this, many contracts contains a so-called saving clause, to the effect that if one clause should be or become invalid, the remaining part of the contract shall remain valid.

## 13. USURY

Usury is the exaction of an exorbitant price for the use of money. An usurious contract is illegal, void and unenforceable. Generally, the courts will not even allow a usurious lender to recover the principal amount of the loan. The legal rate for the lending of money is generally fixed by state law. State laws generally distinguish between civil usury and criminal usury. The rate for establishing criminal usury is higher. Usury laws generally apply only to loans made or credit extended to individuals. For that reason, moneylenders often require individual lenders to arrange for incorporation. The credit is then extended to the corporation, in which case the usury laws do not apply (with certain very limited exceptions).

The usual price for obtaining credit is interest. Mortgage lenders often demand a one-time payment of so-called points, or payment of a finance charge, or an investment charge; or they ask for a premium on early repayment. All these extra charges may be adjudged to be hidden interest, and therefore usurious.

The Federal Law has superseded all state law in cases where a loan is secured by a first mortgage on residential property. In such cases, Federal Law permits the creditor to charge an interest rate in excess of the rate permitted by state law. The statute and the regulations should be consulted for details by anyone who is concerned.

Disregard of the usury laws may have grave consequences for the lender. For instance, in the state of New York an usurious lender not only loses the right to recover any interest, but the entire loan transaction becomes void and the lender cannot even demand repayment of the loan. In other states, the consequence of usury is merely a forfeiture of the interest claim; and in still other jurisdictions, the lender loses only the illegal portion of the interest claim. See also discussion in Chapter 14, Section 11.

## 14. ADHESION CONTRACTS

This term is used for standardized contract forms which parties are offered on a 'take it or leave it' basis. Typical examples are printed conditions of sale, bills of lading, tickets, and franchise agreements. U.S. courts view adhesion contracts with great suspicion. Usually, the parties are of vastly unequal bargaining power, and the courts sometimes invalidate such agreements on the ground that there is no real voluntary agreement between the parties.

## 15. LEASING

The topic here is not the leasing of real property but rather the leasing of equipment. It is mentioned here as a special type of contract, without an exhaustive discussion of the many legal, tax and accounting problems to be considered. Leasing is increasingly popular in the U.S., and it is used for such diverse equipment as machine tools, computers and railroad cars. It spares the lessee the need for capital outlays and it enables the lessor, if he is a U.S. taxpayer, to obtain the investment tax credit. The rental payment is a tax deductible expense, and future rental obligations are often kept off the balance sheet. The latter practice is favored by the accounting profession. The lessor, especially if he is abroad, will want his title (ownership) protected against third parties. This brings the lease within the realm of *secured transactions*, which are discussed in Chapter 15. If the lessee is given the right to acquire ownership at the end of the lease period, either gratis or upon payment of a nominal amount, the question arises whether this is a true lease or an installment sale. See also the discussion of leasing in Chapter 8, Section 7.

## 16. ECONOMIC FLUCTUATIONS

American law does not know the concept of *clausula rebus sic stantibus*, which was developed in the civil law countries. The essence of this doctrine is that one can avoid the enforcement of a contract if, at the time of performance, there has been a radical change of circumstance since the time of the making of the contract.

The present instability of world conditions and wide economic fluctuations, have made this topic important for commercial contracts. The Uniform Commercial Code (see Chapter 10) deals with it in Sec. 2-615, which provides that performance of a sales contract may be excused if there is a failure of a presupposed condition. While the statute applies only to sales, it is not unreasonable to expect that the underlying principle may be applied to all contracts that, by reason of radical changes of the economy, may become frustrated. Increased cost cannot, in itself, furnish an excuse for nonperformance, because that is a foreseeable risk. However, events commonly known as *force majeure* or Acts of God, may well be regarded as an excuse for nonperformance. The law is not well settled.

## 17. INTERFERENCE WITH CONTRACTS

One who interferes purposely with the existing contractual relationship of others commits a tort – an unlawful act which in other countries is known as *delictum*. The perpetrator of the tort is liable for damages. Examples are the stealing of customers and the stealing of a competitor's employee, if the employee is induced to breach an employment contract. Interference with a contract may also constitute unfair competition (see Chapter 20), but unfair competition is not a necessary element of this tort.

## 18. POWER OF ATTORNEY

Strictly speaking, a power of attorney is not a bilateral contract. It is mentioned here because foreigners in their business dealings with the U.S. very often act through a local person who is appointed as a so-called attorney in fact, and whose authority derives from a power of attorney. An international treaty regulates the form of a power of attorney, but in the U.S. no particular form is required except if one deals with the Internal Revenue Service. Some banks also prefer specific written forms. Some states, New York, for instance, have a statutory printed form that is very convenient. A power of attorney may be given by word of mouth, for which reason the signing of another person's name may be perfectly proper. It is recommended, though, that the power of attorney be in writing and notarized. A power of attorney in the U.S. terminates when the donor of the power dies.

CHAPTER 10

# SALES

## *1. INTRODUCTION*

When a sales representative proudly reports to the home office that he has made a sale for $100,000, it is generally understood that the representative has made merely a contract of sale. In daily parlance, the distinction between a contract of sale and a sale is often disregarded. However, if the annual report of a corporation lists annual sales, the report refers to the amount collected on actual sales. The accurate meaning of sale is the transfer of ownership (title) of the property being sold for a price.

Most problems in the field of sales arise in the area of contracts of sale, which, from the viewpoint of the purchaser, is a contract of purchase. This chapter might, therefore, also be called *Purchases*.

The law of sales is generally codified. The Uniform Commercial Code (UCC), a non-official compilation, has been officially adopted by all states in the U.S. (by Louisiana only in part, not including the Sales Article) with some modifications and omissions.[1] Articles 2 and 6 of the UCC cover most of the subject. Internationally, there is the United Nations Convention establishing a uniform Law for International Sales, which has been ratified by the U.S. and, at this writing, by more than twenty other nations. The Convention is a forward step from the 1964 Hague Convention, which adopted an International Sale of Goods Act. In the words of an Hungarian scholar, the 1980 Convention

---

1. e.g. California and North Carolina have omitted Sec. 2-302, which empowers the court to refuse enforcement of a contract that it considers unconscionable. This omission does not mean that unconscionable contracts are allowed in these states. Another example is the omission in New York, Illinois and other states, of the words 'lien creditor' in Section 2-702(c), because these states did not wish to frustrate a seller's reclamation rights (see below) when a buyer becomes bankrupt.

represents a considerable liberalization of rigorous commercial rules. He ascribes this progress to the worldwide participation in the Convention and a growing emphasis on equity in international business. The Convention applies to sales contracts that are made between a party in the U.S. and a party in a country that has ratified the Convention. Even then, it does not apply to sales contracts that expressly provide for application of the domestic law of the U.S. The differences between the Convention and the domestic law of the U.S. do not appear to be substantial. This book is primarily concerned with the domestic law of the U.S.

As mentioned in Chapter 1, the U.S. has developed a substantial body of consumer protection law. That law does not apply to experienced merchants, who are considered to have equal bargaining strength, and, therefore, not to be in need of consumer protection. There is, consequently, a difference between consumer sales law and merchant sales law. This chapter is primarily concerned with merchant sales law.

The term *sale* ordinarily applies to the sale of goods. As a result of decisional law, this has been extended to the sale of services, such as a contract for the delivery of electricity or the sale of blood for a blood transfusion.

In order to sell, one must have a market. That is why some U.S. executives hold the title *director of marketing* or *marketing manager*, instead of the more conventional and more modest title of *sales manager*. Essentially, both titles denote the same function.

## 2. FORMATION OF SALES CONTRACT

The general rule of offer and acceptance applies (Chapter 9). This seems simple. But many lawsuits are fought in this field because of the so-called battle of the forms. An offer may be made subject to printed conditions of sale. It may be accepted subject to printed conditions of purchase that differ from the conditions of sale. Here there is no meeting of the minds, and no contract. However, the law provides that any deviating conditions of purchase are regarded as mere additions to the contract if they do not materially alter the terms of the offer. They are binding unless the offering seller promptly objects. This requires the seller to examine carefully any conditions of purchase to which the acceptance may be subject. The seller can also protect himself by stating in the offer that its terms may not be changed.

The requirement of a signed written form (Statute of Frauds, see Chapter 9) does not apply if the contract is for the special manufacture of goods that are not readily saleable to others. Also, a merchant cannot invoke the Statute of Frauds of he has received a written order and has failed to respond. Finally, the requirement of a signed writing becomes unnecessary where the contract has been performed in part, or where the goods have been accepted.

## 3. *WARRANTIES*

The concept of warranty was explained in Chapter 9. There are two implied warranties in every contract of sale – warranties that are deemed to exist even if not expressed: (*a*) The warranty of fitness for the use which the seller knows is intended by the purchaser, and (*b*) the warranty of merchantability, which means marketability. The statute prescribes minimum standards of merchantability. All warranties can be excluded. A typical exclusion or disclaimer clause reads, 'Seller is not liable for any warranty, express or implied, other than those set forth in this agreement'. However, such a disclaimer clause is not valid with respect to the implied warranty of merchantability, unless the word merchantability is specifically mentioned.

## 4. *PRICE*

A contract of sale in which the price is not fixed or determinable is a nullity. However, the parties may agree to leave the price open. If they subsequently disagree, a reasonable price will be considered as having been stipulated. Somctimes a method by which the price can be clearly determined, such as the publicly quoted market price at time of shipment, is agreed upon.

If several sellers agree to charge the same price, they violate antitrust law. Under U.S. law, they commit the crime of price-fixing. A foreign price-fixer might not be prosecuted unless he comes to the U.S. However, the purchaser may refuse to perform the contract because it is an illegal contract.

The familiar clauses, f.o.b., c.i.f., etc., are pure price clauses that allocate the costs between the parties. They are also regarded as delivery terms, unless the contract contains differing terms.

If the buyer fails to pay the price, the seller may sue for the price, but if the property is still in his possession, he may resell it.

## 5. *TITLE PASSING AND RISK PASSING*

The word *title* denotes ownership. The term *risk passing* refers to the point where the risk of loss or damage passes from the seller to the buyer. Ordinarily, title passing and risk passing occur simultaneously, but not always. For instance, a buyer may request the seller to delay delivery, at his expense and risk. The seller then retains title, but the risk passes to the buyer. In modern legislation, such as the U.S. Uniform Commercial Code (UCC) and the Hague Convention on International Sales, the concept of title has ceased to be important. Stress is placed on what actually happens in commerce. The UCC lays down certain rules that apply when the contract is silent. When the contract calls for shipment, delivery to the carrier passes title to the buyer, unless it is stipulated that the carrier must make a delivery at a specified place, which is the case when the contract specifies 'f.o.b. buyer's plant'. It should be noted that a c.i.f. contract merely requires delivery to the carrier, not delivery at destination. When delivery at destination is required, title passes when the carrier tenders delivery. Title may also be transferred by delivery of a document of title, such as a warehouse receipt or a bill of lading or by a simple delivery order. The foregoing rules do not apply if the seller is in breach of contract – for instance, if he has delivered nonconforming goods.

When the contract to sell and the sale take place simultaneously, title and risk generally pass at the same time. The seller may wish to reserve title to himself until he is paid in full. Such reservation of title does not postpone the transfer of risk to the buyer. Unlike the laws of other countries, U.S. law discountenances secret reservation of title. An unpublished reservation of title may be valid between seller and buyer, but has no force against third parties. If the seller wishes to preserve his title against third parties, he must file a financing statement (see Chapter 15). Other security devices are the trust receipt (Chapter 15), and the so-called documents of title (warehouse receipt, bill of lading). For instance, Schmitz in Dusseldorf contracts to sell Brown in Chicago a machine f.o.b. Hamburg. In the absence of a contrary agreement, title passes when Schmitz delivers the machine to the ship in Hamburg. Schmitz may procure a bill of lading made to his order, which he mails to a bank in the U.S. in order to obtain payment. So long as Schmitz has control over the bill of lading, he retains title to the machine. However, it is only a security title, and the risk of loss has passed to Brown when the machine was delivered to the ship in Hamburg.

## 6. SELLER'S RECLAMATION RIGHTS

The purchaser's insolvency alters the contract. If the contract stipulates the extension of credit, the seller may now refuse delivery unless the buyer pays in cash. If the goods have already been delivered, the seller may demand return; but such demand must be made within ten days after receipt of the goods by the seller. The seller is not permitted to exercise his reclamation right by taking the goods from the possession of the buyer without judicial order.

## 7. BUYER'S RIGHT OF REJECTION

The buyer is entitled to receive perfectly conforming goods, not just substantially conforming goods. The buyer's ordinary remedy is a claim for damages, as discussed in Chapter 9. The buyer also has the right to reject nonconforming goods. The rejection must be prompt; otherwise the goods may be considered as accepted. Acceptance may be revoked, but the law makes this difficult for the buyer. A careful buyer will prefer a prompt inspection or testing and, if indicated, will reject promptly.

## 8. SALE OF A BUSINESS

Contracts for the sale of a business are generally subject to the bulk sales law, which is codified in section 6 of the UCC. A bulk transfer is any transfer of the transferor's business or a substantial part thereof, involving primarily inventory, work in process and equipment. The main purpose of the law is to protect the creditors of the seller. They must be notified in advance by the transferor. If such notice is not given, any creditor may void the transfer and proceed against the transferee. For that reason the transferee is interested that the transferor give proper notice to his creditors. Often this involves considerable work for the transferor, which he can avoid if he is able to satisfy the transferee with an adequate indemnity against future claims by the transferor's creditors. This includes claims by Federal, state and municipal tax authorities.

## 9. 'UNLESS OTHERWISE AGREED UPON'

With a few exceptions, seller and buyer are free to make their contract without regard to the rules of law. It is always advisable to agree on written terms, leaving as little room as possible for later interpretation and disputes. The parties must think of the parol evidence rule in American law (see Chapter 8). It is advisable to stipulate that the contract supersedes all previous discussions, promises and agreements.

## 10. DISTRIBUTION CONTRACT

The distribution contract has aspects that touch many chapters of this book. It is discussed here because effective distribution is crucial to the sale of any product.

There are two types of distributorship agreements. The distributor may be an independent merchant who buys and sells for his own account and bears the concomitant risks. Or he is a sales representative and commission agent, who acts as an intermediary and generally assumes no risks. The distinction is sometimes blurred. Thus, if heavy and costly equipment is involved, even an independent merchant will not hold it in inventory or make a purchase unless he has an order from a customer. Conversely, a sales representative or commission agent will maintain an inventory in order to be able to service his customers promptly. Indeed, if the distributor is to sell foreign machinery or equipment in the U.S., the customer will generally insist that the local distributor have such inventory on hand, because he does not want to experience the perceived delay and risk in procuring spare parts from abroad.

For that reason, a foreign manufacturer frequently will stipulate in the distributorship agreement that the distributor must maintain a spare part inventory that he must buy from the foreign manufacturer. The distributor in such a case will stipulate that upon termination of the distributorship the manufacturer must buy back the inventory. This is generally limited to inventory that is still in saleable condition. It is sometimes overlooked that such inventory has passed through U.S. customs and that a duty has been paid on it. This is no problem if the inventory is purchased by another distributor in the U.S.

The most difficult aspect of a U.S. distributorship is that of exclusivity. For obvious reasons, distributors generally desire to have an *exclusive arrangement*, even if they appoint sub-distributors in different parts of the country. The purpose of an exclusive arrangement is, of course, to exclude potential competitors. This anti-competitive feature brings the agreement in conflict with the antitrust laws (see Chapter 17). The conflict does not arise if the importer is also the first distributor and is owned by the foreign manufacturer or exporter. In that case, the importer needs no agreement that grants him exclusivity and the antitrust problem is avoided. However, he may still have questions under the Tariff Act, with respect to import duties, for which reason the importer may find it advisable to leave the door open for sales from abroad to another importer (see Chapter 22). Exclusive distributorship may also raise trademark questions, which are alluded to in Chapter 20.

From an antitrust standpoint, it is now established that exclusive agreements are illegal only if they constitute an unreasonable restriction. This is ordinarily not the case, as the exclusivity is generally justified by sound marketing policy. The difficulty with the rule is that in the last analysis a court might pass upon the economic effects of the restraint. This introduces an element of uncertainty and unpredictability.

When a U.S. distributor establishes a network of sub-distributors, the latter are generally limited to a specific location in a certain area. Such restrictions are also subject to the rule of reason, which means that they are valid only if they do not unreasonably restrict competition. A sub-distributor in San Francisco may make a sale to a customer who uses the purchased product in Philadelphia. It is not reasonable to forbid this. However, it may be stipulated that in such an instance, the sub-distributor in San Francisco must share his commission with the sub-distributor in Philadelphia.

The U.S. antitrust laws are not concerned with competition in foreign markets. Consequently, if a U.S. manufacturer (who may be owned or controlled abroad) appoints an exclusive distributor abroad, U.S. law is not concerned. However, if the foreign distributor promises to distribute no competing U.S. product, a U.S. antitrust problem may arise. Such exclusivity will not be questioned unless the foreign distributor is such an important outlet in its own country that the exclusivity restricts in an important way the ability of other U.S. firms to export to that market.

Before a U.S. exporter enters into a distributorship agreement with a distributor abroad, he should examine the local laws under which the distributor operates. In many countries, it is difficult to terminate a distributorship agreement. In the U.S., only Puerto Rico has enacted a law that protects a distributor against termination. The Automobile Dealers Franchise Act prohibits automobile manufacturers from arbitrarily terminating distribution agreements with automobile dealers. Domestic as well as foreign automobile manufacturers have been sued under this law; but, so far, no decision has been reported in which the distributor was successful. It does not appear likely that the principle of the Automobile Dealers Franchise Act will be extended.

The motivation for such protective legislation and jurisprudence is that the distributor may have developed local goodwill and a local clientele, and may have invested substantial capital (for instance for an automobile showroom). It is unfair for him to be lightly deprived of the fruits of his efforts. The theory is that the distributor has an ownership interest in the distributorship. Although the theory has not yet achieved recognition in the U.S., it seems prudent to think of it in the preparation of new distribution agreements. A distributor sometimes cuts prices in order to gain a competitive advantage. The competitors are furious and induce the manufacturer to terminate the distributorship of the price cutter. Such a termination violates the antitrust laws and is regarded as illegal.

The following remarks point out the highlights of what should be embodied in a distribution contract. The distributor must be independent if the foreign manufacturer wants to avoid the tax consequences of doing business in the U.S. that were outlined in Chapter 8. Another drawback of the foreign manufacturer dominating the American distributor is that the foreigner is open to suits in American courts, not only by the antitrust authorities (see Chapter 17) but also by aggrieved customers and others. An important part of the distribution contract covers the point where title (ownership) to the foreign product and risk of loss passes to the distributor. It is desirable for a foreign manufacturer to have this occur in his homeland. This does not prevent the U.S. distributor from reselling the product on an f.o.b. foreign port basis, in which case he is not liable for U.S. excise taxes. However, it will generally prevent him from inspecting the merchandise before delivery to the customer, and he should therefore contract for a suitable interval between delivery and acceptance. The contract should also allocate the responsibility for late delivery (a frequent complaint), and for handling problems with administrative agencies, such as the Food and Drug Administration and Customs.

Warranties should be *back to back*, which means that the distributor should obtain from the manufacturer the same warranties that he extends to his customers. Similar congruity ought to be achieved respecting events of *force majeure* and of frustration. If the contract between the distributor and his customer calls for the sale of German chemicals that he intends to obtain from the German factory with which he has a contract, future trade restrictions will not excuse the distributor, and he might be forced to procure the chemicals from local or other outside sources, albeit at a higher price. The problem can be avoided by stating in the contract that shipment from Germany is intended. In the machinery and equipment field, U.S. customers frequently insist that spare parts and accessories be readily available and therefore kept in stock by the distributor. The distributor wants to be assured that the foreign manufacturer will take over the spare parts and accessory inventory when the distributorship ends. Sometimes it is advisable to put the distributor in a position to manufacture the foreign product, in case of interruption of international communications. Trademarks should be assigned to the distributor, not licensed (see Chapter 20). Exclusive agreements should be avoided, even if the distributor is the only U.S. distributor. The reason for this is the Clayton Act (see Chapter 17) and the Tariff Act (see Chapter 22). The need for national distribution throughout the U.S. continent should be considered. Advertising and promotion expenses should be shared between the contracting parties. Before signing a distributor agreement, the foreign manufacturer should acquaint himself with the idiosyncrasies of the American market, some of which are alluded to in Chapter 1.

## 11. PRODUCT LIABILITY

This is a liability against which a seller cannot protect himself in the contract of sale because it is not based on the contract. It is often called *strict liability*. It is based on the notion that anybody who introduces a defective product into the stream of commerce is liable for the damage or injury caused by the product, regardless of whether the introducer knew or could have known the defect. Even reliance on industrial or government standards may not be a defense. The theory is that, as between two innocent parties, the introducer must bear the risk of injury or damage. All parties in the commercial chain of distribution of the products may be held liable for the defect, including the wholesaler, the distributor, the retailer or the commercial lessor; but ultimately the manufacturer of the defective product bears the burden of product liability.

Formerly, this strict liability applied only where the product was inherently dangerous, as, for instance, an automobile or foodstuff that is subject to deterioration. Some states still apply this criterion for design defects as opposed to defects of manufacture. Some states will not apply the strict liability principle if the design of the product was made in accordance with the state of the art and prevailing industry standards. However, it is inadvisable to rely on this limitation. The trend, even in design defect cases, is that state of the art evidence has no place in a product liability case, and that the designer is a guarantor of the safety of the product. Another former limitation was that strict liability existed only in the case of personal injury, not in the case of damage to property. This distinction is no longer made.

Of course, the plaintiff must prove that the product was defective when the defendant sold it. A defect may be due to poor manufacture or to faulty design, or it may be due to an alteration occurring subsequent to manufacture. Some designs are unavoidably unsafe, and the manufacturer may escape strict liability if he issues warning literature. If the intermediate purchaser fails to deliver the warning to his customer, the purchaser may be held liable by the customer and subsequent parties in the chain of distribution. Sometimes, the plaintiff (often a worker) has himself or herself contributed to the injury by careless conduct. If the court is convinced of such contributory negligence (also called comparative negligence) it will generally reduce the award by an amount equal to the degree of the contributory negligence.

The statute of limitations plays an important part in product liability cases. In a recent case in the Federal District Court of New Jersey, the plaintiff had to close its plant for several weeks because the equipment which it had purchased from the defendant proved to be defective. If the plaintiff had sued for breach of contract, the New Jersey statute of limitations would have outlawed the claim, because that statute fixes four years as the limitation for contract claims. However, the New Jersey period of limitations for products liability claims is six years, and that saved the plaintiff. Conversely, in a Texas case, an action based on strict liability was outlawed after two years, whereas the statute of limitations for a breach of contract claim there extended to four years. Consequently, the plaintiff sued for breach of contract rather than relying on the doctrine of product liability.

The statute of limitations raises still another problem. When does it begin to run? This is important in many industrial injury claims, notably the asbestos-related claims which at present loom large in the U.S. (see Chapter 25). The better but not generally accepted view is that the claim arises and the statute begins to run when the illness manifests itself, not when the exposure occurs. Another illustration is the malfunctioning of a body implant. The statute begins to run when the device malfunctions, not when it is implanted.

Most states base their product liability statute on Section 402A of the Restatement of Torts. However, legal scholars disagree on the nature of product liability. That is of little interest to the businessperson who is faced with the harsh reality of the risk of being made a defendant in product liability lawsuits, which are occurring with increasing frequency.

One of the most unsatisfactory features of product liability is the lack of uniformity and the diversity of rules in various jurisdictions. This is sought to be remedied by a Federal statute that would pre-empt the field and supersede state statutes. As of this writing, such a statute has not yet been enacted.

It is expected that such a Federal statute would provide a uniform and sensible method of dealing with punitive damages claims. In 1981, a California jury awarded a product liability plaintiff punitive damages in the amount of $125 million against the Ford Motor Company. The proposed Federal law would prevent such excesses by limiting the role of the jury to the determination of liability, and assigning to the judge alone the determination of the amount of damages.

CHAPTER 11

# CORPORATIONS

## 1. INTRODUCTION

This chapter deals with Business Corporations. Religious Corporations and other Not For Profit Corporations are not discussed. Professional Corporations are a species of the Business Corporation, but the special rules applicable to them are likewise outside the scope of this book.

Like the human body, all American corporations have the same basic structure. There is no variety of structures as in other countries. Foreign business organizations with limited liability such as the SARL, the GmbH and the BV are simply regarded as corporations.[1] The English distinction between a public company and a private company is also not recognized in the U.S. Federal corporate regulations generally apply only to corporations whose shares are publicly traded. There is a growing recognition that a corporation with only one or a few shareholders (so-called close corporations) should be subject to special rules. In Texas, for instance, a close corporation with fewer than fifteen shareholders, may operate without a board of directors. The Internal Revenue Code grants the Small Business Corporation the benefits of incorporation, while eliminating most of the taxation at the corporate level by taxing all profits at the shareholder level. This so-called Chapter S corporation, which is mentioned in Chapter 8, Section 19, is a type of close corporation.

---

1. The Internal Revenue Service states that this is not an absolute rule, and it has in at least two instances asserted that a GmbH or a SARL that is owned by a U.S. corporation is a branch of the U.S. corporation.

The U.S. Congress has chartered a few Federal corporations for public purposes, such as the U.S. Postal Service. Otherwise, all corporations are creatures of one of the 55 American jurisdictions. The most important states in this respect are New York, California and Delaware. In the past, the small state of Delaware succeeded in attracting many corporations, including the giant General Motors Corporation. The reasons for this were low state taxes and flexible corporate legislation. Flexible legislation, as one author has pointed out, means decreased investor protection. Although Delaware was a pioneer in this respect, the Delaware corporation laws today are not much different from those of other states. It is no longer advisable to organize a Delaware corporation if the corporation's business will be conducted in another state.

In the 1960s, the American Bar Association published a Model Business Corporation Act, which since has been adopted by many state legislatures in the U.S. The Model Act fairly represents the prevailing law.

As in other countries, a corporation in the U.S. is an artificial juridical person that is created by the state or jurisdiction in which it is organized. The grant of the corporate charter is almost a fiction, because it can be obtained automatically if the certificate of incorporation (sometimes called articles of incorporation) is prepared so as to comply with some prescribed minimum requirements. The grant can be obtained literally overnight, which surprises many foreigners. In New York, lawyers frequently avail themselves of service organizations, which operate in all parts of the U.S., to organize corporations.

As elsewhere, corporations are availed of an order to limit the liability that may grow out of the operation of the incorporated business. However, individuals who use the corporate structure with fraudulent intent will be held personally liable. One then speaks of 'piercing the corporate veil'.


## 2. FOREIGN CORPORATIONS

A corporation is a foreign corporation outside the state in which it has been organized. Thus, in New York, a French corporation, for all practical purposes, is on the same footing as an Illinois corporation.

The statutes of all states contain special provisions for foreign corporations. A foreign corporation should be *domesticated* in another state by *qualifying* (registering) there. This entails the payment of an entrance fee. The corporation then becomes a resident of that other state. If it is not domesticated, it is generally barred from access to the local courts, although it may be made a defendant there. Failure to register may also entail a fine. A recent decision of the Oklahoma Supreme Court ruled that a Canadian corporation that had registered in Oklahoma was a resident of that state. It was, therefore, not barred from land ownership, as a nonresident alien would have been.

For Federal income tax purposes, an alien corporation is considered a resident corporation if it is engaged in business in the U.S., even if it is not domesticated (see Chapter 8).

If an alien corporation is not domesticated and not engaged in business in the U.S., it is not subject to the jurisdiction of any court in the U.S., even though it owns a subsidiary in the U.S. It is different where the U.S. subsidiary acts as agent for its foreign parent. It is sometimes difficult to draw the line, and foreign owners are well advised to let the U.S. subsidiary operate as independently as possible.

## 3. ORGANIZATION

The first step is to obtain a charter. This is done by submitting the certificate of incorporation to the appropriate state governmental office, generally the Secretary of State. If the certificate conforms to the statutory requirements, and the generally modest filing fee is paid, together with the organization tax, the government approves the Articles, which then become the charter. That is the legal birth of the corporation. Organizational details are contained in the bylaws, which are generally adopted after the corporation has come into existence. The first organizational meeting also elects the directors and officers, arranges for a bank account, and handles other essential matters. All proceedings are recorded in a minute book. It is important that this book be maintained as an accurate and complete record. Auditors and revenue agents will generally examine it.

## 4. POWERS

If a corporation is organized with the specific intent of manufacturing and selling lamps, the article in the certificate of incorporation pertaining to purposes and powers will recite that fact in the first paragraph. The law sometimes precludes a corporation from pursuing certain objectives. For instance, in New York and other states, a corporation may not render legal services and it may not engage in the practice of the engineering profession. In most states, a corporation may not engage in the banking business or act as a trustee, except with the prior approval of the appropriate executive department of the state. The banking business is government-supervised in the interest of the public.

By stating the specific objective of the corporation at the outset of the provision of the certificate of incorporation that refers to the purposes and powers of the corporation, the impression or legal implication may be created that the corporation is limited to that specific objective. To avoid this, and to keep the corporation flexible, it is customary to add any number of *purpose clauses* by which the corporation is empowered to engage in practically any permissible type of trade or transaction. Most states allow such comprehensive clauses. As a rule, a corporation has the implied power to do all things that are necessary in the normal conduct of its regular business. However, there is often some uncertainty as to how far this implied power extends. This is another reason why it is generally advisable to have comprehensive power clauses in the certificate of incorporation. It happens sometimes, particularly when it comes to capital investments, that a party will refuse to make a contract with a corporation unless it is shown that the corporation has the power to make such investments and enter into such a contract. The reason for this is that a contract that goes beyond the power of a corporation is null and void; it is called *ultra vires*.

A party who questions the corporation's power to make a capital investment will generally be satisfied if the board of directors approves the transaction. The concept of an *ultra vires* act still exists, but it is of little practical importance. A disgruntled shareholder may seek to prevent a corporation from engaging in an unauthorized transaction, labeling it *ultra vires*.

An important power is the authority to issue a guaranty for the indebtedness of another party. New York law used to hold that this power is implied only if the guaranty is in favor of a subsidiary corporation. Today, this power is unlimited by express provision of the New York statute. It is generally permissible to include in the power clauses a provision allowing the corporation to issue any kind of guaranty, but the incorporators or shareholders will often hesitate to do this for fear of misuse by the management.

A corporation has no power to make a gift. This prevents the management from transferring property or money of the corporation without adequate consideration. However, the New York Business Corporation Law provides that a corporation has the power to make donations, irrespective of corporate benefit, for the public welfare. Prudent managers will not make any donation of more than a nominal amount without prior approval of the board of directors. The fact that a corporation has the power to act, does not mean that its act is valid for all purposes. For instance, the Internal Revenue Code requires that a qualified stock option plan for the employees of a corporation be approved by the shareholders. If a corporation adopts a qualified stock option plan without prior approval of the shareholders, the corporate action is not *ultra vires*; but it is invalid in the sense that the plan will not qualify for the benefits of the Internal Revenue Code.

## 5. NAME

The name of the corporation must not be confusingly similar to that of any other business organization or trade style. The government officer who reviews the proposed certificate of incorporation will refuse to issue a charter if he finds such confusion with the name of another corporation. However, issuance of the charter under the proposed name does not make the corporation immune to claims by third parties for unfair competition or trade mark infringement. Therefore, a careful lawyer will not submit any certificate of incorporation without first investigating possible conflicts with the contemplated name of the corporation.

## 6. CAPITAL STRUCTURE

Most corporations have a simple capital structure. Some states require a minimum capital, which, however, is never large. Each shareholder of a corporation receives a certain number of shares for the contribution that he makes to the capital of the corporation. The contribution may be in money, in property, or in services. Where property or services are contributed, many states are rather strict as to the valuation thereof. The property may be tangible, such as machinery, or it may be a valuable lease or patent. Each share of stock has a stated value, which may be ten cents, $100, or any other amount. In most states, the shares may also be no par value shares – that is, shares without any par value. In that case, the stated value of each share is the fractional value of the total net worth of the corporation that such share represents. For instance, if the net worth of a corporation is $100,000, and 100 shares have been issued, each no par value share has an initial book value of $1,000. No par value shares are sometimes preferred in order to conceal the true value thereof to the casual observer; or where an initially small capital investment is expected to increase greatly in value by profitable operations. From the viewpoint of corporate finance or corporate organization, there is little practical advantage in having no par value shares. On the contrary, the local transfer taxes in case of no par value shares are frequently higher than the transfer taxes on par value shares.

As a rule, each share entitles the holder thereof to one vote, to a proportionate part of the total amount of dividends that the corporation may distribute, and to a proportionate part of its capital and surplus if the corporation is dissolved.

Frequently, this simple capital structure does not meet the requirements of a business corporation. In that case, several classes of shares may be provided for. This makes it possible to regulate the voting rights of shareholders on an unequal basis, to differentiate among shareholders with respect to the distribution of corporate profits (i.e. dividends), or capital distribution in case of dissolution, and to create priority rights and preferences.

To accomplish this, a corporation may have one or more classes of both common shares and so-called preferred or preference shares. The exact characteristics of the various classes of shares must be described in the certificate of incorporation, which states the amount of the capital and type of shares that the corporation is authorized to issue. This is the so-called authorized capital. The capital stock actually issued may be less than the authorized amount. When a corporation is organized, it is generally advisable to authorize capital stock in such amount as is likely to be issued in the foreseeable future, in order to avoid the necessity of an early amendment of the certificate of incorporation. However, shareholders are sometimes interested in freezing the capital structure and relative positions of the various shareholders at the level that exists at the time of the organization of the corporation. In that case, they will not allow the authorized capital to be higher or different from the capital which is originally provided.

The paid-in capital of a corporation is the *responsible capital* of the corporation, on which people extending credit to the corporation rely. It cannot be reduced unless all creditors are provided for. In most states the capital cannot be used for dividends, which may be paid only out of surplus.

A corporation may buy its own shares, but only with funds which constitute surplus. Such purchases occur, for instance, when a corporation whose shares are publicly traded decides to 'go private', i.e., concentrate the shareholdings in a few hands, and get rid of the public disclosure burdens (see Chapter 18, Section 10).

Shareholders must understand that they are, as a rule, not free to withdraw moneys that they have paid in as capital. If they desire to provide for an easy withdrawal of funds, they can legally do so in either of two ways. Instead of contributing money as capital stock, they may contribute it as *paid-in surplus* which then has the same status as ordinarily earned surplus. Such a procedure is practical only in exceptional circumstances.

A more common way of keeping capital contributions out of the category of *responsible capital* is to finance a corporation by way of loans. These loans may be callable at any time or they may be long-term loans. An additional advantage of such loan financing is that in case of insolvency, the investor is in the same category as ordinary creditors, whereas shareholders are subordinated to creditors. Moreover, as already pointed out, interest payments on a loan constitute a deductible item for corporate income tax purposes, whereas dividends are not in that category.

However, as noted in Chapter 8, Section 6, if the loans result in a *thin capitalization* of the corporation, the government will treat the interest payments as dividends and not allow them to be deductible for income tax purposes.

The disadvantage of loan financing is that it weakens the corporate credit. Moreover, if several shareholders join together in the formation of a corporation, they often want to make certain that none of them can withdraw capital except from earned surplus, and only if a distribution is decided upon by appropriate majority decision.

Sometimes, loans are made to corporations with the provision that the corporation will make no payment thereon – either interest or principal – except from earned income. The notes or bonds issued for such loans are often referred to as *income bonds*. This protects the corporation against the undermining of its financial structure. An income bond often has all the characteristics of a share of preferred stock. The tax authorities may treat it as such, in which case the tax purpose of this method of corporate financing is nullified.

It is important to bear in mind that whether the paid-in surplus or loan financing method is selected, there must be an acceptable minimum of capital paid in.


## 7. THE SHAREHOLDERS

A Delaware corporation was faced with a takeover bid by a Canadian corporation. In an attempt to prevent the takeover, the corporation adopted a bylaw that barred share ownership by aliens. This restriction was held invalid by the court. With the exception of the special industries mentioned in Chapter 6, an alien is not barred from the ownership of shares. The shareholders must meet once a year for the annual shareholders' meeting. The time and place for such meeting is generally regulated by the bylaws. Small corporations at times omit the annual meeting. This has no adverse legal consequences. The shareholders elect and can remove the members of the board of directors. That is their principal function. They have no power to declare a dividend; and unlike the practice in many countries, they do not approve the annual balance sheet of the corporation. It is good practice for the directors and officers to render at the annual shareholders' meeting a general report on the state of the business. It is also recommended that the shareholders pass a resolution by which the management's and directors' actions during the past year are approved.

Any fundamental changes, such as in capitalization, corporate name, and the like, must be reflected in an amended certificate of incorporation, which generally requires the consent of the shareholders. Usually a two-thirds majority consent of shareholders is required if the corporation is to be dissolved or if substantially all of its assets are to be sold or encumbered.

In all ordinary cases, not specifically provided for by law or in the certificate of incorporation or the bylaws, a simple majority vote is sufficient to pass a valid resolution. This applies also to the election of management, the amendment of the bylaws, or any other matter that may be reserved for a decision of the shareholders. Sometimes, directors find it advisable to call a shareholders' meeting, although it is not required, when the management wishes to obtain the express support of the shareholders for a particular decision.

While preferred shareholders ordinarily have no vote, nothing in the law prevents according them voting rights. Sometimes the certificate of incorporation provides that preferred shareholders shall have the right to vote if the corporation fails to pay dividends to its common shareholders.

Shareholders need not vote in person. They can appoint representatives to vote for them. Such a representative is called a proxy. The same name is also used for the written instrument by which the representative is appointed. Proxy instruments are, as a rule, only valid for a limited period of time.

Incorporators sometimes desire to stipulate that shareholders' decisions, on all or on some matters, must be unanimous. This is wholly impracticable; and in some states it is even considered illegal, as a violation of the democratic manner in which a corporation should be governed.

However, there are other ways in which minority shareholders can protect themselves against the overpowering influence of the majority. The need for such protection arises particularly in connection with the main function of the shareholders – the election of directors. If James owns 60% of the shares and Oliver and Donald each own 20%, then James can, under ordinary circumstances, elect all of the directors.

One common way of preventing this is to provide for so-called cumulative voting. This is a method of concentrating votes, devised to give a sufficient minority the ability to secure representation on the board of directors.

Another way is to divide the shareholders into several classes and to give each class the right to elect one or more directors.

Then there are the so-called voting trusts, by which several shareholders transfer their shares to one or more trustees for the purpose of having these shares voted by the trustee or trustees. The law generally limits the duration of such voting trusts, usually to ten years. However, it is possible to extend the duration from time to time by a new agreement.

## 8. SHAREHOLDERS' AGREEMENT

Where shareholders enter into a so-called shareholders' agreement, they often agree that they will vote for each other or other designated persons as directors. While such agreements are not part of the regulatory provisions of the corporation, they are binding on the contracting shareholders and will be enforced by the courts.

The principal function of a shareholders' agreement in a close corporation is to arrange for the case in which a shareholder dies or desires to sell his shares. Frequently the other shareholders are given an option to buy such shares. In providing for death, the shareholders face the difficult question whether it is better to let the family retain the shares, or to buy the family out. It is often undesirable for the surviving shareholders to continue the corporation with the widow or heirs of the deceased, particularly where the deceased was active in the management and must be replaced.

In connection with any option to buy shares, it is customary to stipulate the price to be paid. Book value is a frequently used standard of valuation. It is not always adequate, particularly in the case of large inventories with fluctuating market values, or capital assets that have been written down below their actual value. Consideration must be given to the goodwill value of the shares. If it is exaggerated, it will result in excessive death taxes. On the other hand, share value (which may be the book value) is often fixed in a shareholders' agreement for the express purpose of minimizing death tax problems.

In order to facilitate buying out a retiring or deceased shareholder, some corporations or individual shareholders purchase life insurance policies. In this connection a number of special problems arise. It is not the function of this survey to discuss these problems or other topics which may be covered in a shareholders' agreement. The preparation of a good shareholders' agreement requires more skill and thought than the organization of the corporation.

Even where a corporation is under the control of a faction of shareholders, or where the shares are so widely distributed that there is no organized majority and the management has virtually independent control, a minority shareholder is not completely at the mercy of the majority or the management. Every shareholder, even if he has no voting rights, has a right to inspect the corporate records. This right may be limited by law or the bylaws to prevent abuse. Moreover, if management abuses its power, a shareholder has recourse to the courts, which will protect the legitimate interests of all shareholders in the proper conduct of the corporation's business. However, the courts will seldom interfere with the business judgment of the directors and of the management, even if it is unsound, so long as the directors and the management act in good faith.

Minority shareholders' actions play an important part in U.S. corporation law. The expenses of such lawsuits must be borne by the corporation if the plaintiff wins his case. Unfortunately, minority shareholders' actions have been used to bully corporations into settlements; and corporations frequently agree to settle just to avoid the trouble and expense of litigation. Such abuse has created some antagonism toward this otherwise desirable remedy.

In case of mismanagement, it also may be possible for a shareholder to sue third parties for the damage that such parties have wrongfully caused the corporation.

The most powerful policeman in the corporate field is the Securities and Exchange Commission (see Chapter 18).

U.S. jurisprudence has developed the notion that a majority shareholder owes a fiduciary duty to the minority. A practical application of this doctrine is that a majority shareholder may not sell his shares at a premium price that is not also available to the minority. The question of breach of fiduciary duty by the majority is often raised in cases where the minority claims to have been frozen out. Mergers have been declared illegal in this connection.

## 9. SHAREHOLDERS' ACTION

If a shareholder has suffered an injury by the corporation, he may bring suit against it. He may also sue in the name and for the benefit of all other shareholders who are similarly aggrieved. This is a class action (see Chapter 24).

A class action must be distinguished from a shareholder's derivative action in which the plaintiff asserts that the corporation has been damaged (by the directors or officers) and that the wrongdoers are liable to the corporation. In a derivative action, the corporation is made a nominal defendant in the action, along with the alleged wrongdoer. Some states (for instance New York, but not Delaware) require a plaintiff, unless he owns a substantial amount of shares, to post security for the costs to be incurred by the corporation in defending the action.

## 10. DIRECTORS

U.S. statutes sometimes still state that a corporation is managed by the board of directors. However, directors as such are not managers. The board of directors resembles the supervising board of corporations in many civil law countries, except that in the U.S. the managing officers are generally members of the board of directors. Modern statutes, such as the New York Business Corporation Law, provide that the corporation is managed 'under the direction' of the board of directors. This is a realistic statement of what is true of all American corporations.

Each director must do what he conceives to be in the best interest of the corporation. The independent, good-faith, rational business judgment of an individual board member and of the board as a whole will not be interfered with by any court, even if the court is convinced that the business judgment was foolish. The business judgment rule is frequently invoked when directors make a decision about a takeover bid. Contrariwise, the directors of Signal Corp.

approved the sale of certain oil properties to the Burmah Oil Corp. The court found that the properties were probably worth substantially more, and that the directors had acted in haste and on the basis of inadequate information. The court, therefore, granted a complaining shareholder an injunction.

The board of directors generally must consist of at least three individuals. Most states require that at least one of them be a citizen of the U.S. and a resident of the state of incorporation. New York law does not require this, but it is desirable to elect directors who are close at hand. Foreigners frequently ask their U.S. lawyers to serve as directors of their U.S. corporations. Some overseas owners elect local directors, but require them to sign blank resignations. This is not necessary where the bylaws provide for instant dismissal of directors without need to state a cause. The directors direct policy and make their decisions by resolutions passed at directors' meetings. They must make these decisions according to their unrestricted judgment and, as a rule, are not allowed to bind themselves by contracts with respect to the exercise of this judgment. That means that contracts purporting to obligate a director to vote in a certain manner are invalid. Since directors must use their individual judgment, they cannot delegate their powers to a management company or to others. There are no alternate directors. A director cannot vote by proxy, except in Louisiana and Arkansas. If a director is absent from a meeting, his vote is lost – except where provision has been made for voting by mail or telephone.

One of the most important functions of the board of directors is to declare dividends, if sufficient funds are available. Here, too, the directors are the sole judges of whether or not a dividend should be declared. Even where a preferred stock issue provides for a fixed annual dividend, such dividend does not become payable unless and until the directors declare it. It is only in the rarest instances that court action can be instituted to force the declaration of dividends by the directors. In privately owned corporations, the owners frequently prefer to avoid dividends, which are subject to income tax. They would rather pay themselves higher salaries. In this, they may run afoul of the Internal Revenue Service, which allows tax deductions only for *reasonable compensation*. It is advisable to fix all executive compensation by a directors' resolution that is reflected in the minute book. Unreasonable accumulation of profits is subject to a penalty tax (see Chapter 8, Section 10).

The issuance of shares requires a resolution of the directors. All officers of the corporation are elected, and can be discharged, by the directors, except such officers as under the laws of some states are elected by the shareholders. Banks will generally not open an account for a corporation without written express authority from the board of directors. Outsiders dealing with a corporation often require that important contracts be approved by the directors, and they will then ask for a certified copy of the directors' resolution of approval.

As a rule, directors need not be shareholders. A few states require this, though. In such instances, where it is desired to appoint a non-shareholder as a director, it is customary to transfer one so-called qualifying share to such individual, with appropriate arrangement for re-transfer in case such individual should resign or be discharged.

The amount of work and time that a director, as such, devotes to the corporation is usually small, except in very large corporations where the chairman and certain members of the board may be fully engaged for the corporation. Since the directors are charged with determining policy, and with supervision of the actual management of the corporation, they can be held individually responsible for any act of mismanagement that is due to their own acts or their failure to act. This personal liability can also be asserted in favor of creditors of the corporation, and above all, it exists with respect to securities regulations (see Chapter 18). For this reason, it is often difficult to find outsiders who are willing to serve as directors, although courts are not inclined to hold outside directors as strictly liable as inside directors.

A director can protect himself or herself in four ways: (a) he will see to it that the board meets regularly, once a month or once in every quarter, in order to receive and discuss reports from the management; (b) he will record a dissenting vote, if he disapproves of any corporate action; (c) he will obtain a corporate indemnity against the cost of any litigation and monetary loss suffered as the result of any good faith action or omission on his part (such indemnity is often regulated by statute – in New York it is against public policy to extend the indemnity beyond the statutory limit; in Delaware the public policy is to the contrary, which is one of Delaware's attractions); and (d) he will cause the corporation to cover the risk of director's liability by insurance against various corporate business risks.

Foreign owners sometimes hesitate to confer directorial powers on U.S. residents, even if they are employees of the corporation. Such reluctance can sometimes be overcome by providing that a director may be discharged instantaneously and without stating any cause therefor.

Many states, New York included, allow directors' resolutions to be adopted without a physical meeting. Nonresident alien owners may find this attractive. However, it does away with an oral exchange of views, which is one of the advantages of collegial direction.

A director, as such, is not an employee of the corporation. As stated in Chapter 5, this has a bearing on obtaining an immigration visa. It is also important in connection with the entitlement to employees' benefits (see Chapter 13). However, the bylaws or a contractual arrangement may provide otherwise. As stated below, the chairman of the board of directors sometimes is employed as chief executive officer.

## 11. OFFICERS

Each corporation needs a president, a treasurer, and a secretary. In addition, there may be vice-presidents, assistant treasurers, and assistant secretaries. The bylaws may provide for other officers. A person may hold several corporate offices. However, the offices of president and of secretary should not be held by the same individual.

The officers of the corporation conduct the actual business of the corporation under the supervision of the board of directors. They are elected by the directors, except that in a few states certain officers are elected by the shareholders. As above stated, officers can be, and frequently are, members of the board of directors. The election is for a stated period of time, usually a year, but the officer(s) may be subject to earlier removal at the discretion of the directors.

The right to elect and remove officers cannot be abolished by long-term contracts. It is, therefore, not proper to employ a man as president of the corporation for a term of seven years, because such a contract would restrict the discretion of the directors at the annual elections. However, it is possible to make a long-term employment contract with an executive without reference to an officership. For instance, the president may be employed for seven years as general manager. Then, if the directors fail to re-elect him as president, he may continue to work for the corporation or claim damages for breach of contract, depending on the circumstances and the terms of his employment contract.

The chairman of the board, if one is elected, is, as such, not an officer of the corporation. However, the bylaws may provide to the contrary. It is not unusual for a corporation to have the chairman of the board serve as chief executive officer. In such a case, the president is generally the chief operating officer. In the absence of such an arrangement for the chairman, the president is the chief executive officer of the corporation. All other officers are subordinate to him. In actual practice, with smaller corporations the interested parties frequently distribute the offices among themselves – except where an employee is used to fill an office for which no principal is available.

The legal power of the various officers is of some importance in dealings with outsiders. When one enters into an agreement with a corporation, one has the right to assume that the president has plenary power to bind the corporation so long as the transaction is in the regular course of the corporation's business. With respect to other officers, their acts bind the corporation only if the corporation has, in its conduct, held out such officers as entitled to do such acts. If Smith is Secretary of a corporation, and has always been confined to office management, a purchase contract signed by him may not be binding upon the corporation if it chooses to repudiate it. The corporation cannot do this if the bylaws or a directors' resolution give Smith the power to make purchase contracts. Questions of this type do not arise often in practice. The possibility thereof, however, explains why people doing business with a corporation sometimes inquire into the authority of the officer with whom they are dealing.

## 12. ONE-PERSON CORPORATION

Historically, a corporation is, of course, an association of several persons. For that reason, the one-person corporation is a legal anomaly; but it is a reality that most states in the U.S. recognize. An American corporation may have only one incorporator, one shareholder, one director and one officer – all the same person. Fewer than the traditional minimum of three directors are generally permitted if the corporation has fewer than three shareholders.

A foreign corporation that owns all the shares of an American corporation may need only one director. In practice, the foreign corporation may appoint one of its executives as a member of the board of directors and elect two directors who live in the U.S., one of them usually the local manager in charge. This is not advisable where the foreign owner fears that the U.S. directors will act against his wishes.

In most states, a corporation may act as incorporator of another corporation. Some states, however, among them New York, require an individual as incorporator. This, generally, is a lawyer or an employee in a law office. The incorporator has no power after the directors have taken over and elected the management.

## 13. TRANSFER OF SHARES

American corporations issue no bearer shares. All shares must be registered in the name of the owner. The shares are represented by share certificates. A certificate may be for any number of shares, up to the authorized limit.

The transfer of shares is accomplished by a transfer of the certificate. The transfer of ownership (title) by one person to another is usually accomplished by an endorsement on the back of the certificate and delivery thereof. Instead of the endorsement, the transferor may issue a separate written form of assignment, generally referred to as a stock power. When the new owner has thus acquired title to the shares, he may ask the corporation to record the transfer on its books and to issue one or more new certificates to him. Unless he does so, the corporation will not know of his rights, and all notices of meetings and payments of dividends will go to the old shareholder, who is registered as the last owner in the books of the corporation. However, such registration is not a condition of the validity of the transfer between the parties. Sometimes shareholders refrain from notifying the corporation of the transfer, for instance where it is a temporary arrangement, such as a pledge.

There may be restrictions on the free transfer of shares, generally in close corporations. Such restrictions are binding on a purchaser of shares only if they are stated upon the certificate. Otherwise, an innocent purchaser may acquire title to the certificate regardless of the restriction. The restriction may be based on a private contract between shareholders, as discussed in connection with shareholders' agreements. Sometimes the corporation becomes a party to such agreement. Restrictions on transfer may also be imposed by the certificate of incorporation, or the bylaws of the corporation. For instance, it may be stipulated that shares must always be offered to the corporation before transfer to other parties. Or it may be provided that nobody will be recognized as a shareholder unless he meets certain personal qualifications. Such restrictions will, as a rule, only be legal if they serve a useful purpose. For instance, it might be useful to require that enemy aliens may not be shareholders, but it would not be legal to impose racial restrictions.

When a new shareholder presents a certificate to the corporation in order to have the transfer to him registered and to have a new certificate issued to him, the corporation is obligated to investigate whether the transfer has been validly made. Neglect in this respect makes the corporation liable to the proper shareholder.

That is why it is often so troublesome to effect transfer in case of death, to the surprise of foreign investors who are not used to this sort of difficulty. A corporation may require inspection of the last will of the deceased shareholder, in order to ascertain that the party requesting the transfer is actually entitled thereto. Where an executor or administrator requires transfer, he must furnish proof of his proper appointment. In case of death, most states also require clearance with the state tax authorities before allowing a transfer on the books of the corporation. In a closely-held corporation, there is generally no difficulty in connection with such transfer, as the corporation's officials are aware of the facts. The large corporations, however, employ special transfer agents, usually banks.

Many states impose a tax on the transfer of shares, which is paid by affixing stamps on the back of the certificate to be transferred.

## 14. FEDERAL LAW

Most of the federal regulations of corporations apply only to corporations whose shares are publicly traded. However, Section 10(b) of the Securities Exchange Act of 1934 makes unlawful any manipulative device or action in connection with the sale or purchase of any securities, whether or not they are publicly traded. This is a very broad federal statute. It has been implemented by rulings of the Securities and Exchange Commission and the courts and is discussed in Chapter 18.

CHAPTER 12

# PARTNERSHIPS AND JOINT VENTURES

## *1. INTRODUCTION*

Mr. Smith, doing business in America or with America, may have any or all of the following reasons to familiarize himself with the general principles governing partnerships and similar joint enterprises: He may do business with a U.S. partnership or a member of such a firm. In that case it is important to know who is responsible for what. Or Mr. Smith may engage, in one particular instance, in a joint venture with an American, without wishing to form a partnership. Where is the dividing line and what are the risks, he will ask himself. There are involuntary partnerships under U.S. law; that is, there are situations where one may be treated as a partner against one's intentions. And in certain instances, the law will not recognize a partnership in spite of a valid partnership agreement. Finally, Mr. Smith may wish to know about partnerships as he is interested in organizing one, either because he has a new business or because he wants to convert an existing business into a partnership.

Partnerships are generally governed by the Uniform Partnership Act and the Uniform Limited Partnership Act, which have been adopted (with minor modifications) by all U.S. states (except Louisiana), the District of Columbia and the Virgin Islands. The National Conference of Commissioners on Uniform State Laws recommended in 1976 the enactment of a Revised Uniform Limited Partnership Act, which recommendation has been accepted at this writing by only a handful of states (Connecticut, Arkansas, Minnesota and Wyoming).

In recent years, the organization of partnerships has gained great favor in the U.S. because of certain tax advantages. Some of the tax points are discussed below.

U.S. law knows two types of partnership, the general partnership and the limited partnership. Ordinarily, when we speak of a partnership, we mean a general partnership. We shall therefore consider this type first.

## 2. ORGANIZATION OF PARTNERSHIPS

A partnership is an association of two or more persons to carry on, as co-owners, a business for profit. At one time, it was the general rule that corporations could not be partners, primarily because it would result in divesting the directors of the corporation of management power. However, that rule has been abolished in many states, and many corporate charters expressly provide for the power to become a partner. The common law barred trusts from being a partner, but that is no longer the law. Indeed, aliens may find a U.S. trust a very convenient investment vehicle. A partnership may be a partner in another partnership.

The partnership has a separate identity. It is usually referred to as a *firm*. In contrast to the usage in many other countries, the word *firm* in the U.S. applies generally only to a partnership and not to any other form under which a business is conducted, although the term is often loosely – and carelessly – applied to any business concern. The name of the firm and its partners are generally required to be registered. However, it is not necessary to register the contract by which the parties regulate their relationships to each other. In fact, it is not always necessary to have a written partnership agreement. In most states, no written agreement is required if, at the time the partnership is entered into, the parties do not intend to have it last for more than one year.

Because it is thus possible to have a partnership without a written agreement, it sometimes happens that a person is faced with a claim of partnership where he never intended to be liable as a partner. Such a claim may be made by a business associate, or by a creditor of a business associate. Even if no written agreement is required, it is advisable to reduce to written form all agreements by which one shares profits or risks with another, or otherwise engages in an operation for joint account.

The law has established certain rules that govern the relation of partners to each other. The partners are free to change these rules, although such internal arrangements are not necessarily binding on outsiders who deal with the partnership. Even where the partners desire to adhere to the ordinary rules prescribed by law, practical experience shows the desirability of reciting these rules in a carefully prepared partnership agreement, in order that there be no misunderstanding.

All property brought into the partnership or acquired with partnership funds is partnership property. Each partner is co-owner of that property. He cannot dispose of his interest in any specific piece of partnership property. Nor can the creditors of an individual partner attach such partner's share in a specific piece of partnership property. However, the creditors of an individual partner can seek satisfaction of their claim by attaching the entire partnership interest of such partner – an event which may be of considerable annoyance to the other partners.

A partner may assign his interest in the partnership. That, however, does not make the assignee a partner. It merely gives the assignee the right to receive the profits to which the assigning partner was entitled.

If a partner dies, his rights in specific partnership property do not pass to his heirs, but vest in the surviving partners. The heirs merely have a right to be paid the value of the deceased partner's share, unless other provision has been made by agreement.

In the absence of other arrangements, each partner is entitled to the same share of profits, regardless of his contribution. The contributions, however, must be equal unless otherwise agreed upon. If a partner at any time contributes more than his agreed share, he is entitled to treat this as a loan to the firm, and to demand the payment of interest. If he advances funds or pays partnership debts, the firm must reimburse and indemnify him.

Each partner has equal rights in the management of the partnership business. In case of disagreement, decisions are made by majority vote. This applies only so long as the decision is within the scope of the partnership agreement. If a partnership is organized for the purpose of importing textiles, the majority of the partners cannot decide to engage in the machinery business. Such a change of the partnership agreement requires the consent of all partners.

Partners are held to be in a fiduciary relationship to each other. They must not compete with the business of the partnership. If a partnership operates its business in a leased location and the lease expires, a partner is not permitted to secretly lease the location for himself. If he does, the firm may treat this act of the partner as performed on behalf of the firm. The same is true if a partner attempts to make personal profits for himself in the lines of business in which the firm is engaged.

If disputes of this kind arise, the unfaithful partner must account. An accounting can be compelled by court action. If such an action is successful, the court will do two things: it will direct an accounting and it will decree payment of the amount found to be due on the accounting.

An accounting proceeding is also the usual remedy if disputes arise in connection with the dissolution of a partnership. A retiring party is entitled to an accounting for the entire period during which the partnership was in existence, which is an unwelcome burden on the other partners. This burden can be eliminated by a provision in the partnership agreement. The accounting action may be coupled with an action for dissolution in instances where the right to dissolve is uncertain and a court decision is preferred to a unilateral act of termination.

Each partner may terminate the partnership at any time. This is perfectly lawful if the partnership contains no provision for the duration of the firm or for a prescribed period of notice of termination. If a sudden withdrawal of one partner is in violation of the partnership agreement, such partner is liable to the others for the damage caused by his breach of contract. But the partnership is, in strict law, considered to be dissolved nonetheless. This is so because the existence of a U.S. partnership depends on the continued cooperation of all partners. For that reason, if one partner becomes bankrupt, and his interest in the firm passes to the court-appointed trustee in bankruptcy, the partnership is deemed dissolved

The death of a partner also terminates the partnership, unless the contrary is agreed upon in the partnership agreement.

In view of all this, it has been said that partnerships have a precarious existence due to the serious risk of dissolution and termination.

Prudent businesspeople, therefore, will make provisions in their partnership agreements with respect to termination and dissolution. The arrangement in case of the death of a partner presents difficult tax problems, not discussed in this chapter, but not to be overlooked in the preparation of a partnership agreement. It is often provided that, upon the death of a partner, the partnership shall be continued, with the surviving spouse of the deceased as a successor partner, or it shall be continued only by the remaining partners. In either case, continuity of the business is assured and a 'winding up' operation is prevented. However, it does not alter the fact that death has ended the old partnership, and a new partnership without the deceased partner has come into being. Walter, Weber and Wilcox are the three partners of the firm, Walter & Co. Walter dies. In accordance with the terms of the partnership agreement, Weber and Wilcox continue the firm under the name of Walter & Co. In spite of this, it is not the same partnership. The practical importance of this lies in the termination of Walter's liability for any debt of the firm incurred after his death. If Walter's widow becomes a partner pursuant to the provisions of the agreement, it is still a new partnership and the widow's position is the same as that of any outsider who joins the firm as a partner. However, the continuation of the firm results in liability of the new firm for the debts of the former partnership.

## 3. LIABILITY OF PARTNERSHIP AND INDIVIDUAL PARTNERS

Everybody understands that partnership property is liable for the debts of the partnership. Sometimes controversies arise in connection with the questions: (a) when is a debt a partnership debt?, and (b) to what extent is an individual partner personally liable for debts of the partnership?

Every partner is an agent of the partnership in the conduct of its ordinary and usual business. Therefore, any obligation incurred by a partner in the ordinary course of the firm's business binds the firm and constitutes a partnership liability. It makes no difference whether, by reason of some internal arrangement, the partner had no authority to do what he did. Internal restrictions on a partner's authority to obligate the firm are not binding on an outsider, unless the outsider has knowledge of them.

However, the firm is not bound if a partner makes a commitment which is not 'in the ordinary course of the partnership business'. Perkins is a partner in a firm of New York stockbrokers. He travels in Europe and contracts, in the name of the firm, for the purchase of a shipment of cheese. This is not a transaction in the ordinary course of a stock brokerage business, and the firm need not recognize the cheese contract. The seller in Europe should, therefore, be on his guard; before making shipment or extending credit, he should make sure that all of Perkins' partners consent to the transaction.

The execution of a guaranty is also ordinarily considered as outside the scope of the regular course of business. It is not safe to assume that a guaranty signed by one partner will bind the partnership.

The laws of most states enumerate certain acts that a partner is never authorized to do without the consent of all partners. Anyone dealing with a partnership should be familiar with this list, because his ignorance will not protect him. A partner has no authority to assign partnership property to a trust for creditors, or to dispose of the goodwill of the firm, or to do any other act that, in effect, would make it impossible to carry on the firm's ordinary business.

The statutory restrictions on a partner's authority include a prohibition against submitting a partnership claim to arbitration. The arbitration clause in any contract with a partnership is, therefore, not binding on the partnership, unless all partners have joined in or otherwise authorized the agreement.

The risk of being a general partner is that one may be held liable, with his entire fortune, for the debts of the firm. However, there is a distinction between liability for contract claims and liability for tort claims. The latter, in this connection, are claims based on wrongful acts or a breach of trust. A judgment based on a contract claim must, in the first instance, be satisfied out of partnership assets. Only if these assets are insufficient, may the claimant proceed against an individual partner. But, for a tort claim, each partner can be held directly liable, and the claimant need not first proceed against the firm. For instance, Perkins, a general partner of the Chicago firm of Perkins & Co., injures a pedestrian while he is on a business trip in Paris. If the firm has a partner in Paris, the pedestrian can sue the Paris partner without involving the Chicago firm or any of the Chicago partners.

## 4. LIMITED PARTNERSHIPS

The limited partnership is very similar to the French *société en comandite* and its counterparts in other foreign countries. It consists of one or more general partners and one or more limited partners. The general partners have the same rights and liabilities as in a general partnership. The limited partners (also sometimes called special partners), are only liable for the partnership debts to the extent of their contributions. Once they have made their agreed contributions to the firm, creditors cannot make any further claims against the limited partners. The limited partners share in the profits of the firm, but they are not permitted to participate in its management. They are really investors rather than partners.

If a limited partner takes part in the operation of the firm's business, or even if his name is used in the partnership name, he automatically becomes liable to creditors as a general partner. For this reason, the organization of a limited partnership is of no interest to an investor who expects to be active in the business. It is a convenient device, however, for a foreigner who resides abroad and wishes to invest in a U.S. firm.

The limited partner who participates in management or allows the use of his name becomes liable as a general partner because of the policy of safeguarding the interests of persons who deal with a partnership in reliance on the individual liability of the partners. In pursuance of that policy, it is generally required that full publicity be given to the limitation of liability. A written partnership contract, with complete details regarding the organization of the limited partnership, must be publicly recorded. In many states, including New York, the essence of the contract must be published in a designated newspaper. If this requirement of publication is not met, the limitation of liability is invalid.

## 5. SYNDICATIONS

The limited partnership is a favorite investment vehicle for those who wish to acquire a participating interest in an oil and gas venture, a real estate development, a theatrical production, or some other so-called tax shelter. (A tax shelter is a transaction that accelerates tax benefits and defers or reduces tax burdens.) The advantage of such syndication is that the participant, being a partner, can deduct from his ordinary taxable income a *pro rata* share of the depreciation and other deductions (and, in the case of oil and gas ventures, depletion) to which an owner is entitled under U.S. tax law, without being exposed to the risk of liability beyond the original investment. The promoter of the syndicate is usually a general partner whose liability is unlimited. There may be several general partners. The promoter/general partner usually contributes little money to the limited partnership. He earns his agreed share of the profits of the partnership by selecting and managing the partnership properties.

Attractive as an investment in a limited partnership may be, the investor, in addition to other risks, must be aware of two legal hazards. One is in connection with the tax laws, and the other relates to the securities laws. In syndications, it is customary to address these subjects in a legal opinion that the promoter of the syndicate submits to prospective limited partners. Such legal opinion is, of course, not binding on the government. In many instances the promoter obtains an advance tax ruling from the Internal Revenue Service.

The tax hazard is that the government may consider the limited partnership to be an association, which it taxes as a corporation. In this case, the expected tax advantages do not exist. An organization is taxed as a corporation if a majority of the following characteristics apply: (*a*) continuity of life; (*b*) centralized management; (*c*) limited liability; and (*d*) free transferability of interests. If two of these characteristics are present, and two are not, the Internal Revenue Service will consider other factors that may be relevant, such as the financial strength of the general partner or partners.

A limited partnership interest is a security within the meaning of the Securities Act of 1933 and most applicable state laws. These securities laws are discussed in Chapter 18. Failure to comply with them may have serious consequences. In many instances, exemption from the burdensome registration requirement is available. Even if an offering is exempt from registration, however, the sponsor of a syndication is required to make a full disclosure of all aspects of the contemplated business and its risks. The state of California requires a very extensive and detailed disclosure of the sponsor's performance record during the preceding five years. The California standard is regarded as the most stringent in the U.S.

## 6. INVOLUNTARY PARTNERSHIP

Registration or lack of registration of a partnership is no protection with respect to a person's liability as a partner. Registration and publication are not necessary conditions for the existence of the partnership. In this respect, U.S. law differs fundamentally from that of many foreign jurisdictions. A person may be held liable as a partner in the U.S., although he never intended to be one.

If Smith, by words or conduct, falsely represents himself to be a partner of Perkins & Co., he can be held liable as a general partner of Perkins & Co. by anybody relying on such representation. If Perkins & Co., by conduct or words, consents to such false representation, all partners of the firm will be bound by the acts and agreements of Smith. Such situations do not necessarily arise because a fraud was intended. A person is sometimes introduced as a partner because it appears expedient at the moment, and there is no thought of the further consequences.

Another type of involuntary partnership may arise from a profit-sharing arrangement. If a manufacturer promises an inventor a share of profits because the inventor permits the manufacturer to use the invention, it is generally not intended that the inventor become a partner of the manufacturer. The same is true if, for instance, several persons join in a stock underwriting agreement. The law 'presumes', however, that such arrangements constitute a partnership, unless the contrary can be proved. Consequently, the manufacturer may be faced with a claim by the inventor that they are partners; or the inventor may be confronted by claims of the manufacturer's creditors, who try to hold the inventor liable as a partner. To forestall such situations, many profit-sharing agreements contain a clause stating that the parties are not partners. It is not necessary to have such a provision where the profit share constitutes part of an employee's salary, or a landlord's rent, or other similar instances. Of course, no internal arrangement will prevent partnership liability if an outsider establishes that he was led reasonably to believe that he was dealing with a partnership.

## 7. JOINT VENTURES

The cases just described are known generally as joint ventures. A joint venture is a transaction in which two or more people band together for a specific business purpose that is limited in scope and duration, and that usually does not require the entire time and attention of the persons engaged therein. The parties do not intend to be continuing partners or to form a separate partnership entity. Their liability for each other's acts and commitments is restricted to the particular transaction for which they have joined together.

However, the transaction must be under the joint control of the joint venturers. This should be clearly expressed in a written agreement as the following case demonstrates. A California corporation guaranteed to the creditor of a partnership that the corporation would reimburse the creditor for any losses which the creditor might suffer. For this, the partnership promised the corporation 50% of partnership profits. The business resulted in a loss, and the corporation paid the creditor. The corporation then deducted that payment from its taxable income. The deduction was disallowed because the corporation had no control over the business of the partnership and, therefore, was held not to be a joint venturer.

Joint ventures have gained increased importance in international trade. A U.S. company which in earlier times may have disdained any foreign joint venture – not to mention acquiring a minority interest – may now be having second thoughts. The rise in nationalism in all parts of the world, and the ensuing demands for local participation, have brought about new developments. The need for international cooperation has opened new opportunities for international joint ventures.

A distributor who promises the manufacturer a percentage of the sales profits is not a joint venturer, where the distributor alone controls the sales.

When several joint venturers are engaged in the same line of business, they may run afoul of the antitrust laws. A movement is afoot to make research and development joint ventures, which occur with growing frequency, immune from the antitrust laws.

Sometimes the joint venturers organize a new corporation to pursue their common purpose. Economically this is still a joint venture, but legally it is not.

## 8. TAXATION OF PARTNERSHIPS AND JOINT VENTURES

U.S. tax law makes no distinction between joint ventures and partnerships. The term *partnership* in the tax law embraces all business organizations that are not organized or regarded as corporations.

For income tax purposes, the partnership is not considered as a separate organization. The income of the firm is taxed to each partner, in accordance with his interest in the firm. That means that each partner must include in his annual taxable income that portion of the partnership income to which he is entitled. He may also deduct for tax purposes his proportionate share of any partnership losses.

Partners are taxed on their shares of the firm's income, even if not paid out to them. This may lead to hardship in cases where a partnership has made substantial profits but lacks liquidity, and if the partners themselves are short of cash. Undesirable consequences may also result if the partnership is engaged in international trade, as is illustrated by the following case: Mr. Freudmann in the U.S. was a member of a Canadian partnership. He was unable to transfer his profits from Canada to the U.S. because of Canadian foreign exchange regulations. The Tax Court of the U.S. ruled that Freudmann must, nevertheless, pay U.S. income tax on his Canadian income because the law taxes partners on partnership profits even if not paid out to them.

A nonresident alien who is a partner in a U.S. firm will always be taxed as a person engaged in business in the U.S., as mentioned in Chapter 8. This applies even if he is only a limited partner.

Other tax aspects are discussed in Section 10 of Chapter 8.

## 9. PARTNERSHIP OR CORPORATION?

The principal disadvantage of a corporation, as compared with a partnership, is that the business income of the corporation is taxed twice – first as income of the corporation before it reaches the owners, and then as income of the individual owners when the corporation distributes a dividend to them (see Chapter 8, Section 18).

However, this distinction is purely theoretical in cases where the corporation does not have substantial net profits. For instance, if the profits of the corporation are not greater than the amount that can be reasonably paid as salaries to the owners (the salaries being a deductible business expense for the corporation), there will be no taxable income. In some partnerships, the partners are also paid a *salary*, but such a salary is in reality a part of the partners' shares of the firm's income, and it is treated as such under the tax law. The disadvantage of owners having to pay taxes on profits that are not paid out to them does not exist in the case of a corporation that has a legally recognized reason for accumulating its profits – if, for instance, it lacks sufficient working capital or needs funds to finance an expansion or has substantial debts. In such a situation, the owners may find that the tax on the corporation's income is lower than the tax they would have to pay if the business were operated as a partnership.

Broadly speaking, a low-income business is generally better off as a partnership, while other businesses will operate more profitably as corporations. Whether this is so in any particular case depends on many factors: the business outlook, what salaries can be reasonably paid to the owners, what other income they have, etc. It is impossible to lay down a fixed rule, and businesspeople are well advised to calculate in dollars and cents what the situation will be in their particular case, before trying to reach a conclusion as to which form of organization will be best for tax purposes.

If it is desired to convert a corporation into a partnership, special tax problems arise with respect to resulting taxable gains. Sometimes it is worthwhile to pay these extra taxes because savings will result in the long run. In other instances, the cost of such a change-over is prohibitive.

To transform a partnership into a corporation is less of a tax problem. In fact, even where it has been decided to operate a business as a corporation, it is sometimes found advisable to start out as a partnership and to change over later to corporate form. The primary reason for this is that it is easier for a partnership than for a corporation to obtain a tax benefit from the losses that most new enterprises experience in the early stages of their existence (see Chapter 26, Section 7).

CHAPTER 13

# AGENCY AND EMPLOYMENT RELATIONS

## 1. INTRODUCTION

Hardly any businessperson can handle his affairs without the help of others. He uses agents, employees or independent contractors. The agent and the employee are under his direction, the independent contractor is not. Indeed, agreements with independent contractors often contain a clause confirming this fact. The clause is inserted because the businessperson wants to emphasize that he assumes no liability for any act of the independent contractor. A similar disclaimer cannot be made with respect to agents and employees, who act under the direction of their employer.

Agents are employed to perform specified services for and on behalf of a so-called principal. They are paid as, if, and when the services are rendered. Their compensation is generally called a *commission*. On the other hand, an employee is paid a fixed salary, which may be measured by the time spent (per hour, per week, per month, or per year) or by the work performed (piece workers).

It is inadvisable to enter into an agency relationship or an employment contract without careful consideration to the character of the agreement and its terms.

One of the fundamental questions is the extent of the agent's authority. The principal must determine to what extent he will be bound by the acts of the agent. If that is not properly regulated, it may happen that the law will hold the principal liable beyond the limits that he had in mind when he appointed the agent. Other basic questions concern the compensation payable to the agent or employee, and the duration of the agreement. Disputes on these points between principals and their agents and employees arise all too frequently, mostly because the parties neglected to settle the matters in advance.

Mention should be made of the 1978 Hague Convention on the law applicable to Agency. The Convention has been ratified by the U.S. and is in force. It is of limited interest here because this chapter deals only with situations in which U.S. law applies. It is significant, though, that the Convention takes note of the American concept of an undisclosed agency – that is, a situation where the agent does not disclose to outsiders that he is acting not for himself but on behalf of an undisclosed principal.

## 2. THE AGENT AND HIS AUTHORITY

In the business world, the word *agent* is used in a variety of situations that are not always agency relationships in the legal sense. Conversely, such an agency relationship sometimes exists without the parties being aware of it. The word *agent*, in legal language, describes a person who acts under the authority of and for the account of another, the so-called principal. The acts of the agent bind the principal, provided the agent acts within the limits of his authority. The limits of an agent's authority are not always known to outsiders who deal with the agent. It is, therefore, important for the principal to have a clear understanding of how far the agent's authority goes. Likewise, a third party who deals with an agent frequently faces the question of the extent to which the agent's acts will bind his principal.

In important transactions, the third party will demand written proof of the agent's authority, in order to be sure that the principal cannot repudiate the agent's acts. In ordinary transactions this is usually impracticable. Certain rules have developed, therefore, on which the businessperson can rely. For instance, a sales agent is generally presumed to be without authority to accept payment for his principal. Where this rule applies, the principal need not recognize any payment made by a third party to the agent. That becomes important only if the agent should fail to remit the payment to the principal. The risk of this happening is not confined to cases of dishonesty. The agent may withhold payments from his principal because he has counterclaims. That would not help a third party who has made an unauthorized payment to an agent.   The third party is, however, protected if the agent was given 'apparent authority' on which the third party had a right to rely. In the above example, if the principal has permitted the agent in the past to make collections for him, he cannot suddenly repudiate the agent's act in reliance on some written agency contract that was unknown to the third party. If a corporation appoints a man as its president, he is thereby given the apparent authority to make contracts for the corporation in the regular course of its business; and the corporation will be bound by such contracts, even if there is some internal arrangement that restricts the president's authority. Other officers of a corporation do not have such wide powers merely by virtue of their office and title; but if a corporation allows one of its vice-presidents to sign contracts, it cannot thereafter repudiate a contract made by the vice-president because he lacked authority. The same principal obtains in other situations where one party permits another to act for him. Sometimes the joint ventures organize a new corporation to pursue their common purpose. Economically this is still a joint venture but legally it is not.

In international transactions, the extent of an agent's authority is generally determined according to the law of the place where the agency contract was made. For instance, under U.S. law, an agent usually loses his authority automatically when the principal dies. However, if the agent was appointed in a foreign country, where the law is different, then such different rule will be recognized in the U.S.

## 3. PARTICULAR AGENCY SITUATIONS

Sales agents often insist on being granted an exclusive agency. This does not prevent the principal from making a direct sale if he finds a buyer. But does he, in such a case, have to pay a commission to his exclusive agent? It depends on the nature of the exclusivity agreement. No commission is payable if the agent merely has an exclusive agency, meaning that the principal may not appoint any other agent. However, if the agent is given the exclusive right to sell, he is entitled to a commission if the principal makes a direct sale. The distinction is often overlooked.

The problem of exclusivity also arises in distribution contracts (see Chapter 10, Section 10). Distributors are, in most instances, independent contractors who buy and sell for their own account. Sometimes, however, they are only agents; and sometimes they are both agents and independent contractors. Where the distributor is granted an exclusive territory, the principal, often a foreign manufacturer, will want to reserve to himself the right to sell to certain customers with whom he has established connections. These customers are often called house accounts.

Another exclusivity problem arises when a regional distributor makes a sale in his exclusive territory calling for shipment of the product into the exclusive territory of another regional distributor. This calls for a division of the sales commission, and should be settled by an appropriate contract provision.

Most distributors, even if they are independent contractors, assume agency duties. For instance, they may assume the obligation to promote the business of the principal in a certain territory, or they may make shipping or banking arrangements for the principal.

If merchandise is shipped on consignment, it is necessary for the seller to make a specific agreement with the consignee as to the mutual rights and obligations, and particularly as to the ownership of the merchandise. If nothing is agreed on this point, ownership generally remains with the seller until the consignee has disposed of the merchandise. In this respect, the consignee is an agent of the seller. However, while the merchandise is in the consignee's possession, any creditor of the consignee may be able to seize the merchandise in order to satisfy his claim against the consignee. The most effective method of protecting the seller against this situation is to have the merchandise clearly labeled as the property of the seller, thereby giving notice to the world that the property does not belong to the consignee.

The following example illustrates a problem that arises frequently in international trade: Simon in Chicago sells a machine to Plum in Shanghai. The contract states that the sale is f.o.b. Chicago. In accordance with local usage, Simon makes arrangements for shipment from Chicago to Seattle and from Seattle to Shanghai. Upon arrival of the machine in Seattle, a strike prevents further transportation. Simon then arranges for storage of the machine in a warehouse. The warehouse demands payment of its charges from Simon. Simon then demands payment from Plum for the machine, as well as for the prepaid freight and the warehouse charges. Plum refuses to pay and, in addition, cancels the contract because of the delay in shipment, an event which had not been covered in the contract. Without going into the other questions which this typical case presents, Simon should have made it clear in his contract with Plum that his obligation as seller was fully performed upon delivery of the machine to the railroad in Chicago; and that subsequent acts would be performed by him as agent for Plum. There would then be no question that Plum was responsible for all subsequent expenses and that all subsequent risks, including that of a strike, would be for the account of Plum, the principal. Further, when making the arrangement with the warehouse in Seattle, Simon should have stated expressly that he was acting as agent for Plum. He could thus have avoided personal liability for the warehouse charges. Having failed to disclose the agency relationship, he cannot escape personal liability.

If the agent makes clear that he enters into an obligation on behalf of his principal, he is not personally responsible for the obligation. But if he fails to disclose the agency or the name of his principal, the agent is personally liable. If, later on, the other party discovers the identity of the undisclosed principal, the latter can also be held responsible because the contract was made for his benefit.

Brokers are also agents, in a broad sense. Usually their function is not to act for a principal, but rather to bring two parties together. Generally, a broker has earned his commissions when he has placed his principal in a position to close a desired contract – regardless of whether the principal avails himself of the opportunity.

This should be borne in mind by foreigners, who may not expect to pay the broker unless and until the trasaction is consummated. It is, of course, possible to stipulate in writing that the broker's commissions are only payable if, in the vernacular, the deal closes.

In the absence of a contrary agreement, the broker's commissions must be paid entirely by the seller; the purchaser is not liable. Real estate brokers in most states can enforce a commission claim only if they are licensed in the state in which the real estate is located. Business brokers, as a rule, require no license, except in rare instances. But contracts with business brokers are generally invalid unless they are evidenced by a writing. One may act in good faith as a business broker, only to find, to his chagrin, that he has no enforceable claim against the party for whom he acted.

Brokerage commissions must be distinguished from the so-called finder's fee. Mr X in Kuwait asks somebody in New York to find him a suitable business. Mr X does not realize that by making this request he may incur a financial obligation, which might be substantial. The person in New York is entitled to compensation if the contract between the parties is in writing. The contract need not state the amount. The law presumes that the finder is entitled to a reasonable compensation. What is reasonable is generally determined by custom.

The requirement of a written contract usually does not apply if the services in a real estate matter are rendered by a licensed real estate broker or by a lawyer.

Awareness of the foregoing should suffice to caution anyone doing business in the U.S. Written agreements can avoid such surprises.

In the commodity trade, brokers often act for both parties, and the broker's *memorandum*, if communicated to and accepted by both principals, constitutes the contract between them. In cases of this type, the broker may accept payment from both principals – a practice that is otherwise not permissible for an agent.

## 4. EMPLOYEES

What is generally referred to as an employment relationship is known in the law, archaically, as a *master and servant* relationship. The term *servant* applies in this connection to a cook, a clerk, or even a bank president. All are employed by the *master*, and work for him subject to his direction. An employee may be an agent as well a servant. For instance, the bank president is an officer of the banking corporation and, as such, is an agent of the bank. His acts will bind the bank. For the same reason, a salesman may be an agent of his employer although he receives a weekly salary.

Whatever distinctions may be made as between an employee and an agent, one cardinal principle applies to both, the doctrine of *respondeat superior* ('Let the one higher up be responsible'). That is, if an employee or an agent is acting within the course and scope of his employment or agency when he commits a tortious (wrongful) act (including fraud or misrepresentation), the employer or principal is civilly liable to the injured third person, even if the former had no knowledge of the act, forbade or disapproved of it and it was contrary to instructions. The common law notion that a forged endorsement on any negotiable instrument is a legal nullity and ineffective as to any subsequent holder regardless of good faith is in sharp contrast to the rules under which business operates outside the Anglo-American orbit.

An important feature of the relationship between employer and employee is the employee benefit plan, notably retirement and pension plans. There are a variety of employee stock ownership plans. The subject of employee benefit plans is very complex, and does not lend itself to a discussion within the framework of this book. However, it should be considered by anybody who employs a substantial number of employees. Often, it is also of interest to a small business owner who may be the principal employee and wishes to avail himself of the tax advantages of a retirement plan. This requires compliance with tax regulations. Since these change from time to time, in order to retain the tax advantages the retirement plan will then require amendment.

Trade unions generally have their pension plans. An employer will obligate himself to make financial contributions to the trade union's pension plan, instead of establishing an independent company plan. There are also multi-employers pension plans, which are operated for the benefit for the benefit of employees of several employers. These cause special problems. The selection of a plan requires careful investigation.

Another facet of the employment relationship is the prohibition of discrimination on account of race, religion, nationality, sex, age or physical condition. Many U.S. employers make a special effort to employ members of the protected categories. The president of a U.S. manufacturing company was visited by a Federal official, who inquired how many 'minority' people were employed in the plant. The president answered, with a blank face, 'We employ six English engineers'. That, of course, was not what the official was after. However, he was pleased to learn that the second in command bore a Spanish name. In a recent case, a U.S. employer was sued by an employee in London, who complained that he was discharged because of his age, in violation of the Discrimination in Employment Act. The court dismissed the action because the anti-discrimination Act has no extraterritorial force. If the American employer is a wholly-owned subsidiary of a foreign corporation, it cannot escape responsibility for discrimination because of a treaty. Sumitoro, the New York subsidiary of a Japanese company, employed only Japanese males in executive positions. Some New York female secretaries sued the corporation, alleging unlawful discrimination on the basis of sex and national origin. The corporation asserted that its employment practices were protected by the commercial treaty between Japan and the U.S. The case was appealed to the Supreme Court, which ruled that reliance on such a treaty was misplaced. As a New York corporation, Sumitoro must abide by the U.S. anti-discrimination laws.

One last comment on the employment relationship seems appropriate in light of some foreign practices. The idea that employees or workers should participate in the management of the company is alien to the U.S. system. Enlightened management often finds it desirable to inform the employees of the company's activities and problems. This is believed to increase the employees' interest in the company, to improve productivity, and to boost employee morale. All this is voluntary, and unlike the Vredeling proposal for the European Common Market countries, no legal right to such information is contemplated. Nor does the average U.S. employee like what is conceived to be the Japanese style of management, which is regarded as paternalistic. Lately, there has been movement toward placing a union representative on the board of directors of employer corporations. Such an initiative is under way in the automobile industry, as an example.

## 5. THE WRITTEN CONTRACT

Agency and employment contracts for more than one year must be in writing in order to be valid. Oral agreements extending for more than one year are usually invalid or unenforceable. This is an aspect of what is known as the

'Statute of Frauds'. The strictness of this rule is illustrated by the following case. Windels employed Tyler for a period of eighteen months, at a salary of $350 per month plus 20% of Windels' net profits. Windels paid the salary for each of the eighteen months. At the end of the first year, he also paid Tyler the promised 20% profit share. But six months later, when the agreement came to an end, Windels refused to pay the profit share for the last six months. Tyler sued Windels. Windels admitted everything, including his promise. But since the entire agreement had been oral, the promise was not binding and Tyler lost the lawsuit.

An oral agreement of indefinite duration that is capable of performance within one year is valid – even if the agreement is later extended for a longer period. For this reason, an oral contract whereby Paul hires Adam as a salesman, without any length of employment being specified, is usually valid. Sometimes, the circumstances of the situation disclose that the parties intended a certain, although indefinite, length of time for the contract. For instance, a person may be hired as agent or employee for the purpose of doing a specific job. In these situations, the validity of the contract depends on the question of whether the specific job was capable of performance within one year – a question which may be debatable and, therefore, is likely to result in a lawsuit. The same question arises where an agent is employed for the duration of a certain situation. Oral contracts for the 'duration of the war' have been held valid because the war might terminate within one year. In other instances, the decision may be to the contrary, and no circumspect businessperson will risk such uncertainties arising out of oral contracts.

An agent in New York recently sued his principal for commissions that he claimed to have earned during a six-month period. The agency had been in existence for only those six months. Nevertheless, the agent claimed that under the oral agency agreement he was entitled to commissions not only on orders he had procured during his agency, but also on repeat orders that the principal might receive after the termination of the agency. The principal denied making any such promise. The court found it unnecessary to ascertain the truth on this point. It held that, even if it had been made, the alleged promise of commissions on repeat orders rendered the contract one for an indefinite period, beyond one year. Hence, the contract was invalid. It would have been wiser for the agent not to contend for the commissions on repeat orders. His real mistake was, of course, that he did not insist on a written agreement. This not only would have removed all doubt with respect to the contract's validity, but also would have established the extent of his commission rights.

Employers and principals are often subjected to unfounded claims for salary or commissions, because of the existence of loose oral agreements. They then find themselves compelled to make a settlement to avoid the trouble and expense of a lawsuit. Their decision to compromise an unfounded claim is also based on the experience that courts, and particularly juries, are frequently inclined to favor an employee or agent. Americans incline to the underdog.

It is likewise in the interest of the employee or agent to have a written agreement, as he frequently will be unable to afford a lawsuit against a principal who fails to honor his oral obligations.

## 6. COMPENSATION

The fact that there is no valid contract of agency or employment does not mean, however, that the employee or agent is not entitled to receive any compensation for his actual services. If useful services were rendered and accepted, the agent or employee is entitled to be paid the *reasonable value* of these services. How much that is will be determined by usage, custom, or prevailing rates. The rate of compensation agreed upon in an invalid contract might also be considered as an indication of what is reasonable compensation under the circumstances.

The question of *reasonable compensation* arises not only when contracts are invalid, but also in situations where one is hired as agent or employee without any express agreement regarding compensation. In such a situation, the promise of payment of a reasonable compensation is assumed. This is not always recognized. For instance, if one asks another to find a buyer for one's business or to help one obtain a bank loan, the other person is usually entitled to a finder's fee or a brokerage commission, even if no promise to that effect was given. Some people think it to their advantage to keep silent on the question of compensation when retaining the services of an agent or employee. That is a mistake. In fact, only a specific written agreement will prevent uncertainty and possible disappointment.

This is particularly true in instances where compensation depends on the result to be accomplished, as in the case of commission payments to agents or brokers, or the payment of a percentage of profits to employees. In those cases, the absence of a fixed agreement frequently leads to disputes as to when the compensation is earned, and how it is to be computed. As mentioned, a broker ordinarily has earned his commissions if he has procured a ready buyer or seller for his principal. If it is desired to make the payment of the brokerage fee conditional upon actual consummation of the deal, this must be specifically agreed upon. A sales agent has usually earned his commissions when the sale is closed. The agent's right to receive the commissions is not affected by what happens thereafter, unless the agency agreement provides otherwise. Thus, the principal's inability to ship the merchandise as a result of war conditions does not relieve him from paying the commissions, even if it frees him as against the purchaser. However, if performance of the contract is illegal without a government license, the commissions are not payable before such license is obtained. But the principal must make every reasonable effort to obtain the necessary license. If he fails to do so, the agent may sue him for damages. The agent's right to commissions does not, as a rule, depend on payment by the principal's customer.

Specific agreements between principals and agents usually vary this rule, and make commission payments conditional upon collection. The agreement should also state whether or not the agent's right to receive a commission applies to repeat orders, whether it ends upon termination of the agency and, in case of a territorial agency, whether the agent is entitled to commissions on sales not made by or through him. The U.S. law knows no fixed rules with respect to these questions, and it is therefore essential to have an express agreement thereon.

If an employee is entitled to participate in the employer's profits, it is usually done on a yearly basis. Suppose the employment is terminated in the middle of a year. There are various possibilities of paying the employee a *pro rata* share, and there is also the possibility that the employee is not entitled to any profits unless he is employed for the entire year. Again, there are no fixed rules on the subject, and it must be covered by specific agreement.

How shall the commissions or the profit share be computed – on a gross or on a net basis? An employee's profit share is usually computed without regard to the employer's income tax liability. For instance, Edwards is entitled to 10% of X Corporation's *net profits before taxes*. Suppose X Corporation's net profits are $100,000. Edwards then is entitled to $10,000. X Corporation can deduct this payment as an expense for tax purposes; and its taxable income is $90,000. Assuming a 40% tax rate, X Corporation pays $36,000 in taxes and retains a net of $54,000. If Edwards's profit participation is *after taxes*, Edwards will receive less and the corporation will retain a greater share of its earnings.

Occasionally, employers fix the employee's profit participation as 'before payment of salaries to executives'. This is desirable where the employer wishes to avoid any argument about the amount of salaries paid to executives, who may be the owners of the business. Such arguments are likely to arise where the employee feels that his profit share is unduly reduced by excessive salaries to others. For the same reason, he may question other expenditures. To forestall such arrangements, the employer frequently stipulates that the amount of profits shall be determined by the certified public accountant who audits the employer's books, and that such accountant's statement shall be binding (see Chapter 26).

As a rule, any agent or employee who receives compensation in the form of commissions or a profit share is entitled to demand inspection of the books and records of his employer, if he questions the correctness of the employer's computation. Often this is extremely irksome to an employer or principal, as such request for inspection usually is made after the relationship is terminated. In cases where the ex-employee or ex-agent has become a competitor or works for a competitor, many courts allow only a limited inspection. The employer can protect himself to some extent against such unwelcome inspection by appropriate contract provisions.

## 7. TERMINATION

One of the features of U.S. employment relations that surprises foreigners is the ease with which an employee may be discharged or, in the vernacular, may be fired. The employee may be told at the end of a day, 'Don't come back. You are through'. This applies to a clerk or laborer as well as to the president of a company. The harshness of this state of affairs is sometimes softened by the (not universal) custom that an employee who is paid by the week cannot be discharged until the end of a week; or, if payment is made at other intervals, until the end of the payment period. Recently, a trend has been developing to establish the concept of 'abusive termination'. Abusive termination has been held to exist, and to be illegal, if there is no valid reason for abrupt termination

The highest court of New York has rejected the doctrine unequivocally. The Supreme Court of Wisconsin recognizes a public policy exception to the harsh employment-at-will doctrine. Under the exception, an employee has a cause of action for wrongful discharge if the termination clearly is contrary to the public welfare as expressed in constitutional or statutory provisions. While the concept of abusive termination is not universally recognized, one would do well to reckon with it. The problem can be altogether avoided by a written employment agreement. Executive employees increasingly insist on a written employment contract, with ample advance notice provisions in case of termination.

In a few instances, employees are protected against sudden termination. Discharge is prohibited if it would violate the anti-discrimination laws. The Labor Management Relations Act protects employees from discharge because of union activities. There are a few similar Federal and state statutes; but, as a rule, employees may be discharged at will unless they have a written employment contract, or are protected by a contract between the employer and the trade union of which the employee is a member, or the discharge constitutes an abusive termination in a state which recognizes that concept. The doctrine of abusive termination has been invoked in damages actions by long-time employees who were discharged shortly before they qualified for retirement benefits, or because they revealed illegal acts of the employer.

Executives whose positions are threatened by a corporate takeover sometimes fight to obtain a 'golden parachute', which is the promise of a substantial payment in case of termination. This is supposed to frighten away a potential acquirer. The validity and propriety of the golden parachute are subject to question. The expression comes from England, where the 'golden handshake' at the time of dismissal has a similar meaning.

In Puerto Rico, employees enjoy more protection than in other parts of the U.S. It is very difficult to terminate an agency, and particularly a distribution agreement, in Puerto Rico.

Where an agency or employment contract is made for a specific period of time, the contract is automatically terminated at the end of that period. If, thereafter, the agent or employee continues to work for the principal or employer, the mutual rights are the same as if no contract had been made. Occasionally, courts have held that in such a situation the old contract is considered as extended on its terms, but such is not the general rule.

## 8. COMPETITION BY EX-AGENT OR EX-EMPLOYEE

If the agency or employment relationship is terminated, the principal often is disturbed by the possibility that the ex-agent or ex-employee may use valuable information about the principal's business, either by going into business for himself or by using such information for the benefit of a competitor. To what extent can the principal protect himself?

It is unlawful for any agent or employee to disclose to others or to use for himself confidential information obtained in the course of employment. However, it is not always easy to determine what information is confidential in nature. Moreover, it is difficult for a principal to enforce his rights. If he learns early enough what the unfaithful agent or employee is doing, he may be able to stop him by a court injunction. Otherwise, he can only sue for damages, and that is obviously futile unless the ex-agent or ex-employee is in a financial position to pay damages. If the confidential information is used by a competitor who is aware of the fact that its use is unlawful, the principal may be able to proceed against such competitor (see also the discussion of Trade Secrets in Chapter 20, Part C, Section 3).

Agency and employment contracts frequently provide that upon termination of the contract the agent or employee shall not engage in any competitive business for a certain length of time or in a certain territory. Such clauses are valid only if they do not constitute an unreasonable restraint of trade. U.S. law does not permit a contract by which a person is prevented from earning his livelihood. A chemist cannot be bound to stop working as a chemist after termination of a given employment. However, he may be prevented from taking employment in a particular area or in a specialized industry, provided the stipulated period is not unreasonably long and the stipulated area is not unduly broad. This example does not express any fixed rule, but merely illustrates the general approach to the problem. Each case must be judged in light of its particular circumstances. An invalid non-competition clause may invalidate the entire agreement. For that reason, such clauses must be prepared with care (see Part C of Chapter 20).

## 9. BRIBING EMPLOYEES AND AGENTS

The disloyalty of an agent or employee may be induced by a competitor of the principal, or by people who do business with the principal.

Perkins employs an efficient salesperson. A competitor persuades that individual to leave Perkins' employ for the competitor's. This is lawful, so long as it does not involve any breach of contract by the salesperson. But if the competitor induces the salesperson to breach a contract with Perkins, then Perkins can hold the competitor responsible for damages; and he might even be able to obtain an injunction by which the competitor is prohibited from employing the salesperson.

Sometimes, a supplier of merchandise pays a secret commission or other bribe to an employee of a purchaser, as a means of promoting the supplier's business. This is illegal. The supplier is liable to the purchaser for the amount of the bribe. In many states, he is also subject to criminal prosecution, for the 'corrupt influencing of agents, employees or servants'. The same is true in cases where a customer bribes an employee of his supplier – which happens more frequently when merchandise is scarce. When warned against such improper practices, businesspeople sometimes reply that 'everybody does it'. That is not true; and, in any case, it does not protect the person who is caught.

The Federal Trade Commission may proceed against a party who engages in unfair practices of the kind described, should a complaint be lodged with that agency.

# CHAPTER 14

# BANKING AND FINANCE

## 1. INTRODUCTION

The U.S. has no central bank that issues bank notes. The U.S. dollar bills are issued by the Treasury Department of the Federal Government and signed by Federal Government officials. The Federal Reserve System, which was superimposed on the system of state banks as recently as 1913, performs many of the functions elsewhere performed by central national banks.

The Federal Reserve System consists of twelve regional Federal Reserve Banks and the Federal Reserve Board in Washington, D.C. The 'Fed', as the system is generally called, coordinates and controls the commercial banks and regulates the nationwide money supply and credit conditions. Unlike the central banks elsewhere, the Fed operates independently of the executive branch of the Federal Government and is responsible only to the Congress.

Turning now to private banks, three types stand out: the commercial bank, the savings bank and the investment bank. Investment banks are a special breed, they require neither a Federal nor a state charter. They are discussed in Section 2, below. Savings banks are classified as thrift institutions (also called 'thrifts'), a category which also includes Savings and Loan Associations. All banks accept deposits and make loans. However, one doing business in the U.S. usually deals with commercial banks. Banks are either federally chartered, in which case they are national banks, or chartered by the states in which they are organized. All national banks are members of the Federal Reserve System, and subject to its rules. These rules require bankers to place a portion of their demand deposits with the local Federal Reserve Bank as a reserve. Other rules prescribe credit terms to be observed by banks. stockbrokers and other financial institutions in their lending role.

A substantial number of banks, notably smaller local banks (but also some larger ones, such as Morgan Guaranty Trust Company and Chemical Bank) have merely a state charter and may become, but are not obliged to be, members of the Federal Reserve System. National banks are regulated by the Federal Comptroller of the Currency. In addition, all banks must be licensed by the state in which they operate, usually by the state banking department. All banks, federally chartered as well as state chartered, are subject to the supervision of the banking department of the state in which they operate.

Bank examiners periodically scrutinize banking operations and pass on a bank's solvency. The underlying reason for this supervision is the governmental desire to protect depositors. The Federal Deposit Insurance Corporation is available as an insurer of bank deposits. At this writing, the maximum insured sum for a single account is $100,000. All members of the Federal Reserve System are required to purchase this insurance, and most state-chartered banks do so voluntarily. A depositor whose bank deposit exceeds $100,000 may secure full insurance protection for other accounts in the same bank, provided the additional accounts are not in the same name. For example, one may open one account in his individual name, a second account in the joint names of himself and his wife, and a third account in his name as trustee for another.

Foreign banks that desire to operate in the U.S also require a licence from the banking department in the state in which they want to operate. Some foreign banks wish to accept deposits in the U.S.; others merely want to establish a local representative. In New York, which has become the world's most important financial center, foreign banks that accept deposits are called branches; elsewhere they are called agencies. In either case, the foreign bank applying for a licence must satisfy the State Superintendent of Banks as to its solvency and integrity. If a foreigner, or a group of foreigners, seeks to acquire ownership of an existing U.S. bank, approval must be sought not only from the State Superintendent of Banks but also from the Federal Comptroller of the Currency. Banks in various parts of the country are today owned by foreign interests.

At this time, there is so much turmoil and competition in the world of banking and finance, that it is not possible to delineate the functions and characteristics of a commercial bank in the U.S. Leaders in government and in the Federal Reserve System have called for clarifying legislation.

The confusion and uncertainty about the parameters of the banking business are likely to end in the near future. The Federal Reserve Bank as well as the Congress are actively engaged in making new regulations and laws affecting banking. The Supreme Court has agreed to rule on the legality of the acquisition of the largest U.S. discount brokerage house by Bank America Corp., one of this country's biggest banks. However, no final clarification can be expected before 1985.

As a result of the financial crash in 1929, and the ensuing Great Depression, Congress enacted the Glass-Steagall Act, which separated deposit and loan functions from investment functions. Banks were restricted to taking deposits and making loans. The interest payable on bank deposits was severely limited. No interest was allowed on demand deposits, i.e., checking accounts. Banks remained authorized to continue such traditional functions as trustees, paying agents for bond issues, and dealers in foreign exchange and commercial paper. Banks were not permitted to engage in so-called non-banking activities, such as making investments, or functioning as stockbrokers. Interstate banking was prohibited. The law was strengthened in 1956 by the Bank Holding Company Act. These laws are still in force.

There is a loophole in the Bank Holding Company Act that Enables the Federal Reserve Board to allow a Bank Holding Company to engage in non-banking business, if it is deemed to be in the public interest. The economic developments of the 1980s have made the distinction between banking and non-banking activities nearly obsolete. The wall between pure banking functions and non-banking functions is crumbling. Financial institutions on both sides of the wall are intruding on each other's territory, without hindrance by the authorities. Some banks, some brokerage houses, and some corporations are building what has been termed a financial 'supermarket', in which pure banking is only one department. Other departments are stock brokerage, real estate brokerage, marketing of new securities, money and investment management, insurance services, credit card operations, mortgage financing, money market investments, travel services, and anything else that has a bearing on the public's finances. The American Express Company and the Prudential Insurance Company each merged with a stock brokerage house. Leaders in the trend towards supermarket diversification are Citibank, better known as National City Bank of New York, and Merrill Lynch Pierce Fenner & Smith, the nation's largest stock brokerage house. Separately incorporated money market funds accept deposits and allow checking privileges. The Dreyfus Corp., a large mutual fund manager, has taken over a state-chartered bank. The prestigious Mellon National Bank of Pittsburgh, Pennsylvania, operates in New York City as The Mellon Financial Center.

Commercial banks used to be confined to the locality in which they were organized. The reason for this is that the Federal Banking Act allows national banks to establish branches only to the extent that branching is allowed under state law. A majority of the states prohibit branching altogether, or permit it only within a limited geographical area, such as the county where the main office of the bank is located. A prominent exception has been California. Branches of the giant Bank of America have spread all over that state. At present, the ban against interstate banking is no longer reflected in reality. The ban is avoided by acquiring or organizing another bank as a subsidiary corporation. For example, Citibank purchased a small state bank in South Dakota, because the laws of that state allow local banks to sell life insurance policies. In 1983, Citibank announced the opening of a subsidiary in Portland, Maine. Maine was the first state in the U.S. to allow interstate banking. New York and other states have followed.

Not all banks accept the 'supermarket' trend. In fact, some very prestigious banks shun it, and operate within traditional limits. All of them, though, are conscious of the bottom-line test. The bottom line is the figure that emerges after deducting all operating expenses from income. Banks, as well as stockbrokers, especially in New York, try to minimize their expenses by transferring some of their administrative operations to a location where expenses and taxes are relatively low.

All banks offer a variety of financial services. The most advertised of these services is money management. This is an extension of the trust services that the trust departments of many banks have rendered for a long time. Many banks have traditionally held a charter as a trust company and, conversely, trust companies have held bank charters. In managing funds for their customers, banks today go much farther than trustees. Banks often assist their customers in making business 'deals'. They sometimes act in the manner of merchant banks in England.

In view of all this, one might expect that, more now than ever, the banking business is only for giants. This, however, is not true. Small banks are thriving and are springing up at a surprising rate, especially in Texas and California. According to a report in *Forbes* magazine, the Federal Comptroller of the Currency approved in 1982 as many as 189 new national bank charters, half of them in Texas and California. *Forbes* further reports that 'charters are being approved for virtually anyone with sufficient capital, a decent operating plan and a team of acceptable bankers. That's a result of deregulation'. Regulations formerly required demonstration of an economic need for a new bank, and this protected older banks from new competition.

Deregulation is a growing phenomenon in the banking industry. In various forms interest-paying checking accounts have been developed. Gradually, the distinctions between thrift institutions and commercial banks are being obliterated. Ceilings on interest rates are being phased out. Banking, as conducted today, is a far cry from the era which spawned the Glass-Steagall Act, referred to above.

There are a number of specialized banks. Foremost among them is the so-called World Bank in Washington D.C., whose correct name is Bank for Reconstruction and Development. The bank is an agency of the United Nations, is owned by several governments, and is used to finance new enterprises in third-world countries. It is of limited interest to one doing business in the U.S. The Export Import Bank, also in Washington D.C., is owned by the U.S. Government. Its function is to finance trade with foreign countries. It guarantees commercial loans, and also makes direct loans in aid of U.S. foreign trade (see Chapter 22). The Federal Home Loan Bank, also a U.S. Government institution, makes loans to Federal Savings and Loan Associations in aid of the latters' mortgage loan activities.

Generally, banks are not interested in controlling enterprises, but the present trend toward expanding the scope of commercial bank activities may change this.

Savings banks in Massachusetts, Connecticut, New York, South Carolina and other states sell life insurance policies. The principal business of savings banks is mortgage lending. In this they must compete with the savings and loan associations, the commercial banks and the 'supermarket' institutions.

Next to banks, insurance companies are the most important lending institutions. The pension funds which were established by large companies and trade unions have become important and are much sought after by money lenders. These funds are generally administered by trustees, who, conscious of their fiduciary obligations, rarely take risks. That leaves room for finance companies, which are less regulated than the banking industry. Banks engaged in the financing business often specialize in a particular type of financing to the exclusion of other types. For instance, some banks will finance only big corporate transactions; others specialize in consumer financing, which means the financing of automobile loans and similar small loans.

The field of financing is wide open. A much advertised slogan is 'creative financing'. No matter what one calls it, financing always means lending money for a price. The creativity comes in when one devises a new way to minimize taxes, or to minimize the pain of paying the price of the loan or the price of securing the loan. This last aspect is dealt with in Chapter 15.

The following portion of this chapter deals with particular aspects of the banking and finance business, without regard to the fact that the 'supermarket' institutions may embrace all or some of these particular aspects.

## 2. INVESTMENT BANKS

Investment banking plays an important role in the U.S. economy. U.S. investment bankers are generally stockbrokers who devote all or part of their operations to the marketing of new corporate stock issues. They underwrite, which, in effect, means purchase (sometimes they merely promise to use their best efforts to sell) all shares of a new stock issue. With the aid of other brokers, they resell the shares to the public. A corporation that is interested in marketing its shares will make an underwriting agreement with such an investment banker. This is a complicated and lengthy document.

Investment bankers also act as advisers to corporations, with respect to financing or refinancing. They are often instrumental in bringing about corporate mergers.

Investment banks do not enjoy the advantages, and are not subject to many of the restrictions, of commercial banks.

## 3. STOCKBROKERS

If one wishes to buy or sell shares, bonds or commodities (e.g. silver or cocoa), one will generally do so in the U.S. through a stockbroker, not through a bank. The large American stockbrokers have offices abroad. Foreign individuals should avoid maintaining large cash balances with a brokerage house. A nonresident alien is exempt from death taxes with respect to a deposit in a U.S. bank. the same exemption does not apply to deposits with a brokerage house. This is one of the reasons that (in spite of the confusion regarding the contemporary role of a bank) foreigners should be aware of the difference between a bank and a broker. Stocks and bonds may be purchased on credit. However, in order to prevent an undesirable degree of speculation, the Fed imposes a so-called margin requirement. The customer buying 'on margin' is required to pay a certain percentage of the price of the shares in cash. The balance, or margin, is borrowed from the stockbroker, who will generally require that the customer pledge the purchased securities, and possibly others, as security for the payment of the margin amount. The margin regulations of the Fed change from time to time. At this writing, the margin for shares is 50%, which means that 50% must be paid in cash. The margin for bond purchases is lower, and for commodities it is still lower. Discount brokers are stockbrokers who charge less than the usual commissions for the purchase or sale of shares which are effected through them. They generally do not render the advisory or research service that one expects of an ordinary stockbroker. Some large discount brokerage houses have been acquired by 'supermarket' institutions.

## 4. FINANCE COMPANIES

The following description is taken from a magazine advertisement of a financial services company that bears the name of, and is owned by, a well-known automobile manufacturer: 'Let us show you how we can directly aid your business in the sale of its products with master lease programs, tax benefit transfers, municipal lease purchase financing and uniquely tailored secured or unsecured loans. Our expertise is particularly suited to business with extensive distribution or dealership networks'. Finance companies also render other financial services, such as money management or factoring (see below). Banks compete with them.

## 5. SOME DEFINITIONS AND CONCEPTS

A party doing business in the U.S. should understand the meaning of certain words, expressions and phrases that are current in the world of banking and finance. No more is intended. Specifically, it is not intended to deal with the manifold legal problems connected with the concepts mentioned.

*Compensating Balance*: A lending bank often requires that its customer (borrower) maintain a so-called compensating balance of not less than a stated amount in its checking account, which bears no interest. This, of course, increases the cost of borrowing.

*Non-recourse financing*: This occurs when the financier has no recourse to the party whom he has financed and, in case of default, can seek satisfaction of his claim only from the transaction that he has financed. The primary example is a non-recourse mortgage loan, where, in case of default, the creditor is relegated to the mortgaged property. He cannot make any claim against the borrower. Another non-recourse provision is the direction in a bill of lading whereby the shipper directs the carrier to deliver the goods only upon payment of the carrier's charge by the consignee. The carrier has no recourse against the shipper.

*Equity financing*: This occurs when a party requiring funds obtains them by selling a participation (equity) in its business. Typically, a corporation will sell common shares or preference shares, and use the proceeds to finance an acquisition or a capital outlay; or perhaps, to retire an outstanding debt. Equity financing is sometimes forced upon a borrower. A real estate developer may be unable to obtain a loan commitment unless he gives the financier what is called 'a piece of the action' – which means a share of the equity.

*Debt financing*: This term is used when a party requiring funds borrows the funds. The debtor issues either notes or bonds, also known as debentures. The bonds may or may not be secured. Bonds are of infinite variety. Examples are general obligation bonds, under which the debtor is liable for payment of principal and interest from all available sources; and income bonds, which limit the source of payment to the income earned by the debtor. This distinction is particularly important in the field of municipal bonds. Another bond species is the convertible bond. This is a bond that, at the owner's option, may be exchanged for a stated number of common shares of the issuing corporation. Convertible bonds offer the security of a fixed return plus the option of future participation in the equity of the issuer, if that should become attractive. There are also convertible preference shares, which are preferred shares with the same convertibility feature.

*Warrants*: These are documents that entitle the owner to purchase shares of a corporation at a fixed price. Warrants are sometimes used to make a bond offering more attractive. Warrants may be part of a stock issue or a bond issue.

*Leasing*: This is another form of financing. A company that needs a building or expensive equipment, may find it attractive to lease the building or the equipment. This does not require a heavy capital expenditure. The rental is deductible for income tax purposes. Railroad cars are generally leased rather than purchased. A company sometimes will sell its building and then lease it back, the so-called sale-leaseback. This type of financing involves special tax problems.

*Negotiable instruments*: These are documents, such as checks, that can be transferred from one owner to another by a written endorsement that names the new owner and is signed by the present owner. Sometimes the name of the new owner is even left blank. An endorsement on a check will read 'Pay to the order of X'. Sometimes it reads, 'For Deposit', which means that the endorser wishes to deposit the check in his bank account and wants to prevent any other use of the check.

*Commercial paper*: A typical kind of commercial paper is a ninety-day promissory note of the General Motors Acceptance Corporation, paying interest at the rate of 9% per year. Commercial paper represents a promise to pay a certain amount on demand or at a certain date, to the bearer or order, i.e., to a third party to whom the bearer negotiates the paper. Or it may be an order to pay that is directed to a debtor of the issuer. An order to pay is generally called a draft. A documentary draft is one that, in accordance with the underlying transaction (e.g. a letter of credit, see Section 10 below), requires the draft to be accompanied by documents, such as an invoice or a bill of lading.

The Certificate of Deposit (C.D.), has become a very popular form of commercial paper. It is the written acknowledgement by a bank of a loan made to it. Usually, the interest rate is higher than that on ordinary bank deposits.

Certificates of deposits of various banks are the principal holdings of the so-called money market funds that stockbrokers and other financial organizations have organized as an interest-bearing investment medium for customers' funds that are temporarily idle. The drawback of these funds is that they are not bank deposits and, therefore, are not covered by the insurance provided by the Federal Deposit Insurance Corporation (see Section 1, above). Banks have been quick to point out this disadvantage, and have organized their own money market accounts, which are insured.

*Document of Title*: These are documents the ownership of which represent ownership of the goods covered by the documents (see Article 7 of the Uniform Commercial Code). Warehouse Receipts and Bills of Lading are the most prominent examples. Whoever owns the warehouse receipt for merchandise owns the merchandise. These documents may be, and usually are, negotiable. An exporter in Germany receives a bill of lading and endorses it to his bank or his customer in the U.S. The bank or the customer then becomes the owner of the merchandise. Some documents of title are not negotiable. In such a case, the ownership of the merchandise can be transferred by an assignment.

A word should be said about the concept of *holder in due course*. The law (Sec. 3-302 of Article 3 of the Uniform Commercial Code) defines a holder in due course as one who has acquired a written instrument (*a*) for value, (*b*) in good faith, and (*c*) without notice of any defense against the validity of the underlying claim. To illustrate: Adams fraudulently induces Beck to buy inferior merchandise and receives Beck's check in payment. Adams endorses the check over to Cohn without telling him of the circumstances under which he received the check. Cohn demands payment of the check from Beck. Cohn is a holder in due course. Beck cannot refuse payment to Cohn on the ground that Adams defrauded him.

*Federal Funds*: Contracts, especially contracts that call for the payment of substantial amounts of money, sometimes stipulate that payment must be made in Federal funds. This expression refers to the fact that banks often cover a deficiency in their legal reserve requirements by borrowing from other banks that have excess funds. These bank-to-bank loans are called Federal funds. They are, in fact, bank funds. Originally, Federal funds had to be on deposit with a Federal Reserve Bank. That is no longer necessary. The chief feature is that the funds are immediately available and that quick interest can be earned on them.

*Prime Rate*: This is the rate of interest that a bank generally charges for a loan to its most creditworthy customers. It changes from time to time, depending on the credit market. Each bank sets its own prime rate, but competition generally leads to uniformity of the rate. Ordinary borrowers are generally charged more than the prime rate. Lenders other than banks use the prime rate as a yardstick. Loan agreements frequently provide for an adjustment of the interest rate, depending on the prime rate. For example, an agreement may provide that the interest rate shall be 2% above the prime rate, as it may vary. The parties sometimes overlook stipulating which bank's prime rate shall govern.

*Discount Rate*: Economically related to the prime rate is the discount rate. This is the fluctuating rate of interest that the Federal Reserve System charges banks for loans that the Fed makes to banks. It is the same as what is known in

England as the bank rate, which the Bank of England charges for loans to the banking community. The discount rate is a primary instrument for regulating the money markets.

## 6. CHECKS

Foreigners are often astonished about the apparent carelessness with which Americans send checks for large amounts through the mails, without registering the letter, although the checks are not *crossed*. (Crossed checks, which are only payable to the drawer's bank account, are not known in the U.S.) The explanation for this practice is that, under U.S. law, the drawer of a check will ordinarily suffer no loss if the check is misapplied. It is the bank's responsibility to determine whether the person who presents the check for payment is actually entitled thereto. If the bank pays to the wrong person, the bank, and not the customer, bears the loss. For instance – Adam writes out a check to Brown for $10,000; Coolidge steals the check, endorses it with Brown's name, makes it payable to himself, and presents it for payment. The bank must then determine whether Brown's endorsement is genuine. If it is forged, as in the present example, and the bank pays the check, it is liable and it may not charge Adam's account for the $10,000 paid to Coolidge. Of course, banks are hardly in a position to scrutinize or verify all endorsements, but that is one of the risks that they take (and against which they are usually insured). If substantial amounts are involved, banks may require that endorsements be guaranteed by another bank to which the endorser is known.

Likewise, the bank is liable if it honors a check on which the customer's signature is forged. In that case, however, the customer is obligated to notify the bank as soon as he has had an opportunity to discover the forgery. This opportunity is usually afforded at the end of each month, when banks return to the customer all canceled checks that they have honored. The notion that a forged endorsement on negotiable paper is a legal nullity and ineffective as to any subsequent holder regardless of good faith is in sharp contrast to the rules to which business outside the Anglo-American orbit is accustomed.

The canceled check is, of course, proof of payment. This practice will explain why U.S. financial transactions are generally conducted without a separate receipt.

To issue a check knowing that there are not sufficient funds in the account with which to pay it, is a criminal offense in most states. Such uncovered checks are colloquially referred to as 'rubber checks'. However, the issuance of a 'rubber check' is not a crime if the check is post-dated and it is intended that the account shall be in balance when the check is presented for payment. The very fact that a check is post-dated is taken as a disclosure that, at the date of issuance, the drawer may not have sufficient funds in the bank.

In important transactions, the recipient of a check will not take the risk that the check may be dishonored for lack of funds. He will insist on receiving a *certified check*. A certified check is one on which the bank has indicated by a stamp that there is enough cash in the drawer's account to honor the check if it is presented for payment, and that the amount of the check will be segregated for payment. Such certification is procured either by the drawer of the check before he delivers it to the payee, or by the payee as soon as he has received the check.

Instead of a certified check, parties sometimes use bank checks or so-called cashier's or official checks as a means of greater security. This is a check drawn by a bank on another bank, or on itself.

A check must be presented to the bank for payment 'promptly'. That is, of course, an elastic word. In international transactions, New York banks generally refuse to honor a check that is more than six months old. This is not a fixed rule, but it is bad practice to allow a check to become 'stale'. Many states (New York not included) have passed laws allowing a bank to refuse payment on a check that is presented more than one year or some other period after its date, unless there is an express authorization by the depositor to pay the check.

Sometimes a tricky debtor will send a check for less than the amount owed and write on the back of it, 'in full payment of my debt', or words to that effect. The courts are not agreed as to whether such words on the back of the check have any legal effect. If, however, there is a genuine dispute about the amount owing, such a legend placed on the back of the check will result in discharging the indebtedness, if the check is accepted and paid. The recipient of a check which has such an endorsement should exercise caution.

## 7. *JOINT ACCOUNTS*

While the nature of an account with a bank or other financial institution, in the name of an individual, a partnership, or a corporation, is easily understood, this is not so with respect to so-called joint accounts. In fact, a joint account is sometimes established under a misapprehension about its consequences.

The Spanish Duke and Duchess of Arion deposited funds in a joint account, in both their names, in New York City. When the Duke died, the Duchess demanded that the account be carried in her name. The children in Spain protested. They claimed to have been deprived of the legitimate portion of their father's estate to which they were entitled under Spanish law. In the ensuing lawsuit in New York, the Duchess prevailed. The example illustrates one of the reasons why foreigners sometimes establish joint accounts in the U.S.

Joint accounts are frequently established by husband and wife. However, joint accounts are not limited to married people. Any two, and sometimes even more, persons may have a joint account. It may be a joint checking account, or, if securities are deposited in custody, a joint custody account. Stock certificates can also be registered in the joint names of two or more persons. Usually, joint accounts are confined to two individuals. Typically, such an account will be designated 'Jones and/or Smith, or the survivor thereof', or 'Jones and Smith, joint tenants with right of survivorship'.

Both Jones and Smith have the right to draw on the joint account, and each can act alone. If one of them dies, the survivor becomes the only party entitled to the account. The primary function of the joint account is to establish who can dispose of it. It does not necessarily follow that Jones and Smith are, in reality, co-owners of the funds in the account. Not infrequently, such joint accounts are established merely as a matter of convenience. The funds may all belong to Jones. But it may be desired to give Smith full power of disposition, because Jones is frequently away, or ill. If Jones were to establish an account in his own name, and give Smith merely a power of attorney, the financial institution might, from time to time, question whether the power of attorney is still in effect. Moreover, the power of attorney would, under U.S. law, automatically terminate when Jones dies. This would not happen in a joint survivorship account, although if the bank learns of the death, it may temporarily freeze the account until adequate provision has been made for the payment of death taxes.

Even if the funds in the joint account belonged originally to Jones, the account may have been established with the intention of making a gift of one-half, or some other fraction thereof, to Smith. In that case, a gift tax might have become due upon establishment of the joint account. If it was not intended to make a gift at that time, an estate (tax) might be payable on the death of Jones. The same principle applies if a part of the joint account belongs to Jones, and that part becomes the property of Smith when Jones dies. It is error to believe that one can avoid the payment of gift taxes or estate taxes by establishing a joint account. Under present tax law, no gift or estate tax is generated by joint account transactions between husband and wife.

While a joint account cannot be used to avoid estate taxes, it removes such account from the control of the executor of the party who dies first. Under U.S. law, all property of a deceased party must be administered by an executor or administrator. Joint survivorship accounts pass directly to the survivor without the intervention of such executor or administrator. The establishment of a joint account for husband and wife is, therefore, a device for making funds immediately available to the survivor, which is sometimes found useful in cases where a third party is appointed as executor. However, depending on the understanding between husband and wife with regard to the account, the executor may still claim that the survivor is not the true owner of the funds in the joint account, and that the funds should be turned over to the executor.

It is, therefore, advisable to have a written understanding between the parties to a joint account with respect to their intentions. It should be made clear whether the funds are jointly owned, whether a gift is intended, and who is to be the owner after the death of either party. The absence of such an understanding has led to controversies, and also to difficulties with the tax authorities. It is also possible that creditors of one joint account holder will lay claim to funds that do not belong to him.

Since it happens frequently that there is no such clear-cut understanding between the parties, the laws of some states have laid down certain rules. Thus, under New York law it is presumed that upon the death of one party, it is intended that the other party shall become the sole owner. If the joint account is with a savings bank, this is an absolute rule and nobody can question it or attempt to prove that something else was intended. If the joint account is with a commercial bank, however, the rule is not absolute, and any interested party may seek to prove that the rule is contrary to the intention of the parties.

If it is intended that each of the joint owners shall retain ownership of his share in the account beyond the death of the first to die, the joint account should be entitled: 'A and B as tenants in common.' That simple designation eliminates any right of survivorship.

Unless the joint account serves a definite purpose or a desired convenience, as was true in the case of the Duke of Arion, the establishment of a joint account has little to commend itself to a foreigner doing business in the U.S.

## 8. LETTERS OF CREDIT

When business people speak of a letter of credit, they generally mean a commercial letter of credit by which a bank or other financier agrees to make payment upon the presentation of certain documents. This is by no means the only way in which a letter of credit is used. In the U.S., whose banks are generally forbidden to issue a bank guaranty, the so-called standby letter of credit is not uncommon. It often takes the place of a bank guaranty. Its purpose is to assure a creditor that a debtor will honor his obligations. Two examples will illustrate the use of the standby letter of credit. It has been used to assure a bonding company that the entity for which it issued a bond will have the financial capability to reimburse the bonding company for payments made under its bond. Another standby letter of credit assured a professional athlete that his employer would honor the terms of the employment contract. Unlike the commercial letter of credit, the standby letter of credit generally requires no presentation of documents. It merely requires a draft and a certificate of nonperformance of the principal contract. In reality, it is a security device.

The following discussion is devoted to commercial letters of credit.

The practice of using commercial letters of credit is known in virtually all parts of the world, and they are widely used in international trade. Agreements providing for the issuance of commercial letters of credit are often carelessly prepared, apparently owing to the fact that the import and impact of a letter of credit are not fully understood. It is not uncommon for a seller and a buyer to agree that 'payment is to be made by letter of credit', without in any way specifying what type of letter of credit is intended. Or, if certain details regarding the letter of credit are stipulated, other important specifications are omitted. That such carelessness causes less trouble than might be expected is due to the fact that, in most instances, the parties have the desire to cooperate with each other and iron out difficulties when they arise. However, businesspeople must realize that by making imperfect agreements, they leave themselves open to possible controversies. If the market situation changes, and one party to a sales contract seeks release from a contract obligation, the invocation of some technicality connected with a letter of credit is a favorite means of doing so.

The term *letter of credit* does not necessarily refer to a bank credit. Technically speaking, a commercial letter of credit is a written undertaking to honor drafts drawn by a seller, when such drafts are accompanied by documentary evidence of shipment, such as bills of lading and insurance certificates. The letter of credit may be issued by the buyer himself, or by any other merchant or finance company. Therefore, if a seller expects a bank letter of credit, the agreement should say so in no uncertain terms.

Further, the agreement should state whether the letter of credit is to be *revocable* or *irrevocable*. If nothing is said on this point, U.S. law provides that the letter may be revocable. In fact, this is the rule under the Uniform Regulations for Commercial Documentary Credit, adopted by the International Chamber of Commerce at its Amsterdam Congress in 1929, and subscribed to by most countries. A revocable letter of credit has little value. It permits the modification or cancellation of the credit without notice, and it affords no protection to the seller in whose favor the letter of credit has been established.

In cases where forwarding agents are employed instead of banks to finance shipments, it is not unusual for the forwarding agent to send a letter to the seller along the following lines: 'We have been instructed by our customer in Peru to pay you $10,000 upon presentation of the following documents. . . .' The seller who receives such a letter generally considers this as the equivalent of a letter of credit. He is right. However, it is merely in the nature of a revocable letter of credit. The instructions from Peru may be revoked at any time; if they are revoked, the forwarding agent issuing the letter of credit is not bound to make any payments. The same, of course, would be true for any finance company or other party that issued such a letter of credit. What the seller in whose favor a letter of credit is issued really wants is an irrevocable letter of credit.

The buyer will generally establish a letter of credit through his bank. Assuming the buyer is in Japan and the seller is in New York, the buyer might make arrangements for the establishment of a letter of credit with his bank in Japan. The Japanese bank will then forward the letter of credit through a New York bank to the seller in New York. The New York bank will advise the seller that the credit has been established. In that case, the New York bank merely acts as notifying bank. As such, the New York bank does not assume any direct obligation. If the beneficiary of the letter of credit in New York wants to avoid the necessity of enforcing any claim under the letter of credit in Japan, he must insist on obtaining a commitment by the New York bank. He can do so by requesting a *confirmed* letter of credit. That is a letter of credit in which the New York bank confirms that it assumes the obligation to pay. It must be realized that an irrevocable letter of credit and a confirmed letter of credit are not one and the same, as some businesspeople seem to believe.

The greatest security to the seller is offered by a confirmed irrevocable letter of credit, and this should be stipulated specifically in the underlying agreement between the parties.

Once a bank or finance company has committed itself under a letter of credit, such commitment is entirely independent of the underlying agreement between the buyer and the seller. Thus, if the underlying agreement entitles the buyer to cancel the contract under certain circumstances, that does not give the bank the right to cancel its commitment under the letter of credit, unless such right is specifically stated in the letter of credit. The following example further illustrates the independent nature of the bank commitment. Manufacturers Hanover Trust Company in New York opened a letter of credit in favor of an American importer of Japanese merchandise. The letter of credit required payment upon presentation of the bill of lading. The bill of lading arrived in New York at the time that World War II broke out. There was grave risk that, due to war conditions, the merchandise itself would never reach the U.S. Consequently, the buyer asked Manufacturers Hanover Trust Company not to make payment when the bill of lading was presented. Court proceedings were instituted against the bank to prevent it from making payment. However, the court ruled that the bank was under an obligation to make payment upon the presentation of the bill of lading, regardless of whether the merchandise arrived.

A letter of credit generally has a time limit, after which the obligation therein expires. The buyer who must pay the bank charges for the letter of credit, and who seeks prompt performance, is interested in an early expiration date. The seller wants ample time for performance. Generally, an expiration date of one month after the expected performance date is agreed upon.

The letter of credit should, of course, stipulate what documents must be presented to the bank before it may make payment. The parties are often careless in describing the required documents. In this connection, Article XV of the above-mentioned Uniform Regulations for Commercial Documentary Credit should be noted, as it represents the U.S. practice. It reads as follows:

'Unless otherwise instructed, banks consider themselves authorized to honor the documents which they adjudge necessary, if presented in a suitable form, viz.:
  (a)  In maritime traffic;
       Full set of Sea or Ocean Bills of Lading in negotiable or transferable form:
       Transferable Policy or Certificate of Insurance;
       Invoice.
  (b)  In inland traffic:
       Complete set of negotiable and transferable Inland Waterway Bill of Lading, or
       Inland Waterway Consignment Note, or Railway Consignment Note or Counterfoil Waybill;
       Transferable Policy or Certificate of Insurance;
       Invoice.
  (c)  In Postal traffic:
       Postal Receipt;
       Transferable Policy or Certificate of Insurance;
       Invoice.

The requirement of an ocean bill of lading does not, in U.S. practice, call for an *On Board* bill of lading. It may be a *Received For Shipment* bill of lading. Steamship companies will issue a *Received For Shipment* bill of lading even before the merchandise is placed on board. It has happened that, due to unforeseen circumstances, merchandise could not be actually placed on board and shipped after the issuance of a Received For Shipment bill of lading. The buyer would do well, therefore, to request specifically that the bill of lading to be presented to the bank must be an On Board bill of lading. U.S. exporters, on the other hand, are frequently unwilling to agree to such a stipulation. In fact, they usually want to be paid under the letter of credit when the merchandise is ready for shipment, and they will insist that the buyer be satisfied with presentation of a warehouse receipt or a dock receipt, rather than any kind of ocean bill of lading. This is a matter for negotiation between the parties. In any event, the parties should understand the differences and the risks involved in either situation.

The requirement of presentation of an insurance certificate ordinarily does not include war risk insurance. If war risk insurance is desired, it should be stipulated specifically.

The commercial invoice to be presented to the bank in order to obtain payment under the letter of credit is usually couched in very general language, without a detailed description of the merchandise. If the buyer who arranges for the establishment of the letter of credit stipulates too many details to be contained in the commercial invoice, such as conditions as to size, weight, individual packing, color, quality, etc., U.S. banks will generally refuse to be bound by such conditions. They will rarely undertake to control such details. Banks deal with documents and not with goods, and they will not act as an inspection agency for the buyer.

To make sure that the seller is not paid under the letter of the credit unless there is some assurance that the merchandise is as contracted for, the buyer should stipulate that, in addition to the usual documents, the seller must present to the bank an inspection certificate. He may also stipulate for additional documents, such as an export or import license.

The question frequently arises whether the seller may draw on the credit several times; that is, whether he may perform the contract in installments and make partial shipments. In U.S. practice, a bank is permitted to honor partial shipments under one letter of credit, unless the contrary is expressly stipulated.

It is a well-established principle that the terms of a letter of credit must be meticulously complied with. For instance, if a letter of credit calls for production of a Lloyd's inspection certificate, the bank will not, and may not, accept any other inspection certificate, even if it is issued by a most reliable inspection agency. However, the bank has fully complied with its duty if the documents presented to it appear genuine on their face, and correspond to the description contained in the letter of credit. The bank is not liable if the documents are forged or otherwise defective.

The rule of *meticulous compliance* with the terms of the letter of credit sometimes causes hardship and serious inconvenience. In such a situation, a so-called bank guaranty will often help. Such a bank guaranty may replace the missing part of the documents prescribed in the letter of credit. In the City of New York, it is customary to accept such a bank guaranty, even if it is not provided for or approved by the party who has arranged for the letter of credit. The courts have ruled that this custom overrides the written terms of the letter of credit.

The term *bank guaranty* is a misnomer. Actually, it is merely an indemnity agreement by which the seller's bank agrees to hold harmless the bank that honors the insufficiently documented letter of credit.

In a well-known decision, a bank guaranty was held not to cure non-compliance with the strict requirements of the letter of credit, because the letter of credit had been made subject to specific rules of the International Chamber of Commerce, which left no room for the New York custom of supplying a bank guaranty. While under the letter of credit a bank is not supposed to release the merchandise that is consigned to it unless the bank receives payment, the bank will generally release the merchandise against a Trust Receipt (see Chapter 22, Section 1).

## 9. FACTORING

The standard and common law meaning of 'factor' denotes a selling agent or commission agent. Under trade usage the term has come to mean something quite different, namely, a particular type of financier. This type of factor is of interest here.

The factor purchases a merchant's accounts receivable. He finances the accounts receivable, and thus supplies the merchant with fresh funds to manufacture or acquire new merchandise. The factoring agreement may provide that the factor buys the accounts receivable with recourse or without recourse. In the former case, the merchant must reimburse the factor if the account cannot be collected. If the factor purchases the accounts receivable without recourse, he assumes the credit risk. In such case, the factor generally demands the right to approve every sale in advance. In effect, the factor becomes the credit department of the merchant. The factoring contract provides, generally, that all accounts receivable of the merchant are subject to the factoring agreement. The factor wants to have the benefit of the easy accounts, and does not wish to be limited to the risky accounts. The accounts receivable are assigned to the factor and the debtor is generally advised, by a rubber stamp on the invoice, that payment should be made directly to the factor. Sometimes the agreement forbids notification of the debtor, in which case the merchant undertakes to effect collection and to remit the collected amounts to the factor. Sometimes the factor undertakes to operate the bookkeeping department of the merchant. The extent of the services of the factor determines the price that the merchant must pay to the factor. It is generally a percentage of the amount that the factor finances.

## 10. LONG-TERM LOAN AGREEMENTS

The long-term loan agreement is generally a lengthy document. One speaks of long-term when the loan is extended for more than one year. Many loan agreements extend for fifteen years or more.

Repayment in installments is often stipulated. Self-liquidating loans are loans calling for repayment in equal quarterly or monthly installments. These installments are applied in part to the interest charge, and in part to reduce the loan principal. When all installments have been paid, the debt will have been fully satisfied, with interest.

If the borrower is a corporation with one or several subsidiary corporations, the lender may ask that the subsidiary or subsidiaries join in the obligations imposed by the loan agreement. If the subsidiary is a Controlled Foreign Corporation, which pays no U.S. income tax, any such action will destroy the tax exemption. If a subsidiary is the borrower, the lender will try to obtain a commitment from the parent corporation.

The lender generally extends credit on the basis of the financial condition of the borrower at the time of the loan agreement. The agreement will, therefore, often provide that there shall be no change in that condition, and that the lender will not engage in any activity 'except in the ordinary course of business'.

Frequently, the loan agreement will impose on the lender the obligation to maintain a certain amount of working capital, and a certain ratio of liquid assets and fixed assets. It may also forbid further borrowings and seeking credit 'except in the ordinary course of business'. The lender may require that existing creditors subordinate their claims to that of the lender.

The long-term loan agreement contains a series of affirmative covenants and a number of negative covenants. Affirmative covenants are such obligations as the prompt payment of interest and principal, the rendering of regular financial reports, and the maintenance of the existing property and the insurance thereon. Negative covenants refer to the things that the borrower agrees not to do, such as, not to sell assets and not to incur further debts.

## 11. USURY

Usury (*usure* in French, *Wucher* in German) occurs when a lender demands an illegal price for a loan. This is discussed in Chapter 9, Section 13.

Sometimes, a financier seeks to make a proposed loan palatable to the borrower by stipulating that, instead of any interest payments, he will be satisfied with a percentage of the profits that the borrower realizes when he disposes of the property acquired with the borrowed funds. The trouble with that kind of arrangement is that the profit share may exceed the legal rate of interest, and payment of the profit share may thus make the transaction usurious.

The usury laws have been enacted for the protection of unwary individuals. The laws generally do not apply to loans made to a corporation. As a result, financial institutions often require their individual borrowers to form a corporation. New York does not countenance this easy evasion when the corporation is formed to become the owner of a small dwelling.

A hazard of usury is that it may be alleged at any time either by a borrower or, in case of bankruptcy, by a trustee or receiver – often at the instigation of a competing creditor.

## 12. INTERNATIONAL BANKING

Many loans made by U.S. banks to foreign countries are a matter of grave concern, but of little interest in the context of this book.

A foreign bank desiring to do business in the U.S. has a number of options. In spite of the limitations and restrictions that are placed on banking activities by state and Federal law, the door is open or rather it can be opened by careful advance planning. The *New York Times* reported, in March 1983, the presence of 336 offices of foreign banks in New York City, exclusive of the two New York banks which are wholly owned by the Hong Kong and Shanghai Banking Corporation and Britain's National Westminster Bank, respectively.

Pending before the Supreme Court is a case in which the Federal Comptroller of the Currency allowed two Australian banks to establish branches in Chicago. The Illinois state government is opposed. The Conference of State Bank Supervisors insists that the Comptroller has misinterpreted the International Banking Act and must respect state control.

Foreign banks seeking access to the New York market need not shy away because of high office rents. Many domestic bankers and brokers concentrate their sales activities in New York and, aided by modern technology, conduct their back office or record keeping operations away from New York, in locations where office rents are cheaper.

The dual and overlapping state and Federal legal system complicates matters. A state charter and a national charter each have certain advantages and certain disadvantages. For example, membership in the Federal Reserve System makes cheap loans available. A disadvantage is that member banks must keep a percentage of their deposits, as a reserve, with the Federal Reserve Bank.

New York makes a unique distinction between an agency and a local office of a foreign bank, which is called a branch. Both an agency and a branch require a license from the Superintendent of Banks. An agency is merely a contact point, a public relations outlet designed to 'show the flag'. An agency is not allowed to accept deposits. A branch can conduct a full banking business, like a domestic bank, and it is often separately incorporated.

The backbone of international trade is credit. If the exporter sells 'on open account', he extends credit to the inporter. In most instances, the exporter seeks to minimize his risk by requiring a Letter of Credit, which is discussed above. In the domestic trade, the seller worries only about the solvency of the buyer. Internationally, additional concerns are currency fluctuations and political risks such as war, revolution and expropriation, as well as loss of import or export licenses.

Mention must be made of Edge Act corporations, named after its sponsor, the late Senator Edge. The Act is part of the Federal Reserve Act. It authorizes federally chartered banking corporations to engage in international and foreign financial operations. Its purpose is to facilitate the financing of U.S. exports. The International Banking Act of 1978 has liberalized the provisions of the Edge Act, and has made this banking vehicle available to foreign banks. Very few foreign banks, however, have made use of the Edge Act.

Section 1, above, mentioned the Export-Import Bank and the World Bank, which play an important role in international financing.

## 13. EURODOLLARS AND EUROBONDS

Eurodollars are dollar deposits in Europe, for which a lively and speculative market developed after World War II. Eurodollars are used to finance dollar transactions among Europeans. Foreigners doing business in the U.S. and requiring financing will sometimes find it convenient to obtain financing through a Eurodollar loan from a foreign bank or banking syndicate. This type of financing may be cheaper and simpler than raising a loan in the U.S.

Eurobonds are bonds issued by foreign subsidiaries of U.S. companies. They are not necessarily dollar bonds; some of these bonds are denominated in West German, Swedish, Canadian or even Japanese currency. They are sold mostly in the country in whose currency they are denominated. The Euromarket, as it is called, encompasses transactions as far away as Singapore. The market is not subject to the regulation of the Securities and Exchange Commission. The bonds need not be registered and usually are bearer bonds. This makes Eurobonds attractive.

Eurobonds are a means by which U.S. corporations obtain loans abroad, generally through subsidiary financing companies in the Netherlands Antilles, which in turn lend the funds to the U.S. parent. Because of the existing tax treaty, the interest payments to the subsidiary are not subject to the 30% withholding tax. This is the reason why the treaty with the Netherlands Antilles is likely to be abrogated (see Chapter 8, Section 25). Litigation is pending to exempt Eurodollar interest from the withholding tax.

CHAPTER 15

# SECURED TRANSACTIONS

## *1. INTRODUCTION*

In the business world, a promise to pay is rarely enough. The promisee wants to be secured. This is the basis of the concept of the secured transaction. The best known security device is the mortgage on real (immovable) property. The mortgage secures the promise of the real property owner to repay the loan of the financier. Personal (movable) property is used in a variety of methods to secure an indebtedness or a promise to pay in the future. Most of these methods are regulated by Article 9 of the Uniform Commercial Code (UCC), as amended in 1974, which has been adopted (with some modification) by all U.S. jurisdictions, except Louisiana. The codification has superseded most prior legislation and the earlier common law of secured transactions. Concepts like *conditional sale* (in which the seller retains ownership) and *chattel mortgage* (in which personal property is mortgaged) have become obsolete. This chapter deals with security devices that, in accordance with Article 9 UCC, are created by express agreement, so-called consensual liens. It does not deal with security devices that are created by law, such as a bank's right to set off a customer's balance on deposit against claims that the bank may have against the customer, or the lien that a warehouseman has against a party who owes storage fees, or a mechanic's lien, an innkeeper's lien, or a lawyer's lien. These security rights are created by law, not by agreement between the parties. Practically speaking, they do not arise unless asserted. There is, however, one security device that arises automatically, namely a court judgment. A court judgment creates a lien against the property of the party against whom the judgment is rendered. In most jurisdictions, the lien attaches automatically to real property owned by a judgment debtor, while some further administrative procedures are required to attach the lien to personal property.

145

Article 9 of the UCC is a very complex and detailed piece of legislation. Legal scholars and courts have devoted a great deal of attention to it. This chapter cannot hope to do justice to all those complexities and details. What is attempted here is an outline of the topic in the most general terms.

One who wishes to acquire a piece of property or a business must first inquire whether the property or business is encumbered with a statutory lien, or whether it is the subject of a secured transaction. This search, which must be conducted in various governmental offices, is generally entrusted by the attorney for the buyer to one of a number of organizations that specialize in this field.

If a debtor becomes bankrupt, a secured creditor has a preferential position, as noted in Chapter 25. This is one of the principal reasons for securing a transaction.

The property or property right that is used to secure a promise is called collateral property, or *collateral*, for short. Accounts receivable, chattel paper, and even growing crops may be collateral. The word chattel is an old English word that denotes personal (movable) property. The official comment to Sec. 9-105 of the UCC illustrates the meaning of the term *chattel paper*. It is quoted here because it also illustrates other pertinent concepts.

'A dealer sells a tractor to a farmer on a conditional sales contract. The conditional sales contract is a security agreement, the farmer is the debtor, the dealer is the secured party, and the tractor . . . is the collateral. But now the dealer transfers the contract to his bank, either by outright sale or to secure a loan. Since the conditional sales contract is a security agreement relating to specific equipment, the conditional sales contract is now the type of collateral called chattel paper.'

Any property having value may be used as collateral. If the purchase of a property is financed, the very property may be used as collateral. For instance, if the shares of a corporation are sold, the seller may retain ownership of the shares until they are fully paid for (in which case he is said to have a purchase money security interest); or, if the purchase is financed by a third party, the shares may be transferred as collateral to such third party.

A security agreement must be in writing in order to be binding between the parties. In order to be binding on third parties, it must be publicly disclosed by filing a financing statement (see Section 3, below) or by physical manifestation of delivery.

The subject matter of secured transactions is of interest to foreigners doing business in the U.S. in two instances: (*a*) if they wish to finance a transaction with or in the U.S., and (*b*) if they are unsecured creditors and find themselves in conflict with creditors who claim to be secured.

## 2.  GUARANTY

The simplest security is a guaranty. It is not even mentioned in UCC Article 9. In many parts of the world, a creditor will ask for a bank guaranty. As noted in a prior chapter, American banks generally are not allowed to issue a guaranty. Instead, they will issue a standby letter of credit, which is even better than a guaranty because it constitutes a primary obligation of the bank (see Section 8 of Chapter 14). The Federal Comptroller of the Currency, who forbids bank guaranties, has expressly approved the standby letter of credit. If the obligor is a subsidiary of a financially strong parent company, the guaranty of the parent company may also be used as a security device. U.S. parent companies do not readily issue such guaranties because they expect their subsidiaries to stand on their own financial feet. A corporate guaranty is generally not available, and might not be valid under applicable state law, unless the obligor is a subsidiary. A related security device, also not covered by UCC Article 9, is the performance bond. A performance bond is generally available from a type of insurer known as a surety company. The bond insures that the obligor will perform in accordance with its agreement. It is generally coupled with a penalty provision in case of delay. The bond issuer is liable if the obligor defaults. Performance bonds are customary in the construction industry, but they can also be used in other fields of business.

The rest of this chapter refers to security transactions embraced by UCC Article 9.

## 3. PERFECTION OF THE SECURITY INTEREST

In order to have a security interest that is good against third parties, (i.e., against other secured parties, attaching creditors, and/or a trustee in bankruptcy), the security interest must be perfected. This can be done in different ways, depending on the kind of collateral involved. A security interest may be perfected when it attaches, or it may require the transfer of possession from the debtor to the secured party. Transfer of possession is necessary if, for example, one pledges stock as security for a loan. The usual manner of perfecting a security interest is the filing of a financing statement (see Section 4, below). Sometimes, there are conflicting perfected security interests. In that case, the question of priority arises. The manner of resolving that issue is addressed by the statute.

When either filing or the transfer of possession of collateral is necessary for perfection, that act may occur prior to the *attachment of the security interest*. The security interest is perfected when the last of the events necessary for attachment and perfection has occurred. As there is an advantage in securing priority by an early filing of the financing statement, the financier sometimes does not part with any value until after the filing has occurred.

The statute provides that a security interest will attach only if three requirements are met: (*a*) there must be a security agreement, (*b*) the financier must give value, and (*c*) the debtor must have rights in the collateral. This last requirement seems simple. But recently a British bank ran afoul of this provision. The case involved the purchase of a yacht in California. The yacht dealer's inventory was financed by Chrysler Corporation, which held a security interest in the inventory. The dealer sold the yacht to an individual, who financed the transaction through the British bank. Actually, the individual had no assignable rights in the yacht as it was part of Chrysler's collateral security. The court ruled that the British bank had acquired no security interest and, therefore, no interest that was capable of being perfected. This ruling contradicts the general rule in inventory financing, (stated below in Section 7), but it serves as a cautionary signal to interested parties.

## 4. FILING

Where filing is required to perfect a security interest, the document filed is called a financing statement. Printed statutory forms are available and generally used.

The financing statement is simple. It need contain only the names, addresses and signatures of the debtor and the secured party, and a description of the collateral. If the secured party is entitled to the proceeds of any sale of the collateral, or of the products that are manufactured with the collateral, this also should be stated in the financing statement. The 1974 revision of the UCC has abolished the requirement that this be mentioned. It is now presumed that proceeds are always covered by the financing statement. However, not all states have accepted this change.

The sufficiency of the description of the collateral has sometimes been challenged in litigation. It is therefore advisable to make the description as specific as possible. It is also advisable to avoid attaching separate description documents to the financing statement. The statute says that minor errors in a financing statement will be overlooked if they are not seriously misleading. This has led to conflicting decisions in cases where an error occurred in the description of the name of the debtor. The description is misleading if it impedes a searcher – if, for instance, a debtor corporation is listed under the name of its division.

The rules for filing a financing statement vary in different states. Generally, local filing in the county of the debtor's residence or place of business and central filing in the state capital are required.

A financing statement loses its effect five years after filing. However, a continuation statement may be filed, which extends the effectiveness for an additional five-year period. There is no limit to the number of continuation statements that may be filed.

Additional filings are made when collateral is released or the entire security agreement is terminated. An assignment of the security agreement may also be filed. If a debt is paid, a diligent debtor will see to it that the public records so indicate.

## 5. PROCEEDS

The term, 'proceeds', includes whatever is received when collateral is sold, exchanged, collected, or otherwise disposed of. Typical proceeds are accounts receivable arising from the sale of collateral, and money, when the accounts receivable are collected. A secured creditor is entitled to a security interest in the proceeds, even if that is not expressly stated in the security agreement. That raises the question whether the debtor is automatically authorized to sell the collateral. An Illinois court concluded that such automatic authorization does not exist. Logic, as well as the realities of the market place, would seem to lead to the opposite conclusion. If the secured creditor does not wish to permit the debtor to sell the collateral, it is best to so provide in the security agreement.

Under the original version of UCC Article 9, it is doubtful whether the proceeds of insurance constitute *proceeds* of lost or damaged collateral. There are court rulings to the effect that insurance proceeds do not qualify. The 1974 version of Article 9 now provides that such insurance proceeds are covered by the security agreement.

What is the situation if a dissatisfied customer returns the goods to the seller? Clearly, the returned goods are not proceeds. And yet, the financier has a legitimate interest in the goods. The rights of the financier in such a situation are regulated by statute (UCC Section 306.5).

## 6. PRIORITY

One of the primary purposes of UCC Article 9 was to insure certainty in the procedure for creating security interests, by clearly establishing priority among conflicting interests in the same collateral. The basic rule is that priority is accorded to the creditor who files first. There are qualifications of this basic rule, as, for example, in the case of purchase money security interests, which generally have priority even over prior secured creditors.

## 7. INVENTORY FINANCING

This is one of the most important areas of secured transactions. But it is hardly of great interest to one who is doing business with the U.S. For that reason, it will be given only passing mention. The characteristic of inventory is that it changes frequently. The debtor must have freedom to dispose of the inventory, and to transfer unencumbered title to a *bona fide* purchaser. The secured creditor will be satisfied with having a security interest in the resulting accounts receivable (proceeds). He will allow the debtor to keep the accounts receivable, and to use the collected funds to buy or produce new inventory, to which the security interest will attach. That is the concept of the so-called 'floating lien'. The secured party obtains and retains a security interest in constantly changing collateral.

A field warehouse is a device whereby a debtor fences off an area of his own premises in which he stores property that serves as collateral for a loan. An employee is installed as a warehouseman. He is authorized to release collateral if adequate substitution is made. Floor planning is a similar device, used primarily by automobile dealers. The automobile manufacturer finances the dealer's inventory, which is generally located on the floor of the dealer's showroom. The dealer is allowed to sell the financed automobiles, and to substitute the proceeds as collateral.

## 8. *TRUST RECEIPTS*

Trust receipts were first used in connection with importing. Today, they are also used for other purposes, notably in the financing of automobile dealers. The lender entrusts the collateral to the borrower in order to enable the lender to dispose of the collateral. To illustrate, Jones in New York has purchased a quantity of cocoa in Brazil and resold it to a customer in Chicago. A bank in New York has financed the purchase by establishing a letter of credit in favor of the seller in Brazil. Consequently, the cocoa is consigned to the bank. The bank, however, allows Jones to take possession of the cocoa and to ship it to Chicago, against issuance of a trust receipt by Jones to the bank. Jones, as trustee, agrees to act for the entruster (the bank) and to pay the bank out of the proceeds of sale, which Jones will collect from the customer in Chicago. The trust receipt may also be issued for the more limited purpose of enabling Jones to clear the merchandise through Customs and the necessary inspection by the Food and Drug Administration – activities with which the bank does not wish to be burdened.

## 9. *LEASES*

A lease may constitute a secured transaction. For instance, a debtor induces a bank to purchase industrial equipment which the debtor needs. The bank then leases the equipment to the debtor. The bank collects its finance charges, generally in the form of rent. At the end of the rental period the debtor buys the equipment from the bank at the original cost price. Another illustration is the case of a manufacturer who sells equipment to a finance company and then leases it back. This is called a sale and leaseback. The finance company is the owner, but its title is only intended to be a security interest. The manufacturer obligates himself to buy the property eventually. The rental charges may be so high that the debtor is allowed to purchase the property at the end of the rental period for a relatively low price. In such a situation complex tax questions may arise.

The distinction between a true lease of personal property (such as equipment) and a lease that is, in reality, a secured transaction, is frequently litigated.

## 10. *ENFORCEMENT*

How does a secured creditor enforce his rights in the collateral in case the debtor defaults? The statute (UCC, Section 9-504) allows a secured creditor wide latitude in disposing of the collateral, but whatever is done must be commercially reasonable. What this means is illustrated by a case in which a New York court found the enforcement action of the secured creditor commercially unreasonable. The finance company never inspected the construction equipment collateral and, therefore, did not know that it had special features that significantly enhanced its value. The newspaper in which the finance company advertised the sale was not appropriate for reaching potential buyers. Further, the finance company rejected as too low a tentative offer that was substantially higher than the price ultimately received, and it made no attempt to pursue this higher offer. As a result, the finance company was liable to the debtor.

The UCC also gives the secured party, in case of default, the right to take possession of the collateral by peaceful means (Section 9-503). In light of recent pronouncements of the Supreme Court, it has become doubtful whether this statutory authorization for self-help is constitutionally permissible. In any event, it is not advisable to rely on this provision of the statute.

CHAPTER 16[1]

# INSURANCE

## *1. INTRODUCTION*

The insurance business is an important segment of the U.S. economy. A number of insurance companies are financial institutions, which derive a substantial part of their revenues from real estate transactions and long-term financing activities. The U.S. Government acts as insurer in fields that are deemed of public importance. The Federal Deposit Insurance Company is mentioned in Chapter 14. The Federal Housing Administration and the Veterans Administration insure or guarantee mortgage loans. Similar governmental guaranties exist in the export field (see Chapter 22).

This chapter deals only with private insurance arrangements by which one doing business in the U.S. seeks protection against certain risks, or is required to procure such insurance protection.

Insurance is a complex business in any country, but even more so in the U.S., where insurance companies or underwriters, and their policies and operations, are controlled by the laws, rules and regulations of the individual states, as well as decisions of the various state courts. From a practical point of view, however, property, liability, life, accident and health policies generally have identical basic conditions, modified according to the requirements of the place where the risk is located.

## *2. INSURERS, AGENTS, BROKERS*

All insurance companies (also referred to as insurance carriers or simply as

---

1. The material for this chapter was contributed by Henry Salfeld, Consultant, Frenkel & Co., Inc., Insurance Brokers, New York, N.Y.

insurers) and their agents must be licensed by the states in which they operate. Insurance brokers must be similarly licensed. Insurance brokers occupy a peculiar position. Primarily, they are agents for the insured, employed to procure appropriate insurance protection for their principal. The principal, or customer, relies on the guidance of the broker in selecting a suitable insurer. The broker also acts as agent for the insured in helping to settle any claims that the insured may have against the insurer. On the other hand, the broker acts as agent for the insurer when he collects insurance premiums. Often, a broker is authorized to act for the insurer in issuing a temporary *binder* (see Section 3, below).

The principal function of the insurance broker is to select the most suitable insurance company or companies. In making this selection, the broker will not only consider the cost of the insurance, but also the financial strength of the insurer, and its practice of settling claims. Some insurers have a reputation for being difficult in paying claims. It is obvious that the use of an experienced insurance broker is important for one seeking insurance protection. It is also important that the broker carry enough weight with the insurance carrier when it comes to seeking a satisfactory settlement of any claims. One doing business in the U.S. will find it almost indispensable to use the services of a local insurance broker.

The commission of the broker is included in the premium that the customer pays for the insurance. Brokers are not allowed to charge any additional fee for their services, except when they procure insurance from an insurer that pays no commissions. This applies to insurers who prefer to deal directly with the insured, and to State Funds for Workers' Compensation Insurance (see below). Brokers are not permitted to share their commissions with lawyers or other non-brokers, nor is it legal for them to rebate any part of their commission to the customer.

Information on competent and trustworthy insurance brokers is generally available from any of the following sources: the domestic insurance broker or agent in the home country, a business associate with experience in the U.S., the U.S. Chamber of Commerce in the home country, the local consulate of the home country, or the American lawyer who may be engaged.

While the use of an insurance broker is recommended, it is not required. One can purchase insurance directly from an insurance carrier, or from an insurance agent who acts for a particular insurer.

When insurance is not available from an insurer who is licensed in the jurisdiction where the risk is located, insurance from another carrier can be procured through a so-called excess line broker who is licensed as such. If one's broker is not so licensed, he will use an excess line broker. This is how one buys insurance from Lloyd's of London, and other carriers that are not licensed locally.

In addition, there exist in the states of New York, Illinois and Florida, Insurance Exchanges, modeled after Lloyd's of London, through which large and unusual domestic and foreign risks can be insured without the restrictions of the local laws.

## 3. INSURANCE POLICIES

Insurance policies constitute contracts between the insurance company and the insured, and are subject to the laws and rules applicable to contracts in general. A basic concept is that a valid insurance contract requires that the insured have an insurable interest in the insured hazard. An insurable interest exists if the contemplated hazard would cause a loss to the insured. For instance, an employer or a creditor has an insurable interest in the continued life of an employee or a debtor. The owner of a winter resort hotel has an insurable interest in the occurrence of snow at Christmas. A person who has no intention of skiing at Christmas has no such interest, and if he were to buy insurance against rain at Christmas, he would be making a mere bet, which is not legally enforceable. An insurance policy is an adhesion contract (see Chapter 9); if any of its provisions are ambiguous, they are interpreted by the courts in favor of the insured, as a consumer. Many states recently have passed laws requiring policies to be written in easily understandable, rather than legalistic, language. The policies must, therefore, clearly state conditions, exclusions, restrictions and limitations; and if, for instance, an exclusion neither has been properly explained nor is readily understandable, the insurance company may not use it to deny liability.

Prior to the issuance of a policy, coverage may be temporarily provided by a binder, which is subject to the same conditions as the final policy.

Policy conditions in the U.S. are generally required to be filed in each state, for approval by the supervising authority. Such filings are made either by a rating organization acting for its insurance company member, or by individual insurers.

An alien cannot assume that insurance coverage in the U.S. is identical with that in his home country, where the insured may be covered for similar risks. Nor is it safe for an alien to rely on the insurance coverage that he carries in his home country. For instance, a foreign liability policy may not cover liability to a claimant in the U.S. In the case of product liability insurance, there are other problems, which are discussed below.

## 4. TYPES OF INSURANCE

The risks for which insurance should or must be carried depend upon the method by which the foreigner decides to do business in the U.S. (Chapter 2).

The insurance field is sometimes divided into four broad categories: Life Insurance, Property Insurance, Casualty Insurance and Marine Insurance. Health and Accident Insurance and Pension Plans fall, generally, into the category of Life Insurance.

The term *Marine Insurance* is misleading, in that it is not limited to maritime traffic. Marine Insurance includes, of course, the insurance of a ship and of a ship's cargo. It also includes overseas shipments by airplane. Shipments should be insured *warehouse to warehouse*, which means from the point of shipment to the point of destination. If the risk continues after arrival at the port, it is necessary to make sure that the policy also covers domestic transportation.

After the shipment arrives at the consignee's place of business, it is important to make arrangements for inspection, in order to avoid a dispute, should hidden damage be discovered after arrival, and it is not certain when and where it occurred. The insurance of inland transportation from Montreal to, say, Mexico City, or even from Chicago to San Francisco, is generally referred to as Inland Marine Insurance. The better term is inland transportation insurance. There are various policies of Marine Insurance and Inland Marine Insurance, which an insured should endeavor to understand and discuss with his broker. The preferred type of policy is the so-called All Risk policy. The terms of a marine insurance policy for international shipments are competitive, and not subject to state regulation.

One who makes frequent shipments may buy a so-called 'Open Policy', which automatically covers all shipments and relieves one of the need to insure each individual risk. In either case, if the shipper makes the arrangement with a foreign insurance company, he should make certain that proper representation of the insurer is available in the U.S., in case of need for adjustment of a damage claim, or security arrangement in case of a *general average*.

Liability Insurance against third party claims for personal injury and damage to physical property arising in the U.S. is a branch of casualty insurance. Liability Insurance is an absolute requirement for anyone doing business in the U.S. Liability claims may spring up from the most unexpected sources. If a person stumbles on your property, he or she may haul you into court. You may be sued because the smoke from your chimney allegedly impairs your neighbor's health, or damages the vegetables in his garden. There are, of course, many more serious risks, to which even a careful person or company is exposed. The advantage of Liability Insurance is that, in addition to paying or settling the claim against you, the insurer will handle your legal defense, and bear the cost thereof. There are many special aspects of liability, some of which are mentioned below. The prudent businessperson will buy a Comprehensive Liability Insurance policy.

Property insurance policies are written today on a so-called 'All Risk' basis. In spite of the All Risk terminology, the policies always contain certain exclusions, restrictions and limitations. For instance, damages due to surface water and flood, earthquake, and volcanic eruption are excluded unless they occur in transit; and insurance against such risks must, therefore, like war risk insurance, be separately arranged. The policy should also provide for reimbursement of loss of earnings and continuing cost of overhead in the case of business interruption resulting from an insured occurrence.

Fire Insurance is, of course, property insurance. If a plant is a so-called highly protected risk (HPR), fire insurance, either separately or as part of a package, may be available at substantially reduced rates from insurance carriers specializing in such risks. The engineering department of the broker should be consulted on any construction plans before they are finalized, in order, if feasible, to avoid designs that may cause unnecessarily high insurance costs.

Flood Insurance on a limited scale, for businesses in flood-prone communities, is only available through the National Flood Insurance Association, a pool of private companies organized under a Federal law.

Losses resulting from burglary, theft, holdup, kidnapping and payment of ransom are usually insurable, either by inclusion under a package or by a separate policy. This also applies to losses caused by damage to, or malfunctioning of, data processing equipment.

Fidelity Insurance, covering losses due to dishonest or fraudulent acts of executives or employees, should be part of the insurance program, especially where absentee ownership is involved.

Product Liability Insurance (see Chapter 9) presents special problems. Sometimes, the manufacturer abroad includes in its own products liability insurance policy claims made against its U.S. importer or distributor. The problem in such case is that the limit of liability (see below) may not be adequate, owing to the size of U.S. verdicts. Also, the foreign insurer may not be sufficiently familiar with lawyers in the U.S. to mount an adequate defense in the locality in which the product liability claim is made. On the other hand, if the U.S. importer or distributor procures insurance from a U.S. insurance company, and the case is lost, the foreign manufacturer is exposed to an indemnity claim by the U.S. insurance company, by reason of what is known as subrogation. This can be avoided if the U.S. importer or distributor includes the foreign manufacturer in its insurance coverage, or the U.S. insurance company waives the right of subrogation.

Federal and state laws for the protection of the environment may require careful attention, due to possible liability for pollution of land, air or water. Insurance may be required not only for sudden, unexpected events, but for gradual pollution as well.

Whereas officers, directors and shareholders of corporations are automatically covered under the corporation's liability policy for personal injury and property damage caused in the performance of their duties, separate policies must be arranged to insure officers and directors against claims for other wrongful acts causing financial loss to the corporation or shareholders. These are Directors' and Officers' Liability policies, which have become important for public as well as nonpublic corporations.

Discrimination on account of color, race, religion, national origin, physical condition, or sex is illegal and, if committed intentionally, may result in a liability claim for monetary damages. Coverage of this risk is frequently excluded from liability insurance policies as being against public policy (see Chapter 1) but separate Discrimination Liability Insurance may be available.

There is no uniformity in court decisions as to whether liability policies automatically cover punitive damages (see Chapter 9, Section 11), or whether such coverage would be in violation of public policy. Insureds should try to avoid specific punitive damage exclusions in liability policies. Irrespective of policy conditions, insureds should always report such claims to the insurance company.

## 5. LIMITS OF LIABILITY

It was previously emphasized that Americans are rather litigious and, therefore, the scope and limits of liability insurance are of utmost importance. The insurance company generally is obligated to defend the insured against any third party claim based on an occurrence covered by the policy, and to pay the cost of litigation as well as any judgment or settlement within the policy limits. In the U.S. the cost of legal defense generally is not charged against the limit of liability. As property values and awards by juries in accident cases constantly increase – million-dollar verdicts are no longer unusual – high limits of liability should be carried either under the basic liability policy or under excess or broader so-called umbrella policies. How high the limits should be is difficult to determine. The inherent danger of a product to the public and the financial condition of the insured must be considered.

Where property is insured, one may insure either the cost of replacement or the actual depreciated value. Some policies contain a co-insurance clause, requiring the insured to carry at least 80%, 90%, or some other percentage of the value of the property. If, in case of a loss, it turns out that the insured has violated this provision, he is underinsured. In case of a partial loss, he will collect only the percentage of the loss equal to the ratio of the amount insured to the amount that should have been insured in compliance with the co-insurance requirement. In case of total loss, the co-insurance clause does not apply, but the insured can never collect more than the amount insured.

## 6. AUTOMOBILE INSURANCE

Although this insurance is subject to the jurisdiction of the individual states, the principal policy conditions are standard. Automobile liability coverage is compulsory in most states, but the prescribed minimum limits are low, considering the high jury verdicts in accident cases. Anyone using an automobile, whether a passenger or commercial vehicle, should, therefore, arrange for automobile liability insurance with high limits. He might also carry comprehensive physical damage coverage for the vehicle itself. Due to the large number of uninsured or underinsured motorists, automobile policies must be extended to protect the insured and his passengers in case of injuries caused by such motorists. In most states, policies also provide no-fault insurance, to reimburse the insured and others for medical and similar expenses, and loss of earnings, irrespective of liability.

## 7. RENTAL CARS

When a vehicle is rented, the rental agency has usually arranged for liability and physical damage insurance on the rented car, subject to a sizable deductible amount in case of collision damage. However, as the insurance carriers, conditions, and limits of liability of the policy are mostly unknown, the renter is well advised to carry his own insurance as well. Rental agreements generally contain various restrictions, for instance with regard to the persons permitted to drive the car.

## 8. WORKERS' COMPENSATION INSURANCE

All states have enacted statutes requiring employers to insure their employees for medical and hospital expenses, and loss of earnings, resulting from accidents or diseases arising out of, and in the course of, the employment. Death benefits are also included. There are, however, differences in the required minimum number of employees, maximum payrolls on which the premium is to be based, classification of employees according to their work, and the rates applicable thereto.

In Ohio and five other states, the insurance must be placed with a State Fund organized for that purpose. New York, California, and some other states, also have a State Fund, but one may also place Workers' Compensation insurance with a private insurance company. In the majority of states there is no State Fund, and Workers' Compensation insurance must always be placed with a private insurance company.

In New York, New Jersey and several other states, the law also requires employers to provide disability insurance for non-occupational accidents and diseases.

Benefits and their duration vary by state. Premium rates are state-controlled, and frequently based on the past experience of the particular employer.

Employees entitled to Workers' Compensation may not make a claim against their employer, or, in most states, against fellow employees. However, the recipient of Workers' Compensation benefits is not precluded from suing outsiders, such as a manufacturer who is claimed to be liable on the basis of product liability. In such a case, if the worker wins, he must reimburse the State Fund or the insurance carrier that has paid the Compensation benefit.

## 9. GROUP INSURANCE

In addition to legally required social insurance for the benefit of employees, voluntary life, health, accident and sickness insurance, as well as pension plans, have become common in the U.S. The conditions vary widely as to the minimum number of employees constituting a group, the minimum period of employment required for entering the group, the scope of the coverage, the benefits provided, whether the benefits extend to employees only or to their families as well, and other provisions. Strict legal rules forbid discrimination. Whereas policies may only be written by licensed insurers, pension plans can also be developed and serviced by actuarial firms, or by the employer itself with the advice of actuaries. The income tax aspects of these plans are of considerable importance.

## 10. COST OF INSURANCE

Mention has been made of some of the ways to reduce the cost of certain insurance.

Premium rates differ and are often negotiable. This is particularly true in the field of Marine Insurance, which one's broker may cover in the U.S. or abroad.

In recent years, states have permitted individual insurance companies to fix their own rates. The rates are not uniform. Most types of domestic policies may now be written at differing premiums.

A rather simple means of reducing cost is the acceptance of substantial deductible amounts, to be borne by the insured in case of loss. The amounts depend upon the type of insurance, the financial condition of the insured, and the saving to be achieved.

Large insureds have organized insurance subsidiaries, called captives, either in certain states or in tax haven countries. The purpose is to save in premiums by being able to deduct them from the taxable income of the insured's parent company. Most captives are in Bermuda; another favorite location is Guernsey.

Similarly, insureds with high premiums, payable under specific policies, may consider self-insuring the risk wherever legally permitted, and limiting the purchase of insurance to an amount in excess of the maximum limit they are prepared to bear themselves. Unlike premiums paid to insurance companies, reserves established by insureds for future losses may not be deducted from taxable income under Federal and state laws. Tax deductibility has sometimes been challenged successfully.

## 11. SUBROGATION

If an insurance company pays the loss or damage which the insured has suffered, it is subrogated, to the extent of its payment, to any claim which the insured may have against the wrongdoer. In other words, it takes over the position of the insured. It is sometimes overlooked that by virtue of the subrogation, the insurance company may now bring an action against the party that caused the damage or loss. For instance, if the American distributor of a German-produced machine is held to be liable to a purchaser of the machine on the ground of product liability, and the distributor's insurer pays the claim, the insurer is entitled to seek reimbursement from the German manufacturer.

Landlords and tenants generally purchase insurance against damage to the leased property and its contents. Leases usually require that the insurance policy provide that if the insurer pays for the damage, it shall waive its right of subrogation.

CHAPTER 17

# ANTITRUST LAWS

## 1. INTRODUCTION

The antitrust laws are a collection of statutes that are designed to assure the U.S. of an unfettered economy where free competition flourishes and monopolistic power is suppressed. On the other hand, and therein lies a certain inconsistency, the law prohibits selling at a price that represents predatory pricing, that is a price established (sometimes below the seller's cost) for the purpose of driving a competitor out of business or a market. This rule, which is subject to certain exceptions, is aimed at maintaining a healthy competition in the market place. 'Free competition' and 'no restraint of trade' are the hallmarks of the antitrust laws.

The antitrust laws are generally subject to the rule of reason, but certain violations are considered so evil that they are absolutely prohibited. They are illegal *per se*, and no argument about possible reasonableness will be heard. Examples of this are agreements for price-fixing and the division of territories or termination of a distributorship in order to lessen intrabrand competition (see Chapter 10, Section 10).

It all started in 1890, with the so-called Sherman Act, which outlawed any contract, combination, or conspiracy in restraint of domestic or foreign commerce. The best known subsequent enactments, named after their sponsors in Congress, are the Clayton Act and the Robinson Patman Act, both of which are primarily directed against price discrimination. Many antitrust decisions are based on Section 5 of the Federal Trade Commission Act, which outlaws, in general terms, unfair methods of competition. There are over seventy other Federal statutes that are designed to refine and to implement the antitrust laws. In addition, interpretive court decisions are an important source of antitrust law. The difficulty with those decisions, however, is that they generally have a retroactive effect. They may declare unlawful a common business practice that theretofore was considered proper. This creates a climate of uncertainty in the antitrust field. In 1969, the Supreme Court ruled that an exclusive regional distributorship was illegal *per se*. In 1977, the Supreme Court overturned this ruling and reversed itself, holding that an exclusive regional distributorship may well be legal, if reasonable under the circumstances (rule of reason). In cases where the Supreme Court has not laid down the law, the lower court judges are often driven to interpret the law according to their own understanding of economics. This also creates uncertainty.

The chief deterrents against the violation of the antitrust laws are criminal sanctions and the risk of treble damages claims. Other remedies for antitrust violations include civil penalties and a simple cease and desist order. The latter is relatively harmless if it is not coupled with an award of damages to a private claimant. The courts may fashion other remedies which fit the situation. For instance, if a business acquisition or a business merger is held to be violative of the antitrust laws, the court may order divestiture, i.e., undoing of the arrangement. If a contractual arrangement is held to be of excessively long duration, the court may shorten the duration. The enforcement rules in the U.S. are rather severe, in contrast to the policy to which the Common Market is accustomed under Sections 85 and 86 of the Treaty of Rome. The (Webb-Pomerene) Export Trade Act of 1918 exempts export associations from the strictures of the Sherman Act. There are also a few other exemptions, which are of little interest to one doing business in the U.S.

The government and private plaintiffs may also utilize the Racketeer Influence and Corrupt Organization Act (RICO), which is part of the Federal Organized Crime Control Act of 1970. This statute has been invoked in antitrust suits against some highly reputed pillars of the business world. One of the features of this law is a ten-year statute of limitations, whereas under the general antitrust laws, actions are outlawed after four years.

Most of the antitrust laws are Federal laws and they do not apply to business conduct that is confined to the area of a single state. However, most states have their own antitrust laws. Intrastate business is, therefore, also barred from anticompetitive and monopolistic practices. This chapter is limited to Federal law because one doing business with the U.S. is primarily concerned with the rules affecting interstate and foreign commerce.

The antitrust laws are administered by the Antitrust Division of the Department of Justice, as well as by the Federal Trade Commission (FTC), which is an independent administrative agency. They have concurrent jurisdiction. They are staffed by very competent lawyers, accountants and economists. The FTC has field offices throughout the country. The Antitrust Division of the Department of Justice is aided by over ninety U.S. Attorneys in all parts of the country, as well as by the Federal Bureau of Investigation (FBI). When the FTC initiates an investigation (sometimes spurred by an aggrieved competitor or customer), it sometimes holds hearings which result in an order. Such an order is subject to review by a Federal Appellate Court. In other instances, the FTC may not hold hearings, but instead may go directly to court. When the Department of Justice starts a proceeding, the U.S. Government is the plaintiff. Often, an aggrieved competitor or customer is the plaintiff. In that case, we have a private antitrust suit. Private parties sometimes raise an antitrust issue in a lawsuit that is not primarily an antitrust suit. Antitrust may be one of several claims or one of several defenses.

The question whether an antitrust issue may be raised is often litigated. The question posed is: Does a particular party have 'standing' to raise the issue? Recently, the Supreme Court decided that a foreign government has standing to claim treble damages from its U.S. supplier. The antitrust laws do not compel anyone to do business with anyone else. Generally speaking, one has a basic right to select one's customers, and to refuse to deal with others. There are some qualifications to the right, dependent on the context in which it is asserted. This is of some importance because the question arises at times in antitrust and antitrust-related litigation.

In these introductory remarks, it seems appropriate to caution people doing business in the U.S. not to be intimidated, without careful examination, by a charge of antitrust violation. Such charges are often made frivolously. The experience of Brunswick Corporation illustrates this. Brunswick is a large and financially strong manufacturer of bowling equipment. The bowling alley business had a recession in the 1960s and Brunswick found it difficult to collect payment from some customers. It was forced to repossess some bowling alleys, many of which it succeeded in reselling. When a resale was not possible, Brunswick took over the operation of the bowling alley. This incensed some existing bowling alley centers. They sued Brunswick, asserting that it had violated the anti-merger statute and was illegally interfering with competition, depriving the plaintiffs of the profits that they would have made if the defaulting bowling alleys had closed. They sued for treble damages (see Section 6). Brunswick appealed to the Supreme Court to quash this frivolous resort to the antitrust laws, and was successful.

Mention has been made of the fact that enforcement of the antitrust laws is sometimes sought outside the territorial limits of the U.S. (see Chapter 1, Section 13). This appears legitimate when it is done in order to protect the U.S. market from violations of the antitrust laws. Thus, if a nonresident alien participates in what is regarded as a conspiracy to monopolize the U.S. market, the nonresident should not complain about an investigation of his conduct, even though he may be immune from prosecution. Nevertheless, a U.S. litigant (be it the government or a private party) must expect to encounter obstacles in seeking pre-trial discovery of evidence, especially in Great Britain and Switzerland.

The protection of the antitrust laws does not extend to foreign markets. Sales to foreign markets are not subject to the restrictions of the antitrust laws.

The Export Trading Company Act of 1982 has somewhat loosened the antitrust restrictions for U.S. exporters. Title IV of the statute bears the subtitle Foreign Trade Antitrust Improvements Act. As early as 1918, Congress exempted export associations from the antitrust laws by passing the Webb-Pomerene Act.

## 2. PRICE-FIXING

Price-fixing is a crime. It is sometimes perpetrated at a golf course, where competitors meet for a 'friendly' game on a Saturday morning. Each of them is convinced that he has a superior product. The competitors, therefore, think it proper that their products should compete on quality, and that price competition should be eliminated. Price-fixing has a strong appeal in the business community, and it is hard to stamp out. The golf course is not essential. Sometimes one or more telephone calls are sufficient. Some years ago, several executives of a giant electrical equipment producer were sentenced to jail terms for price-fixing. In a recent case, some of the major U.S. plywood manufacturers were convicted of price-fixing. The companies denied that their parallel behavior, in quoting prices according to a similar formula, constituted a price-fixing conspiracy. They argued that their pricing method was based on good business judgement, which they exercised independently of each other. This business conduct is known as conscious parallelism. A corporation, of course, cannot be put in jail. However, it is specifically provided that if a corporation violates any of the penal provisions of the antitrust laws, the individual directors, officers and agents of the corporation may be held criminally liable.

The word, 'conscious', is perhaps misleading; it does not denote evil intent. Anticompetitive conduct need not arise out of an agreement. It may be held to violate the antitrust laws because it is an unfair trading practice within the meaning of Section 5 of the Federal Trade Commission Act. But, as the FTC said recently, in a case involving gasoline additives, 'Unilateral prices that affect price uniformity are suspect only when they occur in a market that is conducive to price coordination, where the effects on competition are clearly discernible, and where no mitigating circumstances exist sufficient to offset the harmful effect of the practice'. The FTC then further explains, 'Structural factors that suggest a market conducive to price coordination include high concentration, a small number of dominant firms, inelastic demand, homogeneous products and significant barriers to entry'. The language is quoted to demonstrate the difficulties that a businessman and his professional adviser sometimes face in determining what is lawful and what is not. It is like walking through a booby-trapped minefield.

Another example of price-fixing is resale price maintenance. A manufacturer or other seller used to be allowed to prescribe the resale price for products sold under a brand name. This is no longer permitted. A seller may not dictate the price at which the buyer resells. An exception applies to patented articles. The patent owner, who has a legal monopoly, can determine the resale price of the patented article.

## 3. PRICE DISCRIMINATION

Price discrimination occurs when one customer is allowed a better price or better payment terms than other customers, or when a customer is granted a special concession. It is unlawful only if the discrimination may have the effect of substantially lessening competition or creating a monopoly or injuring competition. These are the words of the Clayton Act. It is not necessary to show that the price discrimination actually has the injurious effect. The Robinson-Patman Act, which outlaws discriminatory discounts, services and allowances, was enacted because the Clayton Act strictures were found to be insufficient to prevent anti-competitive discrimination.

In order to establish a case of price discrimination it is necessary to show that the discrimination occurred with respect to products of 'like grade and quality'. It is not unlawful to charge a different price if changed conditions justify it. The prohibition against price discrimination cannot be circumvented by payment of a buyer's commission to a favored customer. Quantity discounts, though, are allowed. A seller who grants a quantity discount must be prepared to prove why the sale of a larger quantity justifies a lower price. The FTC may review the price computation that led to the quantity discount. Introductory discounts for new products are allowed for a limited period of time.

It should be noted that the strictures of the law apply not only to the party who discriminates, but also to the party who asks for or receives the benefit of the discrimination. This should deter businesspeople from asking for a special concession; or if it is offered, from accepting it. The Robinson Patman Act dictates that all discounts, rebates, and allowances must be non-discriminatory.

An important exception to the rule against price discrimination is hidden in a section of the Clayton Act. A seller may lower his usual price in order to meet the lower price charged by a competitor, provided the seller acts in good faith. He may meet the lower price, but he may not better it by charging a still lower price. This exception puts a seller in a difficult position because it is often hard to obtain reliable information about a competitor's pricing. The customer who says the competitor's price is lower may not be telling the truth. A seller tries to avoid a direct exchange of information with the competitor because that may lead to a charge of price-fixing. The seller's only resort is his good faith belief. In a recent case, a brewer in Kentucky invoked the meeting competition defense when it was sued by one of its distributors in Indiana, who complained that he was charged a higher price than the distributors in Kentucky. One of the novel features of the defense was that the brewer claimed the meeting competition defense on an area-wide basis. The Supreme Court upheld the brewer, and stated, 'The prudent businessman, responding fairly to what he believes in good faith is a situation of competitive necessity, might well raise his prices to some customers to increase his profits, while meeting competitors' prices by keeping prices to other customers low'. In the same decision, the Court said, 'Congress did not intend to bar territorial price differences that are in fact responses to competitive conditions'. The decision represented a departure from the previously held view that the law permitted differential pricing to meet competition only on a customer-by-customer basis. It constituted a significant application of the rule of reason in the law of price discrimination.

## 4. MONOPOLIZATION

When the Sherman Act of 1890 made monopolizing unlawful, it did not outlaw monopolies. Monopolization must be understood as the anticompetitive use of

monopoly power. This is convincingly explained in the recent decision of the
Second Circuit Court of Appeals in *Berkey Photo Co.* v. *Eastman Kodak Co.*,
which supplanted earlier court decisions that tried to explain the meaning of
unlawful monopolization. The following excerpt from the court decision will
help in understanding the concept of monopolization:

> 'A large firm does not violate the law simply by keeping the competitive
> rewards attributable to its efficient size, nor does an integrated business
> (Kodak produced cameras as well as film) offend the Sherman Act whenever
> one of its departments benefits from association with a division possessing a
> monopoly in its own market. . . . More efficient production, greater ability to
> develop complementary products, reduced transaction costs, and so forth
> are gains that accrue to any integrated firm, regardless of its market share,
> and they cannot by themselves be considered uses of monopoly power.'

A monopoly as such is not illegal. It may even be created by law as, for
instance, a patent. The patent owner can exclude anybody else from the use of
his patent, and he may license its use as he pleases. Bigness as such is not illegal,
although a big organization such as IBM is more vulnerable than a smaller
enterprise. A big organization is subject to increased temptations to misuse its
power in an anticompetitive manner. When the Dupont company acquired a
patent on its product called Cellophane, it was anxious for a competitive
product to come on the market, lest Dupont be charged with improper
monopolization.

A crucial element in determining whether monopoly power exists that is
likely to be misused is to determine what is the so-called relevant market. For
instance, a manufacturer of steel is not in a position to monopolize the entire
steel market. It can, however, acquire a monopoly in the market for a special
kind of steel. Courts dealing with the charge of monopolization must first
determine what is the relevant market.

How far the courts will go to safeguard competition against abuse by
monopolistic power is illustrated by a decision of the Supreme Court involving
a lawfully constituted public utility company. The company refused to permit
other utilities access to its transmission lines. The purpose was, of course, to
keep out the competition of smaller power companies. The Supreme Court
ruled that this was a violation of the antitrust laws, and that the defendant utility
company must grant its competitors access to its transmission lines.

## 5. MERGERS AND ACQUISITIONS

It is obvious that corporate mergers and acquisitions are a potential danger to
free competition. It is not unusual for a company to acquire or merge with
another company in order to gain access to that other company's market. This
may be an insignificant horizontal acquisition. Whether it is insignificant
depends, often, on the share of the market that each of the competitors has
captured. Acquisitions have been invalidated where the combined share of the

relevant market was as low as 8%. The acquisition by a substantial company in one market of another independent company in a different market, where each is a leading producer in the same line of commerce in its market, has increasingly been condemned, on the theory that some form of potential competition between the parties has thereby been restrained, and a trend towards industry-wide concentration has been accelerated. If it is found that the merger or acquisition prevents the acquiring party from entering the market as an independent competitor (which is indeed sometimes the purpose of the acquisition or merger), the acquisition or merger will be held to be a violation of the antitrust laws. This is illustrated by the *Falstaff Brewery* case. Falstaff, the nation's fourth largest brewer, is located in the West. It purchased the shares of a leading brewer in New England. The Supreme Court invalidated the acquisition on the ground that it tended to lessen competition in New England, although Falstaff disclaimed any intention to enter the New England market. The possibility that Falstaff, at some future time, might enter the New England market to compete there, was enough to outlaw an acquisition that would eliminate such possibility of enhanced competition.

The antitrust aspect of acquisitions and mergers merits the attention of foreigners who seek to enter the U.S. market. The contemplated joint venture between the Toyota Motor Corporation of Japan and General Motors Company illustrates the problem. Toyota and General Motors intend jointly to produce a subcompact car in California. The two leading competitors of General Motors, Ford Motor Company and Chrysler Corporation, have protested that the joint venture violates the antitrust laws. They contend that it would eliminate competition between Toyota and General Motors. The FTC has approved the merger, and the matter is now pending before the courts. It may take a long time before the issue is ultimately decided by the Supreme Court. Few market entrants can wait that long, or can afford the expense of protracted proceedings.

The FTC has established a pre-merger clearance bureau, to which businesspeople may turn for an expert, though not binding, opinion.

## 6. TREBLE DAMAGES ACTIONS

The present source of the dreaded treble damages claim is Section 4 of the Clayton Act, which provides that 'any person who shall be injured in his business or property by reason of anything forbidden by the antitrust laws . . . shall recover threefold the damages by him sustained, and the cost of suit, including a reasonable attorney's fee'.

The provision for reimbursement of litigation expenses and attorneys' fees is unusual in U.S. practice, and tends to encourage the commencement of a treble damages action.

Treble damages claims are usually made in private antitrust suits. However, a government or a government agency may also sue for treble damages; and in 1978, the Supreme Court ruled that even foreign governments can demand the payment of treble damages.

A treble damages claim presupposes, of course, that the plaintiff has suffered damage as a result of an antitrust violation. The damage may, for instance, consist of an overcharge due to illegal price-fixing or an anticompetitive monopolistic practice. The claim can only be made by the original victim of the antitrust violation. If the victim resells the product and passes on the overcharge to his customer, the customer cannot make a treble damages claim against the antitrust violator. This may not appear logical, but the Supreme Court has so interpreted the law.

## 7. TYING ARRANGEMENTS

During World War II, Scotch whisky was scarce. Some liquor store owners would, therefore, require a customer to buy one or two bottles of gin with every bottle of Scotch whisky. This is an illegal *tie-in*, although a local liquor store owner is not subject to the Federal antitrust laws. The gin is called the tied product, which one really does not want. The whisky is known as the *tying* product, the product one wants. Tie-in sales and leases are generally illegal *per se* if, in the words of the Supreme Court, the violator possesses 'sufficient economic power' over the tying product to 'appreciably restrain' competition for the tied product. The vice of the arrangement is that it denies competitors free access to the market for the tied product, not because the seller has a better product but because he has superior power with respect to the tying product.

One of the earliest tying decisions concerned IBM. That company used to lease its computing machines on condition that the lessees buy from IBM all the punch cards needed for the use of the machines. This was held to be an illegal tie-in. It is not uncommon for a party possessing dominant power to use it for the purpose of promoting the use of freely available products which it also sells. This is not always illegal. For instance, Daimler Benz AG was held to be justified in requiring that automobile spare parts for its Mercedes cars be purchased from an 'approved source'. This was a legitimate way to make sure that only approved spare parts were used, and it was not an illegal tie-in. The case of *United States Steel Corp.* v. *Fortner Enterprises* offers an interesting illustration. Fortner was a real estate developer. It purchased expensive prefabricated homes from U.S. Steel. It also borrowed from a credit corporation that was a division of U.S. Steel the funds needed for the purchase of vacant land and the houses. The credit was very cheap, and only available to purchasers of the prefabricated homes. Fortner brought suit against U.S. Steel Corp., on the ground that the arrangement was an illegal tie-in. The tying product here was the loan, and the question was whether the credit corporation possessed sufficient economic power to promote the sale of prefabricated homes. The Supreme Court concluded that the credit facilities which were granted to Fortner were not so unique as to allow Fortner to invoke the rule of *per se* illegality.

Tying arrangements occur often in agreements for the licensing of a patent or a trademark. This is discussed in the next section of this chapter.

Tying arrangements have occurred in the franchising of fast food stores. The franchisor, not content to collect a franchise fee for the use of its recipes and its operating methods, would also compel the franchisee to buy from him paper goods, such as napkins and plates. It is proper to prescribe standards, which can be maintained without a tie-in. A franchisor's desire for quality control is legitimate, and does not offend the antitrust laws.

## 8. PATENT, TRADEMARK AND COPYRIGHT MISUSE

As previously stated, patents, trademarks and copyrights are a legal monopoly. The owner is privileged by law to exclude others from the enjoyment of the monopoly power, and to parcel out pieces of the monopoly power through licenses. However, the monopoly may not be misused by an antitrust arrangement. Utilization of a patent in violation of the antitrust laws constitutes patent misuse and will not be tolerated by the courts. This simple statement raises a number of complicated questions, which cannot here be dealt with exhaustively. One of the questions is whether misuse leads to the invalidation of the patent. It is a much debated question, and one doing business in the U.S. must assume that such a risk exists. Generally, the question is answered in the negative (see below).

In an old case involving General Electric Company, the Supreme Court ruled that a patent owner could fix the resale price of the patented product. This rule is still valid, but it is sometimes disregarded. In one case the Supreme Court said that the rule does not apply where the patent license covers an entire industry. In still another case, a Japanese patent owner marketed the patented camera through a U.S. distributor. The patent owner prescribed the resale price and limited the U.S. territory in which a U.S. distributor could operate. When the distributor balked, the Japanese patent owner terminated the distribution agreement. The court forbade this, and annulled the termination.

Territorial limitations in a patent license are ordinarily legal. Thus, a German citizen who owned a number of U.S. patents licensed a U.S. corporation. It was stipulated that the German was not to sell to customers in the U.S., and that the U.S. licensee was not to export. That was held perfectly legal.

Patent infringement suits frequently have been dismissed because the patent owner tried to extend the patent monopoly by requiring the patent licensee to buy one or more unpatented products. This was, of course, an illegal tying agreement (as described above in Section 7).

The pooling of patents and cross-licensing are not unlawful if a party to the pooling or cross-licensing agreement is not precluded from contracting outside the pool or agreement. But this type of arrangement constitutes an antitrust violation if, in effect, it amounts to a restraint of trade, or if it is designed to create a monopoly. More about this in Chapter 21.

Package licensing represents a problem. It occurs when a party owns many patents and charges its licensee one flat fee for the use of all patents. This is considered an antitrust violation if it compels a licensee to pay a fee for patents that have expired. It is legal if the flat fee arrangement is for the mutual convenience of the parties, who want to avoid a complicated accounting.

Patent misuse is generally a complete defense in an action for patent infringement. However, when the patent misuse has terminated, the patent owner can enforce the patent. In other words, patent misuse bars enforcement, but does not destroy the patent.

As is noted in Chapter 20, trademarks also are a legal monopoly. If a trademark is used in violation of the antitrust laws, it is an illegal misuse, and the trademark will be ignored. One of the most well-known decisions in the field of international trade is the *Timken* case, involving a division of markets between American Timken and its subsidiaries, British Timken and French Timken. They agreed not to sell in each other's market and American Timken licensed the two other companies to use the name Timken.

The license was held to be no shield against the antitrust violation, but rather an ineffective pretext for implementing the market division, which was illegal *per se* under the antitrust laws. An earlier case illustrates the situation further. The General Electric Company marketed an incandescent lamp bulb under the trademark Mazda. It licensed its chief competitor, Westinghouse Electric Company, to use the trademark. No other manufacturer received a license. The court found that General Electric and Westinghouse together had engaged in a campaign to exclude competition. This was held to be a violation of the antitrust laws.

Copyrights are in the same category. It is an abuse if the owner of a copyright uses his copyright position to violate the antitrust laws. It is improper for a copyright owner to control the resale price of a copyrighted book. It is likewise a copyright abuse if the copyright owner of a film tries to control the admission price of a motion picture theatre.

## 9. BOYCOTT

A trade boycott is, by definition, a restraint of trade, and therefore, a violation of the antitrust laws.

The Arab League attempts to boycott anyone dealing with the state of Israel. U.S. law forbids not only participation in such a boycott, but also responses to inquiries related to the boycott. Disregard of this prohibition may lead to severe tax penalties. The prohibition is found in the Export Administration Act, which is administered by the Secretary of Commerce. At this writing, the incumbent is Malcolm Baldrige. Mr. Baldrige is the defendant in a number of lawsuits that attack the prohibition. The most comprehensive attack, on constitutional grounds, was launched by a manufacturer of electrical equipment, which asserted substantial damage because it was blacklisted by the Arab League as a result of compliance with the anti-boycott law. The court ruled that the law and the regulations issued thereunder do not violate the Constitution.

## 10. STATE LAWS

Prohibition of restraint of trade, and freedom of competition, are almost articles of faith throughout the U.S. It is, therefore, not surprising that the principles of Federal antitrust law discussed in this chapter have been enacted into law in the various states. The state laws apply only to intrastate business, i.e. business that is confined within the borders of a state. In California, the applicable law is found in the Business and Professional Code. Illinois has a statute called the Antitrust Act. In New York, the so-called Donnelly Antitrust Act is part of the General Business Law (Sec. 340 *seq*).

# CHAPTER 18

# FEDERAL REGULATIONS AFFECTING BUSINESS

## 1. INTRODUCTION

Businesspeople everywhere resist government interference. And yet, in their role as private citizens they usually would not want to do without government regulation. That is probably why, loud protests notwithstanding, business everywhere is subject and subjected to numerous regulations, from the licensing of plumbers to the supervision of power plants. Pursuant to a pre-election promise of President Reagan, the executive department of the U.S. Government is at present engaged in a program of deregulation, which has met with mixed reaction. It is characteristic of U.S. Government controls that great emphasis is placed on the welfare of individual persons. American ships are frequently chartered in Panama, Liberia, or elsewhere, because the ship owners desire to avoid the safety regulations imposed on ships that are chartered in the U.S. Some pharmaceutical products obtainable elsewhere are not permitted to be sold in the U.S. because the Federal Food and Drug Administration (FDA) does not consider them safe or effective. All new drugs require pre-clearance by the FDA. No foodstuffs can be imported unless the FDA has inspected and cleared the goods. This is a hazard as well as a burden for food importers.

The desire to protect the ecology and the environment is not uniquely American. However, it is noteworthy that no dam or waterway or power plant may be built in the U.S. unless the government agency involved first proposes and publishes an environmental impact statement, which is subject to court review. The Environmental Protection Agency (EPA) is charged with protecting and enhancing the physical environment and controlling pollution through regulations and surveillance. It is concerned with air and water quality, solid waste disposal, toxic substances, pesticides and noise. EPA limits the amount of radioactivity in the environment, reviews proposals for new nuclear facilities and coal-burning facilities, regulates chemical usage, and establishes tolerance levels for pesticides in foods. Since its inception, in December 1970, EPA has issued an average of ninety regulations each year.

OSHA legislation affects many small and medium-size businesses. OSHA is the acronym for Occupational Safety and Health Administration. It is part of the Federal Department of Labor. It is probably the most disliked regulator. OSHA standards fill about 1,500 pages of fine print in the Code of Federal Regulations. In 1980 the standards for workers' exposure to benzine were reviewed by the Supreme Court, which pointed out that 'OSHA is not given unbridled discretion to adopt standards designed to create absolutely risk free places'. A typical OSHA measure is a regulation requiring chemical manufacturers to communicate to their workers any hazards of their products. OSHA has numerous offices in all parts of the country, through which it supervises plants, imposes fines for violations, and not infrequently battles business in the courts.

Business is regulated by many other laws, regulations, ordinances and rules imposed by Federal, state and municipal authorities. They are too numerous to discuss here.

The best known governmental regulations are the antitrust laws, which are discussed in Chapter 17, and the laws and regulations pertaining to the securities markets, to which the rest of this chapter is devoted.

## 2. SECURITIES REGULATIONS

While most of the securities regulations are Federal law, virtually all states have also legislated in this field. This is referred to in section 11 of this chapter.

The Federal law is policed by the Securities and Exchange Commission (SEC), a highly respected government agency. It was created early in the administration of President Franklin D. Roosevelt, because it was found that wild and irresponsible stock speculation had been one of the causes of the Great Depression. The first chairman of the SEC was a wealthy businessman who had been a successful securities trader. The second was a former law professor who helped draft the Federal securities laws, and then went on to become the Dean of Harvard Law School. The third chairman was a young law professor who thereafter became a long-time member of the Supreme Court. The major Federal securities laws are the Securities Act of 1933, the Securities Exchange Act of 1934, the Williams Act (an amendment of the 1933 Act, pertaining to tender offers), the Public Utility Holding Company Act of 1935, the Trust Indenture Act of 1939, and the Investment Company Act of 1940.

Persons doing business in the U.S. are primarily interested in the first three of these enactments, and it is, therefore, appropriate to concentrate on them.

The 1933 Act is primarily concerned with the initial issuance of securities. The 1934 Act focuses upon the trading of securities, the markets where securities are traded, and the filing of reports.

Three great principles permeate the securities regulations. The first is disclosure. Full disclosure of all pertinent business facts is required at the time when securities are issued to the public, and regularly thereafter. Disclosure of all important events, as they occur, is to be made to the securities market, to a buyer of securities, and to all potential buyers. The second great principle is restraint. The person of superior knowledge (the 'insider') is restrained from taking competitive advantage of his knowledge. The third principle is increased responsibility of corporate managers and directors, as well as their professional advisers.

A violation of any of these principles will lead to a charge of securities fraud. The harsh word *fraud* does not necessarily mean a criminal offense, although the SEC does not shy away from urging the Justice Department to seek criminal indictments in appropriate cases. The ordinary remedy for securities fraud is civil in nature. The rules of the game are constantly changed and refined by the SEC and by judicial interpretation.

Although the SEC is the chief enforcer of the Federal securities laws, it supports private actions to supplement its own efforts to police the securities market. The SEC also supervises and regulates the stock exchanges and the so-called over-the-counter market, as well as the activities of stockbrokers and securities dealers. The largest stock exchange is the New York Stock Exchange. It accounts for more than 75% of the dollar volume of all organized stock exchanges. The other major exchanges are the American Stock Exchange in New York, and the exchanges in Boston, Philadelphia, and San Francisco (Pacific Stock Exchange). The stock exchanges are independent bodies with their own rules, which must be complied with to obtain listing for a security. The over-the-counter market handles transactions that are not conducted on a national stock exchange. The stockbrokers and dealers who operate in the over-the-counter market are organized as the National Association of Securities Dealers, and are subject to the discipline of the SEC.

The securities regulations are so complicated that businessmen and their advisers are sometimes uncertain whether a planned action is permissible. They may then turn to the SEC staff for advice. If the SEC finds no objection to the proposed transaction, the inquirer will receive a so-called no action letter, stating that no action by the staff of the SEC will be recommended. This is not a legally binding commitment, but a no action letter may generally be relied upon.

## 3. DEFINITION OF A SECURITY

When speaking of securities, one usually thinks of stocks and bonds. However, for the purposes of securities regulation, the Securities Act of 1933 and the Securities Exchange Act of 1934 have established a much broader definition. Included, for instance, are participation in any profit-sharing agreement, any oil, gas or mineral royalty arrangement or lease, and any investment contract.

The principal significance of this broad concept of securities is that aggrieved parties may assert a claim for securities fraud under SEC Rule 10b-5, as hereafter discussed. Oil and gas leases often appear in SEC decisions. A franchise, such as a franchise for a Kentucky Fried Chicken outlet, has been held to be a security.

## 4. REGISTRATION OF SECURITIES AND PERIODIC REPORTING

A company that plans to offer a security for public sale must first file a registration statement with the SEC, and prepare a sales prospectus that summarizes the data in the registration statement. Certain transactions and securities are exempt, as noted below. The purpose of the registration is to provide disclosure of financial and other information about the offering party. The offering party is generally called the issuer, because it seeks to raise capital by issuing new shares of stock or bonds. But there is also the so-called secondary offering. We speak of a secondary offering or a secondary distribution when the owner of a block of securities wishes to distribute this block among the investing public. If the securities are unregistered, the owner of the shares must file a registration statement, and he is then the issuer. The disclosure in the registration statement is supposed to enable the prospective purchasing public to evaluate the offered security.

The registration statement is prepared on forms prescribed by the SEC. The forms vary, depending on the type of issue involved. However, all forms have in common a demand for information, such as (*a*) a description of the business of the issuer and its properties, (*b*) a description of the capitalization of the issuer if it is a corporation, and the role of the proposed new securities issue in that capitalization, (*c*) information regarding the management of the issuer, and (*d*) financial statements for the last three years, certified by independent public accountants. The SEC will examine the registration statement, to see whether it is in proper form and contains all required information. The SEC does not examine the merits of a proposed offering. If the SEC is not satisfied, it will require one or more amendments or corrections. If there is no objection by the SEC, the registration statement becomes effective, which means that the sale may begin. Although the law says that a statement becomes automatically effective twenty days after filing, it is customary to give the SEC more time to review the filing. The registration statement, as well as the prospectus, are generally prepared in cooperation with the underwriter, i.e. the investment banker who has agreed to buy or to market all offered shares. In practice, this means cooperation between the lawyers for the issuer and the lawyers for the underwriters.

While they work on the registration statement, the lawyers generally also prepare such so-called Blue Sky compliance measures as may be required by applicable state laws (see Section 12).

Information must be kept up-to-date by the filing of quarterly reports (on SEC Form 10-Q), and periodic reports (on SEC Form 8-K) with respect to important business events, such as the fire loss of a factory, a prolonged strike, a take-over bid, changes in management, and acquisitions and dispositions of assets. Financial results and information about important events, must be disseminated to the public as and when they occur. This is generally done by a press release. After the end of each calendar year, a comprehensive report about the state of the business must be rendered on SEC Form 10-K. This is generally done in conjunction with the annual proxy statement (see Section 10, below). At the heart of the annual report are the financial data for the past year, which are reviewed by independent certified public accountants after preparation by the corporation under the supervision of its chief financial officer. However, the directors are responsible for reviewing the financial statements before they are filed with the SEC. Since 1980, the annual reports on form 10-K must be signed by a majority of the directors, which entails a duty of increased diligence and increased liability. The registration statements and the periodic reports are freely available for inspection at all SEC offices. These reports are more valuable and more reliable than credit bureau information, and more detailed than the public register on which one must rely in other countries. If a security is to be traded on a national stock exchange, registration is also required under the Securities Exchange Act of 1934. Securities of corporations that are not traded on a national stock exchange but that have total assets exceeding $1,000,000 and more than 500 shareholders must also be registered. In addition, proxy statements must be filed. The SEC has announced that it will provide for an integrated registration form under the 1933 and the 1934 Acts. This has not yet been achieved. However, the registration under the 1934 Act contains much the same information as the registration under the 1933 Act.

## 5. EXEMPTIONS FROM REGISTRATION

There are several exemptions from the registration requirements. The most important is the private placement exemption, provided by Regulation D under the 1933 Act. It became effective in 1982, and is now the controlling Federal regulation with respect to non-public and limited offerings. Offerings made in compliance with Regulation D are not required to be registered with the SEC. Rules 504, 505 and 506 of Regulation D set forth three types of exempt offerings. Rule 504 exempts certain issuers who raise no more than $500,000 from an unlimited number of investors during a twelve-month period. Rule 505 exempts certain issuers who raise no more than $5 million from thirty-five *non-accredited*, and an unlimited number of *accredited*, investors during a twelve-month period. Rule 506 exempts any issuer who raises an unlimited amount of dollars from no more than thirty-five experienced, non-accredited, or an unlimited number of accredited, investors. Among the eight categories of accredited investors are purchasers of $150,000 or more, individuals with annual income of at least $200,000, and individuals who have a net worth of at least $1 million, either alone or together with their spouses. In each case, Regulation D provides certain limitations on the manner in which the offering may be made. The SEC must be notified of the offering. The issuer will also have to either register under, or find an exemption from, state 'Blue Sky' laws (see Section 12, below). The issuer must make sure that purchasers will not redistribute the securities to a wider public. To this end, the issuer generally demands a so-called investment letter, in which the purchaser confirms that he is making the purchase for investment and not for distribution. Additionally, the certificate(s) involved will be marked with a legend, indicating that the securities are not registered for distribution. Certificates so marked are generally referred to as *letter stock*. From an excess of caution, some issuers also instruct their transfer agent about the transfer restriction.

The letter stock restriction remains effective for at least two years. Thereafter the purchaser may resell the securities gradually, within narrowly defined limits.

The private placement exemption is often used by financial institutions, such as insurance companies, which buy a corporate bond issue in connection with debt financing. Debt financing is one of the most frequent applications of the private placement exemption.

So-called Small Business Investment Companies are exempt from registration, but are subject to SEC regulations. Intrastate offerings are exempt from registration. To qualify for this exemption, both the issuer and the offerees (and purchasers) must be located within one state. The issuer must also be doing business in the state. To meet this requirement, the issuer must derive at least 80% of its revenues from within the state and have at least 80% of its assets located there. At least 80% of the proceeds of the offering must be used in the state. Since most issuers operate in more than one state, it is obviously difficult to qualify for this exemption.

Finally, a registration exemption prevails for securities that are issued by governmental bodies, by banks, by charitable institutions and by public carriers that are governed by the Interstate Commerce Act.

## 6. PROXY STATEMENT

Another disclosure tool is the proxy statement. Few shareholders attend a shareholders' meeting. It is, therefore, customary to attach to any call for a shareholders' meeting a form of power of attorney, called a proxy, in which the holder of the proxy is empowered to vote on behalf of the absent shareholder. Ordinarily, the proxy is solicited by the management of the corporation. But one or more dissenting or hostile groups may send out different proxies. In each case, the request for the proxy must be accompanied by a proxy statement containing detailed information about the finances and the condition of the business; and if directors are to be elected, personal data about the individuals proposed for election. The agenda of the shareholders' meeting must be submitted, and every shareholder must be given the opportunity to indicate whether he wants to vote yes or no on the various items on the agenda. If any shareholder has advised the management that he wishes to submit a resolution, the proxy statement must include it. These resolutions often deal with general political questions, such as nuclear energy or the apartheid policy in South Africa, and they are often remote from the business of the corporation.

Management, therefore, discourages such resolutions, which are rarely adopted by a majority of the shareholders. It has been proposed to limit the right to submit such resolutions to shareholders who own some minimum number of shares.

The proxy statement must first be submitted to the SEC, which will examine it to determine whether all disclosure requirements have been met. Only after the SEC has so satisfied itself, may the proxy statements be sent out.

## 7. SECURITIES FRAUD

This is the most litigated subject in the field of securities transactions. The litigation may be initiated by the SEC as part of its enforcement efforts, or it may be commenced by an aggrieved private party who seeks the recovery of damages.

It will help in the understanding of the concept to know the basic law. It is Section 10(b) of the Securities Exchange Act of 1934, which reads as follows:

'It shall be unlawful for any person, directly or indirectly, by the use of any means or instrumentality of interstate commerce or of the mails, or of any facility of any national securities exchange, ... to use or employ, in connection with the purchase or sale of any security registered on a national securities exchange or any security not so registered, any manipulative or deceptive device or contrivance in contravention of such rules and regulations as the Commission may prescribe as necessary or appropriate in the public interest or for the protection of investors.'

The statute is supplemented by SEC Rule 10b-5 which reads:

'It shall be unlawful for any person, directly or indirectly, by the use of any means or instrumentality of interstate commerce, or of the mails or of any facility of any national securities exchange,
(a) To employ any device, scheme, or artifice to defraud,
(b) To make any untrue statement of a material fact or to omit to state a material fact necessary in order to make the statements made, in the light of the circumstances under which they were made, not misleading, or
(c) To engage in any act, practice, or course of business which operates as a fraud or deceit upon any person, in connection with the purchase or sale of any security.'

One of the basic questions is whether, in order to make a claim of securities fraud, it must be shown that either the seller or the purchaser of securities was defrauded. This has never been an issue in an enforcement action by the SEC. But in a private action it is of some importance. More than thirty years ago a court decision established a doctrine (the so-called *Birnbaum* doctrine) that the plaintiff must be either the seller or the purchaser of securities. The *Birnbaum* doctrine is still valid, but has declined in vitality. The courts now hold that the purchaser may be one who has a contract to purchase, and the concept of seller includes one who has contracted to sell. Thus, the holder of convertible preferred stock who alleged that defendant's misrepresentation caused him not to convert, was held to be a purchaser who could sue under Section 10-b. Similarly, the holder of an unexercised option to purchase shares was held to be a seller for purposes of Section 10-b. Shareholders of a defrauded corporation have been allowed to sue for damages under the statute. There are other interpretations. Suffice it to say that it is not safe to build one's defense against a security fraud action on the *Birnbaum* doctrine.

The courts take an expansive view of the scope of Section 10-b. The application of the statute is not limited to fraud with respect to the securities sold. It also covers fraud relating to the consideration received in exchange for the securities. To illustrate, if the consideration consists of the licensing of technical know-how, and the value of the know-how was misrepresented, an action for securities fraud may be maintained.

Some courts hold that the transfer of a controlling stock interest in a business is not a securities fraud. This is the so-called sale of business doctrine. In a recent case, a purchaser bought all of the outstanding shares of a trucking business, and then assumed managerial control of the business. Thereafter, he sued for securities fraud under Rule 10b-5, alleging that the sellers had furnished inaccurate, incomplete, and misleading financial information. The defense argued that the securities fraud law applies only to investment fraud, not to the purchase and sale of a business. This argument was rejected.

The misrepresentation must be intentional. The technical legal term is *scienter*. The Supreme Court has made it clear that there can be no action for securities fraud unless there is *scienter*, an intentional misrepresentation.

Mere negligence cannot support an action under Section 10-b. It must be remembered that Section 10-b applies to all corporations, whether or not their shares are required to be registered.

## 8. TENDER OFFERS AND TAKE-OVERS

The tender offer (a legal term which is a linguistic redundancy) concerns take-overs. A take-over occurs when a company acquires all or the majority of shares of another company. The applicable rules are of particular interest to a foreign company that wishes to enter the U.S. market by acquiring a publicly owned U.S. company.

Take-overs are usually friendly arrangements between the acquirer and the other party, often called the target company. Sometimes, the take-over, or attempted take-over, is hostile, and then the target company fights back. Generally, take-overs are based on sound economic reasons, but sometimes they stem from a desire for vain aggrandizement. Tender offers are necessary when the shares of the target company are held by a large number of people who are not readily available for friendly negotiations. The Williams Act, which regulates take-overs, was not designed to prevent changes in control. Its aim is to compel reporting to the SEC and disclosure to the shareholders of the affected corporations of what is probably going to happen, so that they can decide intelligently whether to keep or to sell their shares. Bearing in mind this fundamental purpose of the statute, the Supreme Court overruled a lower court injunction against an offering corporation that, out of ignorance, had filed too late the information that was required by the Williams Act. The lower court issued an injunction prohibiting the offeror from acquiring additional shares of the target company, and ordered the defendant not to vote or pledge the shares which it had acquired, and to divest itself of those shares. The Supreme Court overruled the lower court, pointing out that the delayed filing had cured the earlier lapse and did not result in irreparable harm. The Court held that no injunction was necessary to protect the interests of shareholders who had sold their shares at pre-disclosure prices, not knowing that a take-over bid was imminent. Such persons, the Court pointed out, are not barred from an ordinary damages action, if they suffered actual damages. The reference to this decision should not be taken as a recommendation for laxity in the observance of the Williams Act.

The disclosure requirements of the Williams Act are very detailed, and more complicated and comprehensive than those for a registration statement.

At this juncture, it is worth noting that the Williams Act also amended Section 13 of the Securities Exchange Act of 1934. Section 13 requires that any person acquiring 5% or more of the outstanding securities of a corporation must notify the SEC, as well as the corporation. For that reason, persons who secretly prepare for a take-over by purchasing in the open market shares of the target company, sometimes limit these purchases to just under 5% of the outstanding shares. A 5% shareholder must disclose personal data about himself or itself. An acquirer wishing to preserve anonymity cannot hide under the shield of a bank or other third party. The law requires identification of the real party in interest. If the purchase was financed by a loan, the loan arrangement must likewise be disclosed. If the acquirer plans a merger or further purchases, or a sale of his or its interest, that also must be disclosed.

The disclosure requirements for a tender offer are similar. The tender offer must, of course, state the terms of the offer. It must also disclose any dealings with the target company during the past three years. The offeror's own financial condition must be described, and if it is a subsidiary, the financial condition of its parent. All material facts must be disclosed, and it is sometimes debatable what is material. The question must be primarily judged from the viewpoint of a shareholder who is in doubt whether he should accept the tender offer. When the Gulf and Western Corp. made a tender offer for a minority interest in the Atlantic and Pacific Tea Corporation, it was held to be a suppression of a material fact that Gulf and Western did not disclose its history of transforming a minority position to a position of complete control. Triumph American Inc., a subsidiary of a British corporation, made a tender offer for shares of General Host Corp. The court held that the tender offer should have disclosed that Triumph American's only other acquisition had paid an extraordinary dividend, which, in effect, permitted Triumph American to pay for the acquisition with the acquired company's own funds. Also, it was not disclosed that the British Government had the power to exercise control over the target company. If a court issues an injunction on such grounds, it is not necessarily fatal to the contemplated take-over. The injunction does not prevent correction and amendment of the tender offer. Application for such an injunction is one of the weapons of a resisting target company. However, suppression of a material fact may also be claimed in a fraud action for damages by anybody who can prove injury.

The tender offer that is filed with the SEC must be accompanied by a copy of any solicitation material that is intended to be used, and a copy of any intended newspaper advertisements.

The tender offer may be for cash; the cash amount offered frequently is higher than the book value or the quoted stock exchange price of the shares of the target company. The tender offer may also be for shares of the offering company, or it may be a mixed offer. If shares are offered, they are generally not registered shares, and, in that case, the offering corporation must also file a registration statement and prospectus.

A tender offer is generally valid for a stated period of time. It is not unusual to obtain an extension of the deadline, but one cannot count on it.

The tender offer is often conditioned on the receipt of a minimum number of offers. Also, the offeror may state that it will not accept more than a stated maximum number of the shares of the target company.

While a tender offer is pending, the offeror is not allowed to acquire shares of the target company by any other means.

## 9. INSIDER INFORMATION

In accordance with the general disclosure principle, information that is not available to the general public may not be used to make a profit. Section 16 of the Securities Exchange Act of 1934 provides that if insiders make such a profit, it may be recovered by the corporation. Action for such payment may be instituted by the corporation or any of its shareholders. Insiders are defined as directors and officers, and all shareholders who own more than 10% of any class of equity security registered under Section 12(g) of the 1934 Act. The statute is limited to profits made within any six-month period, and the profits are known as *short swing profits*. Short swing profits are recoverable only if they result from a sale by the insiders. The significance of this is demonstrated by a Supreme Court decision, which is mentioned here because it involves a factual situation that also illustrates other aspects of the U.S. securities law and practice. Occidental Petroleum Company sought to merge with the Kern County Land Company. The negotiations came to naught, primarily because the management of Kern County Land Company did not wish to be absorbed by Occidental. Occidental then made a tender offer to the shareholders of the target company. This was again unsuccessful. Occidental acquired slightly more than 10% of the shares of Kern, just enough to be in the category of an insider. The target company, anxious to avert further advances by Occidental, proposed a merger to Tenneco Corp. This merger would be achieved by the target company's selling its assets to Tenneco, which would place the assets in a new Kern company. Occidental now was in an awkward position. It was afraid that if the merger succeeded, it would be locked into a minority position in Tenneco. It, therefore, made an agreement by which Occidental granted

Tenneco an option to buy the shares of the new Kern Company to which Occidental would be entitled in the exchange following the merger. After the merger was consummated, Tenneco exercised the option. Occidental received more money for the shares of the new Kern company than it had paid for the shares of the old Kern company. The new Kern company then sued to recover this profit. The Supreme Court held that Occidental had not abused insider information, and that the sale was not in violation of Section 16.

Beyond the provisions of Section 16, it is illegal to use undisclosed information for the purpose of making a profit. How far this goes is illustrated by two examples: A director of a corporation tipped off a friend (such people are often called tippees) that the price of his corporation's shares were likely to rise because of an imminent, yet undisclosed, tender offer. The tippee bought some shares and sold them at a modest profit of less than $1,000. A few weeks later, he was summoned by the local office of the SEC that had started an investigation. In another case, an employee of a printing concern, which was engaged in printing certain prospectuses, took advantage of the information that he read in the prospectuses. He made some purchases and sales, resulting in a profit of about $30,000. Criminal proceedings were instituted, but the Supreme Court held that the printer was not an insider covered by the statute.

## 10. GOING PRIVATE

If a privately owned corporation sells shares to the public, and in connection therewith files a registration statement, it is said to be 'going public'. Going private is the reverse procedure. The controlling shareholders of a publicly owned corporation desire to eliminate the minority shareholders by buying them out, and making the corporation a private business. The motivation for such a step is generally the desire to get rid of the strictures of the SEC reporting requirements imposed on a corporation whose shares are registered.

The technique frequently used in going private is to merge the public corporation into a private corporation that is owned by the controlling shareholders.

The SEC regards such transactions with suspicion, especially when the controlling shareholders have sold their shares to the public at a high price and, in the going private transaction, pay a lower price for the minority shares. However, the SEC will generally only intervene when and if the proposed transaction is unfair to the minority. In that case the SEC may initiate a securities fraud action under Section 10-b, as discussed above. The Second Circuit Court of Appeals stated in one case: 'We hold that when controlling stockholders and directors of a publicly held corporation cause it . . . to force elimination of minority stockholders' equity participation for reasons not benefiting the corporation but rather serving only the interests of the controlling shareholders, such conduct will be enjoined pursuant to Section 10-b and Rule 10b-5(b).' Of course, an injured shareholder also can initiate a securities fraud action. If there is no securities fraud, there is no basis for Federal action. However, in some cases state courts have condemned going private transactions, on the ground that they constitute a breach of warranty. The warranty that these state courts implied is a warranty of the controlling shareholders when they sold shares to the public, to the effect that the purchasers would acquire a security that is traded publicly. This is important to many shareholders, especially in connection with estate planning, i.e., the planning for distribution and taxation of one's property after death.

## 11. THE FOREIGN CORRUPT PRACTICES ACT

This statute, which was enacted in 1977 as an amendment to the Securities Exchange Act of 1934, concerns the commercial bribery that a number of U.S. corporations practice abroad. The payment of foreign bribes is generally not disclosed in a corporation's financial statement. That is why the SEC becomes interested. Non-disclosure tends to weaken the confidence of the investment community in the financial integrity of the corporation involved. The argument that such bribes are necessary or customary in certain countries did not impress Congress as relevant. The statute makes it a crime for any citizen or resident of the U.S. and for any U.S. business organization to bribe foreign government officials for the purpose of obtaining business. Bribe payments are referred to as *questionable and illegal* payments. They are illegal even if permitted in the country where payment is made. Questionable and illegal payments must be clearly reported, if the reporting corporation wants to avoid a claim for securities fraud.

The Foreign Corrupt Practices Act also contains provisions that address internal accounting controls (see Chapter 26).

## 12. STATE LAWS

Most states require the registration of securities that are newly offered in that state. This is in addition to the Federal registration discussed above. The state laws, which are generally older than the SEC legislation, are popularly known as Blue Sky laws. This quaint name stems from the fact that the laws were enacted to protect the public against speculative schemes that had no more substance than so many square feet of blue sky. Blue sky filings are generally prepared simultaneously with the Federal registration.

In some states, the Blue Sky laws are interpreted to apply also to tender offers. Most states, however, have enacted separate take-over and tender offer legislation. In a number of instances, the state legislators have been overzealous. They have decreed waiting periods of varying length that would make a tender offer effective only so many days after its announcement. In effect, these laws make a tender offer even more difficult than do the provisions of the Williams Act. This may well be an unconstitutional intrusion into a field that has been preempted by Federal legislation, namely the Williams Act. It also imposes an unconstitutional burden on interstate commerce, as has been held in an authoritative court decision.

The penal statutes of the various states are generally adequate to deal with securities fraud occurring in intrastate transactions.

## 13. FOREIGN ISSUERS

Since the basic objective of the SEC legislation is the protection of the investing public in the U.S., it is clear why, generally speaking, the strictures of the such legislation are applicable equally to domestic issuers and to foreign issuers. However, there are some differences.

Foreign securities are available to the U.S. investor in four forms: (*a*) as shares issued abroad by foreign issuers, (*b*) as shares issued specifically for the U.S. market (known as American shares), (*c*) as so-called American Depository Receipts (ADRs), and (*d*) as shares of a U.S. investment fund which holds foreign securities.

The ADR functions as follows: The foreign issuer deposits original shares with a U.S. bank, which then issues and sells a corresponding amount of ADRs. The bank receives dividends from abroad and disburses them to the holder of the ADRs. The bank votes the original shares. The ADR holders may sell the ADRs in the U.S. market or exchange them for the underlying securities.

A foreign issuer may raise new capital in the U.S. by private placement or by a public offering and registration under the Securities Act of 1933, as above described. This applies also if the new capital is raised through the sale of ADRs.

The registration statement may be more burdensome for a foreign issuer than for a domestic issuer. The greatest burden is that the financial statements must be submitted in accordance with U.S. accounting principles. A foreign corporation may employ accounting practices that are very different from U.S. practices. For instance, depreciation may be calculated on replacement cost instead of historical cost, or inventories may not be verified by physical verification, as required by U.S. practice (see Chapter 26). More important, SEC rules require that the auditors must be independent, and the foreign auditors may not meet U.S. standards of independence. Another difficulty for foreign issuers is that the registration statement may be misleading, unless supplemented by special material in the prospectus. For instance, foreign tax or exchange control laws may have a bearing on the dividend distributions which the U.S. investor expects. One of the matters that foreign issuers often find objectionable is disclosure of the remuneration of the managers. This difficulty arises particularly in connection with registration under the Securities Exchange Act of 1934.

The SEC has prepared special forms for registration and reporting by foreign parties. It is sympathetic to the problems that a foreign party has in complying with the U.S. securities laws, but it is bound by the basic legislation and the objective stated at the beginning of this chapter.

The periodic reporting requirements under the Securities Exchange Act of 1934 are eased for foreign issuers. Foreign corporations need not file periodic reports (except the annual report) if they have fewer than 300 U.S. shareholders. If they have more than that number, they can obtain an exemption from the SEC if they supply the information which the home country requires, in the original language, and other minimal information.

The SEC has a special office of International Corporate Finance which deals with registration and reporting by foreign companies. Like other U.S. Government offices, it is easily accessible.

Reference has been made in Section 4, above, to the role of the underwriter. If a foreign issue is involved, the underwriter will often sell the securities to a dealer abroad. The foreign dealer should be prohibited from selling in the U.S. market. This will prevent an unregistered foreign dealer from selling in contravention of the Securities Exchange Act of 1934.

A foreign issuer must consider whether he wants the issue listed on a U.S. stock exchange. If so, he must, of course, comply with the listing requirements of the stock exchange. Also, the foreign issuer may object to registration under the Securities Exchange Act of 1934, which is required for any class of securities traded on a national securities exchange. Many domestic issuers avoid this by being content with having their securities traded 'over the counter'.

# PATENTS

## 1. INTRODUCTION

U.S. patent law is national in scope and is based upon statutes enacted by Congress pursuant to the U.S. Constitution. The current statute is the Patent Act of 1952. The patent grants to the patentee a legal monopoly. It is issued as an incentive to disclosure of the invention. It is not a certificate of merit. The U.S. Patent Office does not guarantee the value or the practicability of the patented invention.

A patent is issued for a period of seventeen years from the date of issuance.

Article I, Section 8, Clause 8 of the Constitution reads: 'The Congress shall have power . . . To promote the progress of . . . useful arts by securing for limited times to . . . inventors the exclusive right to their . . . discoveries'.

In 1851, the Supreme Court held that to be patentable an invention must not only be new and useful but also must involve 'more ingenuity and skill . . . than were possessed by the ordinary mechanic acquainted with the business'.

The different subjective interpretations of various U.S. courts as to what was obvious to a man skilled in the art or business inevitably led to confusion and uncertainty. To many attorneys specializing in the law of patents, it has appeared that certain of the Circuit Courts of Appeal set a much higher standard of invention (i.e. ingenuity or non-obviousness) than other Courts of Appeal. This wide discrepancy led to the abuse of so-called forum shopping,

---

1. This chapter was contributed by Daniel H. Kane, Esq. and Gerald Levy, Esq., of Kane, Dalsimer, Kane, Sullivan and Kurucz, Patent Attorneys.

where attorneys would try to initiate their litigation in a circuit most favorable to their side of the case.

In addition to the discrepancy between the decisions of the courts of the various circuits, the high fatality rate of patents (more than 82% in one circuit) indicates a wide difference between the viewpoints of the Patent Office and the courts on the question of patent validity.

Patent cases cannot be appealed as a matter of right from the various Circuit Courts of Appeal to the Supreme Court. A complicated procedure involving a petition for a writ of certiorari must be filed with the Supreme Court to obtain review of the decision of the Court of Appeals, and very few of these petitions are granted.

The lack of uniformity in the decisions of the various circuits has been aggravated by the fact that the Supreme Court itself has been far from uniform in its decisions. Depending on the composition of the Court and the prevailing economic philosophy, the Supreme Court has varied between a reasonable standard of ingenuity or unobviousness, on the one hand, and the unreasonable requirement of a 'flash of creative genius', on the other. As an example, the Supreme Court held valid a patent for a dry cell flashlight battery where the improvement consisted simply of substituting a metal sheath for a paper sheath encasing the battery. In another case, involving a patent for the rather ingenious automatic cigarette lighter of the pop-out type commonly used in automobiles, the Court held the patent invalid. In this case, it set an apparently higher standard of invention, stating, 'That is to say, a new device, however useful it may be, must reveal the flash of creative genius . . .'.

To insure a uniform standard of invention throughout the country, Congress has created a new Court of Appeals which is national in scope and known as the U.S. Court of Appeals for the Federal Circuit. Since October 1, 1982, appeals from all Federal District Courts throughout the country in most patent related litigation will be heard by this new Court rather than by the various Circuit Courts of Appeal. The new Court will also hear appeals from the Patent Office. Accordingly, this new appellate forum should not only assure uniformity in the decisions of the courts throughout the country but also between the Patent Office and the courts.

So far, we have referred only to the law affecting patents for inventions in the popular sense of the word, namely, new and useful processes, machines, manufactures and compositions of matter. The Patent Act also provides that a patent may be obtained for plants (see below) and any 'new, original and ornamental *design* for an article of manufacture'. Design patents are not uncommon in the garment industry. Under certain circumstances, copyright protection may also be obtained for designs.

## 2. PATENTABLE INVENTIONS

The types of inventions that can be patented and the conditions for patentability are outlined in general terms in the Act: 'Whoever invents or discovers any new and useful process, machine, manufacture or composition of matter, or any new and useful improvement thereof, may obtain a patent therefor. . . .'

The word *process* means a method that produces a beneficial result, including chemical, mechanical, metallurgical and electrical treatments.

*Composition of matter* indicates a new chemical compound or mixture and may be in solid, liquid or gaseous form.

Certain types of inventions or discoveries are not patentable. As an example, scientific principles and products of nature are not patentable. The use of ether as an anesthetic by Dr. Morton was held to be not patentable for this reason. Some of the claims of the patent of Samuel Morse for the telegraph were held invalid as simply claiming a scientific principle. Abstract ideas that have not been reduced to a concrete form are, likewise, not patentable; and systems or methods of doing business have been held to be not patentable.

With modern changes in technology, new types of subject matter have been presented to the Patent Office and to the courts, and these have required new interpretations of the language in the statutes. As an example, the Supreme Court has held that a genetically engineered bacterium in which four different plasmids were transferred into a single *Pseudomonas* bacterium, which is useful for degrading oil and oil spills, was not simply a product of nature but was a manufacture created by man and accordingly patentable.

Computer programs have presented a problem, and the law with respect thereto is at present in a state of development. A computer program that is a mere mathematical algorithmic formula has been held not patentable. The program in question involved a method of programming a general purpose digital computer to convert signals from binary coded decimal form into pure binary form. The Court found the program to be a mere mathematical formula and not patentable. Since that time, a number of different computer programs have come before the Patent Office, and that tribunal has distinguished some of the programs from those considered purely mathematical algorithm by the Supreme Court, and has found these programs to be patentable. As an example, a computer program designed to prepare a complete set of printed architectural specifications was held to be patentable. In addition, a program that converted a computer from a sequential processor to a processor that was not dependent upon the order in which the computer received the input data was also held to be patentable. More recently, a computer program for controlling the cash management account of a brokerage firm, which involved operating the computer so as to selectively transfer funds between various accounts and automatically make short-term investments, was held to be patentable. The claims for the computer programs in these patents sometimes were cast in the form of a process and sometimes in the form of a machine.

Previous reference was made to the patent of Dr. Morton on the use of ether for anesthesia. This case sometimes has been cited as establishing the principle that a patent cannot be obtained for a scientific principle; but it also has been cited for the proposition that a patent cannot be obtained on a method of treating human beings. However, in recent times this question has been reconsidered. Patents have been granted and have been sustained for various methods for the general therapeutic treatment of human beings and for treating specific health problems. Thus, a patent was granted for inducing artificial fevers in human beings by means of a high frequency field. Also, a patent was recognized for the treatment of the disease of scarlet fever.

However, it should be recognized that patents in this area of the treatment of human beings will also have to meet the other conditions of patentability, namely: utility (effective without detrimental side-effects) and non-obviousness to a person skilled in the art.

In addition to identifying the classes of inventions or subject matter that can be protected by patent in the U.S., the law also specifies that the inventions must be (*a*) new, (*b*) useful and (*c*) not *obvious at the time the invention was made to a person having ordinary skill in the art to which said subject matter pertains*. The statutes also specify that *patentability shall not be negatived by the manner in which the invention was made*.

*New* and *useful* are fairly simple concepts and the Patent Office and the courts have had very little trouble in interpreting them. The Patent Act provides that a person shall be entitled to a patent (*a*) unless the invention was known and used by others in the U.S., or patented and described in a printed publication in any country, before the invention thereof by the applicant for patent; (*b*) unless the invention was patented or described in a printed publication in the U.S. or a foreign country, or was in public use or on sale in the U.S., more than one year prior to the date of the application for patent in the U.S.; (*c*) unless the invention was first patented or caused to be patented by the applicant, or his representatives or assigns, in a foreign country prior to the date of application in the U.S., by an application filed more than twelve months before the filing of the application in the U.S.; (*d*) unless the invention was described in a patent granted on an application for patent by another, filed in the U.S. before the invention thereof by the applicant for patent; and (*e*) unless, before the applicant's invention thereof, the invention was made in the U.S. by another who had not abandoned, suppressed or concealed the invention. Thus, it will be seen that the meaning of *new*, or the characteristic of novelty, is defined in specific detail in the Patent Act. The Patent Act's descriptions of the requirements for the condition of novelty are so complete that there has been no substantial modification thereof by decisions of the Patent Office or of the courts.

It is probably worth noting at this point that U.S. patent law has a nationalistic aspect. Thus, inventions in public use or on sale, or which are made in a foreign country by someone other than the patentee prior to the filing date of the U.S. application, do not affect the validity of the U.S. patent. Also, in establishing priority of invention, inventive activity outside of the U.S. (other than filing a foreign patent application within twelve months prior to the filing of a U.S. patent application) cannot be used to establish a date of invention, except activities by a military or civil employee of the U.S. serving abroad.

Generally speaking, the requirement that an invention be useful is so self-evident that few, if any, problems have arisen with respect thereto. To be useful within the meaning of the statute, it is not necessary that the invention be the best or most useful product or method of its kind. It is only necessary that the invention accomplish some function having an indicated utility. Some of the earlier U.S. decisions have held that inventions that accomplish an illegal or immoral function are lacking in utility. Thus, a patent for a game of chance or gambling device was held invalid. However, with the changing mores on matters of this type, it is doubtful whether patents would be declared invalid today for that reason. An interesting development on the question of utility involves a Supreme Court decision which held that a process for producing a new chemical compound was lacking in utility, even though proof of the production of the compound was complete, unless it was also proven that the compound produced by the method had a useful result (in this case inhibiting the development of tumors).

The statute also bars patentability if the alleged invention is considered an obvious application of prior art. The requirement of non-obviousness is the statutory language for the requirement of 'ingenuity and skill', which the Supreme Court developed in 1851 (see Section 1, above).

The Supreme Court adopted an unreasonably high standard of invention in the case of *Cuno Corp.* v. *Automatic Devices Corp.* when, in 1941, it held that the patent on the standard cigarette lighter used in most U.S. automobiles was invalid because an invention had to reveal a 'flash of creative genius'. This decision resulted in a number of decisions by the lower Federal courts quoting the 'flash of creative genius' statement of the Supreme Court and holding patents invalid.

To counteract the decision of the Supreme Court, and in order to restore a more reasonable standard of invention, the Patent Act of 1952 established the *non-obvious* standard.

This provision of the Patent Act was dealt with by the Supreme Court in 1966, in connection with several patent cases. One of the cases considered by the Supreme Court at that time involved a patent for a rather simple invention representing a small margin of novelty over the prior art, and the Supreme Court held the patent valid. The patent related to a wet cell battery having two electrodes, one made of magnesium and the other of cuprous chloride, in which the electrolite used could be either plain or salt water. The individual elements of the battery were all old, but the specific combination was new, and the court held the patent to be valid.

It is believed that this provision of the Patent Act, setting forth non-obviousness as a condition for patentability, along with the establishment of the new U.S. Court of Appeals for the Federal Circuit will establish a more reasonable and uniform standard of invention and validity for patents than has existed in the past.

Patents may also be obtained for new, original and ornamental designs for articles of manufacture. Design patents are not intended for pure works of art, which are normally protected by copyright, but rather for industrial designs for articles of manufacture. The distinction between patents for designs and patents for utilitarian inventions resides in the word *useful* in utilitarian inventions, and the word *ornamental* in design patents. The statute provides that the provisions for a utilitarian patent should also apply to design patents, except that the right of priority for foreign patent applications in the case of design patents requires that the U.S. application be filed within six months of the foreign application, instead of one year.

Patents may also be obtained for asexually-reproduced plants. Sexually-reproduced plants other than fungi, bacteria or first generation hybrids are protected under the Plant Variety Protection Act of 1970.

## 3. THE APPLICANT

Patents can only be obtained by or on behalf of actual inventors. The applicant must file an oath or declaration that he or she believes himself to be the first inventor of the subject matter of the application. Where the invention has been made jointly by two or more persons, they are required to apply jointly and to make the required oath. If a joint inventor refuses to join in an application or cannot be found after a diligent search, the remaining inventor may apply on behalf of himself and the missing co-inventor.

When an inventor refuses to execute an application for a patent, or cannot be found after a diligent search, a person to whom the inventor has assigned or agreed in writing to assign the invention may make application for the patent on behalf of the inventor. For this purpose, the person making the application must prove the pertinent facts as to his interest, and must show that the action is necessary to preserve the rights of the parties and to prevent irreparable damage. In this connection, if an invention has gone into public use in the U.S. or has been described in a printed publication, failure to file a U.S. application within one year will result in loss of U.S. patent rights. This justifies the filing of the application by an assignee on behalf of the inventor.

When an application is thus filed on behalf of an inventor, upon a proper showing, the Commissioner of Patents may issue a patent to the inventor, not to the party filing on behalf of the inventor. To obtain an assignment of the patent, the person filing on behalf of the inventor must pursue his remedy by means of an appropriate civil action in the courts.

## 4. THE APPLICATION

The patent statutes and the Rules of Practice in Patent Cases of the U.S. Patent and Trademark Office specify the form and content of a U.S. patent application.

In brief, a U.S. patent application must be in writing, addressed to the Commissioner of Patents and Trademarks, and signed by the applicant. It must include a specification and claims, a drawing (when necessary for the understanding of the invention), and an oath (or declaration); and it is to be accompanied by the fee required by law. For purpose of establishing a filing date in the U.S., the application need not be in English, although an English translation will eventually be required.

The specification of the application is a written description of the invention, and the statute requires that it be in such full, clear, concise and exact terms as to enable any person skilled in the art to which it pertains to make and use the invention. A special provision of the statute, which has received some attention from both the Patent Office and the Federal courts in recent years, is the provision that the application 'shall set forth the best mode contemplated by the inventor of carrying out his invention'.

The purpose of this provision is to restrain inventors from applying for patents while at the same time concealing from the public preferred embodiments of the invention that they have in fact conceived. The following is an example of a case in which a patent was held invalid for failure to disclose the best mode involved in an injection molding process. The specification and drawings of the patent disclosed an extruder with a particular type of valve. In the trial of the case it was shown that the valve disclosed in the patent was unsatisfactory, and discharged a slug into the mold. A valve that solved this problem had been developed prior to the filing of the patent application, but was not disclosed therein. The court decided that the patentee had failed to disclose the best mode in his patent application, and declared the patent invalid for that reason. It is well established, however, that the best mode provision does not require a detailed description of well-known techniques. The specification of the application terminates in one or more claims which are definitions of the monopoly to be granted by the Patent Office.

The U.S. is a party to the Patent Cooperation Treaty. The effective date of the treaty in the U.S. was January 24, 1978. Under the treaty, the U.S. Patent and Trademark Office may act as a receiving office for international applications filed by residents or nationals of the U.S. The international patent application may designate various countries that are parties to the Patent Cooperation Treaty as countries in which a patent is sought. An international patent application designating the U.S. as one of the countries in which a patent is sought will have the same effect as a national application regularly filed in the U.S., provided that the requirements of form and content for national applications of the U.S. have been met.

## 5. PATENT OFFICE PROCEEDINGS

The process of obtaining a patent begins with the filing of a patent application. One unique aspect of the U.S. patent system is a two-tier fee structure under which a *small entity* need only pay one-half the normal fee. A *small entity* is defined as an independent inventor, a business having less than 500 employees, or a non-profit organization.

From the time the application is filed, until such time as the application either issues in a patent or is abandoned, the application is pending and the article covered by the patent application claims may be marked *patent pending* or *patent applied for.*

The application is assigned to a patent examining group having expertise in the field to which the application pertains. The groups are broadly divided into chemical, electrical, and mechanical arts, and further divided into subgroups within each of the broad general categories. Prior to assigning the application to a particular group, the Patent Office will review the application to assure that the various formalities required for filing an application have been complied with.

Applications are taken up within the examining groups in the order in which they are received. Once examination begins, the examination process is relatively fast (usually lasting less than one year). However, the time from the filing of an application until it is taken up for examination varies from one to three years, depending upon the art involved.

The Patent Office examiner, trained in the art to which the application pertains, will receive the application and conduct a search for pertinent prior art.

After completing his search, the examiner will issue an *Official Action* in which he either allows, rejects, or objects to each claim of the application. The examiner must set forth the specific reasons for objecting to, or rejecting, a particular claim. The prior art may be applied as either a direct anticipation, or, what is more common, as the basis for an *obviousness* rejection. That is, the examiner may determine that the exact invention had already been made by another; or he may consider that the subject matter of the application, taken as a whole, would have been obvious, at the time the invention was made, to a person having ordinary skill in the art to which the subject matter pertains. Very often, the examiner will combine two or three prior art references as the basis for an obviousness rejection.

The applicant is given a period of time (usually three months, but extendible up to six months upon payment of a fee) in which to respond to the Official Action. The response may include argument as to why the examiner misconstrued the prior art or the invention, as well as amendment of the claims in order to overcome any objections raised by the examiner.

The examiner usually responds to the amendment (generally within three months) by either allowing the amended application and claims, or by issuing a second Official Action. In most cases, if the second Action is also a rejection, the rejection is made final. The applicant may then again amend the application, but he must either convince the examiner to withdraw his final rejection within the allotted time period for response or, if the examiner maintains his rejection, the applicant must either accept the rejection or file an appeal with the Board of Appeals. If the examiner does not withdraw his final rejection, and an appeal is not taken within the allotted period, the application becomes abandoned.

The Board of Appeals is made up of at least three senior examiners, who decide the case on the basis of briefs filed by the applicant and the examiner. The applicant may also request an oral hearing before the Board. The Board of Appeals may reverse the examiner's decision and instruct him to allow the application, or it may affirm the examiner in whole or in part. In addition, the Board of Appeals may affirm an examiner's rejection of an application but set forth a new ground for rejection. In the latter case, the applicant would be entitled to respond to the new rejection.

If the applicant is not satisfied with the decision of the Board of Appeals, he may request reconsideration; or an action may be commenced in the Federal courts to compel the granting of a patent, by bringing a civil action against the Commissioner of Patents in the U.S. District Court for the District of Columbia; or an appeal may be taken directly to the Court of Appeals for the Federal Circuit. The latter is the customary route. Should the applicant be dissatisfied with the Court of Appeals decision, a petition for a writ of certiorari may be filed with the Supreme Court. However, such writs are very rarely granted.

If the application is granted, either by the examiner during the examination proceeding, or following an appeal, the issue fee must be paid in order to have the patent issued. The issue fee will keep the patent in effect for four years. An additional fee must be paid to keep the patent in effect beyond four years; yet another fee must be paid to keep the patent in force beyond eight years, and still another fee must be paid to keep the patent in force beyond twelve years. At present, the issue fee is $500 and the four-, eight- and twelve-year fees are respectively $400, $800 and $1,200. Small entities need only pay half the issue and maintenance fees.

## A. INTERFERENCE PROCEEDINGS

On very rare occasions, two applications are filed with the Patent Office at substantially the same time, relating to the same invention. In the U.S. a patent is awarded to the first inventor, who may not necessarily be the first to have filed his patent application. To determine which of the applicants is entitled to the patent, a proceeding known as an *interference* may be established. In some cases, one of the applications may have already issued as a patent while the other application is still pending, or even before the other application has been filed.

To determine who is the first inventor, evidence is presented in deposition form and filed with the Board of Patent Interferences, and, subsequently, briefs and oral arguments may be presented.

## B. REISSUE

After a patent has issued, the patent owner may find that, through error, the patent is wholly or partly inoperative, or that the patentee claimed more or less that he had a right to claim in the patent. In such case, upon the offer to surrender the original patent and the payment of fees (which correspond to the fees for the original patent), the patentee may apply to reissue his patent with the error corrected. A reissued patent lasts for a term commensurate with the unexpired part of the term of the original patent. During the prosecution of the application for a reissue patent the entire application is reviewed by the Patent Office and, theoretically, the examiner may raise any grounds for rejecting the application that he deems proper. In addition, an interested party may participate in the prosecution of the reissue application by filing a *protest* to the reissue. The protestor participates in the prosecution by submitting prior art to the Patent Office, and commenting on the arguments and amendments raised by the applicant. A third party may not, however, precipitate a reissue application.

## C. REEXAMINATION

After a patent issues, either the patent owner or a third party may request the Patent Office to reexamine the patent in the light of prior art not previously cited, and more pertinent than the art considered by the examiner. Unlike a reissue proceeding, which may only be precipitated by the patent owner, any member of the public may request a reexamination of any patent.

## D. DISCLAIMER

If a patentee discovers that he has failed to make the necessary disclosure to the Patent Office, he may formally disclaim a portion of the patent. The disclaimer may be directed to specific claims or to a portion of the term of the patent. Terminal disclaimers are generally filed where a patentee has two or more patents with overlapping claims. The terminal disclaimer limits the life of the later patent to expire with the expiration of the earlier patent. In most cases, the filing of the disclaimer will purge any earlier failure to disclose material to the Patent Office, as long as the failure was inadvertent.

## 6. TRANSFER OF PATENT RIGHTS

A patent (as well as a patent application) is a tangible property right that has all the attributes of personal property. A patent may be sold, leased, devised, or otherwise conveyed or transferred.

The transfer may be in whole or in part. If in part, the partial interest may be for an undivided share of the entire patent rights, or a specific divided interest. The partial transfer may be drawn along geographic or field-of-use lines. The two most common forms of transferring patent rights are *assignments* and *licenses*.

An assignment conveys to the transferee the entire right, title and interest of the transferor in and to the patent. The Patent Office will record any assignment, grant, or conveyance of a patent.

Employees may be required to assign their inventions to their employer. Thus, a written contract may spell out the employee's obligation to assign his inventions. In addition, if the employee is hired to make inventions in a specific field, he is obligated to assign them to his employer even in the absence of a written contract. Where an employee is not obligated to assign his inventions to his employer, the employer may, nevertheless, acquire a royalty-free, non-exclusive license, known as a 'shop right', if the employee made the invention on the employer's time and using the employer's material.

Transfer by license is dealt with in Chapter 25.

## 7. ENFORCEMENT OF PATENTS

## A. CIVIL ACTION

A U.S. patent gives the patent holder the right to exclude others from making, using and selling the patented invention within the U.S. during the term of the patent. The unauthorized practice of a patented invention constitutes patent infringement. The remedy for infringement of a patent is a civil action brought in the Federal courts. The civil action must be brought in the judicial district where the defendant resides, or (a) where the defendant has committed acts of infringement, and (b) has a regular and established place of business (see Chapter 23). If either the plaintiff or defendant makes a timely demand, the factual issues in the case will be tried before a jury; otherwise the action is heard by a judge. There are no special patent courts or judges at the trial level.

If it is found that the patent is infringed, the patent owner is entitled to damages adequate to compensate him for the infringement, which in no event may be less than a reasonable royalty. When the patentee makes and sells goods under the patent, he may mark the goods with the word 'patent', or the abbreviation 'pat', followed by the patent number. If the goods have not been so marked, damages cannot be collected except on proof that the infringer was actually notified of the infringement and continued his infringing act. For this reason, it is good practice to place a patent marking on patented goods. The court may also enjoin the defendant from future infringement. Where the infringement is found to be willful, the court may increase the damages up to three times the amount found or assessed.

The principal defenses usually raised in a civil action for patent infringement are (a) that the patent is invalid, and (b) that the patent has not been infringed. In determining the merits of the invalidity defense, the court must determine whether or not the Patent Office properly issued the patent. The patent is presumed to be valid and, thus, the burden of proof is on the party alleging invalidity. The court normally will not overturn a Patent Office decision of validity unless it is provided with evidence that was not before the Patent Office at the time of the examination of the application for the patent. The evidence may be in the form of prior art, which the Patent Office did not consider, or details of a sale or public use which were not known to the Patent Office. The defendant may also argue that the patent is unenforceable against him because of misuse of the patent (see Chapter 17 and Section 8, below); or he may offer a personal defense, such as a license, estoppel or laches.

To establish infringement, the patent holder must show that every element of at least one claim of his patent is present in the accused structure or process. If a minor element is lacking, the court may still find infringement if it was replaced by equivalent structure. A party may also be found guilty of patent infringement if it *induces* the infringement of a patent by another. This would happen, for example, if one were to sell a piece of equipment which could only be used to practice a patented process, along with instructions for practicing the process. In addition, the sale of a product that has no use other than as a component of a patented machine or apparatus for use in practicing a patented process, constitutes *contributory* infringement. The liability and remedies for inducing infringement and contributory infringement are the same as for direct infringement.

A very important part of patent litigation is the discovery proceeding, which is discussed in Chapter 23, Section 1.

When discovery is completed, a pre-trial conference is held to simplify the issues at trial and attempt to reach a settlement. If the case is not settled, it will go to trial. The time from the filing of the complaint to the trial is generally three or four years.

A final decision from the District Court may be appealed to the newly established U.S. Court of Appeals for the Federal Circuit. Very rarely, a decision of the Court of Appeals may be reviewed by the Supreme Court, by means of a petition for a writ of certiorari.

An alleged infringer need not wait until it is sued by a patent holder in order to have the issues of patent infringement and patent validity determined by the court. If an accusation of infringement is made, the accused infringer may file a *declaratory judgment* action on the issues of patent validity and infringement. Before a declaratory judgment action may be filed, there must be an actual 'controversy' between the parties. The controversy would arise if the patent holder made an accusation of patent infringement. For this reason, a patent holder should consider carefully before he charges anyone with infringement.

The declaratory judgment action may be filed in the judicial district where all the plaintiffs and/or defendants reside, or in which the claim arose. A corporation may be sued in any judicial district in which it is incorporated, or licensed to do business, or is doing business. If a foreign patent holder does not have a residence in the U.S., a declaratory judgment action may be filed in the District of Columbia, unless a resident is appointed as an agent for receiving process relative to the patent, in which case the residence of the appointee becomes the district in which the declaratory judgment action may be filed.

Patent litigation is notoriously lengthy and expensive, due primarily to the broad pre-trial discovery proceedings available in the U.S. The courts will tolerate discovery on virtually any subject that is related to the issues involved in the suit, or that may lead to information relating to the issues.

If a patent is found to be invalid, the holding of invalidity generally applies with regard to all third parties. However, if a patent is found to be valid, any third party may again challenge the validity of the patent in a later litigation – although the initial holding is usually given considerable weight in any later proceeding.

## B. ALTERNATIVE REMEDIES

In recent times, two alternatives to the filing of a patent suit have gained in popularity: (*i*) arbitration, and (*ii*) International Trade Commission proceedings.

### I. ARBITRATION

The parties to a patent dispute may agree to have the dispute arbitrated (see Chapter 24). The arbitrator may be given authority to decide the questions of infringement, validity, or any particular issue, which would then be taken as a fact in a subsequent or concurrent legal proceeding. The advantages and pitfalls of agreeing to arbitration in a patent-based dispute are the same as those associated with agreeing to arbitration in any other dispute. If the parties have agreed to arbitration, however, the courts will enforce the arbitration clause, and compel arbitration. The award of the arbitrator may be reduced to a judgment, which would have the same effect and enforceability as any other judgment (see Chapter 24).

## II. INTERNATIONAL TRADE COMMISSION PROCEEDING

The USITC is a six-member administrative tribunal that has the authority to protect U.S. manufacturers from unfair methods of competition and unfair acts in the importation of articles the 'effect or tendency of which is to destroy or substantially injure an industry efficiently and economically operated in the United States'. Infringement of a U.S. patent, or the practice of a method that would infringe a U.S. patent if practiced in the U.S., are designated as unfair methods of competition and unfair acts.

The principal remedy available through an ITC action is an exclusion order, which bars the infringing articles from entry into the U.S. The exclusion order is enforced through the Customs Service and its effect is *in rem* (i.e., against the articles themselves regardless of the manufacturer, the exporter, or the importer). The ITC also has the authority to issue cease and desist orders directed against individual violators.

An ITC proceeding is initiated by the filing of a complaint by the injured party. The complaint, in addition to proving that it has suffered as a result of an unfair act must prove that: (*a*) a domestic industry exists in the U.S. which practices under the patent; (*b*) the domestic industry is efficiently and economically operated; and (*c*) the actions complained of have injured the affected domestic industry, or have a tendency to injure the domestic industry or prevent an industry from being established.

The ITC proceeding takes place under rules of discovery which closely parallel those that apply in Federal court actions. The time limits, however, are very greatly reduced.

Once the ITC decides to act on a complaint, it must render its final decision within one year (in some more complicated cases, up to a six-month extension may be granted). The trial of the ITC action is normally completed within seven months of the institution of an investigation, and the initial determination is rendered a month or so thereafter.

The hearing and all motions concerning pre-trial discovery matters come before an Administrative Law Judge. The trial procedure is informal. The findings of the Administrative Law Judge are presented to the full commission in the form of a *recommended determination*. Although the full Commission has the authority to review the underlying facts *de novo*, in most instances the Commission will accept the recommended determination.

In addition to deciding the usual infringement and validity questions, the ITC must determine whether there is any 'public interest' aspect of the case that might preclude the issuance of an exclusion order. Various government agencies, such as the Department of Justice and the Federal Trade Commission, may participate in the public interest aspect of the case. After the ITC renders its decision, it is subject to review by the President of the United States. If the President does not overturn the Commission decision within six months, it becomes final.

Appeals from the Commission may be taken to the Court of Appeals for the Federal Circuit. Thus, the patent issues will be reviewed in the same manner as they would had they stemmed from a conventional litigation. If the exclusion order becomes final, it is sent to each port of entry into the U.S., along with instructions to the Customs Service to bar the excluded article from entry into the U.S.

The principal advantages of an ITC action from the standpoint of the patent holder are:

(a) the relatively short time involved from the initiation of the proceedings until the final decision;

(b) the *in rem* nature of the relief, so that it extends against all infringing articles so long as they are imported;

(c) the more favorable attitude of the ITC towards the validity of patents as compared with the attitude of the Federal courts;

(d) the cost of the proceedings is generally lower than the cost of a comparable civil action, although it must be borne in mind that in a District Court action the costs are spread out over a far greater time period.

In view of the very pro-patent nature of the ITC as a forum for settling patent disputes, the decisions of the ITC should be very closely followed by exporters to the U.S.

## 8. PATENT USE AND MISUSE

Under U.S. law, a patentee cannot ordinarily be compelled to grant licenses under his patent. Thus, if the patentee chooses to do so, he may exclude the world from practicing the patented invention for the term of the patent. However, the patentee may not use the patent to extend his control and monopoly beyond the patent grant. Any attempt to use a patent to extend the granted monopoly could constitute a misuse of the patent. If litigated, a finding of misuse could render the patent unenforceable or, in an extreme case, might constitute an anti-trust violation. The implications of antitrust violations are discussed in detail in Chapter 17, Section 8.

Another form of misuse occurs when an applicant for a patent fails to divulge pertinent information to the Patent Office, such as the facts concerning an early public use of publication, known prior art, or the like. The Patent Office has recently required that inventors 'acknowledge' this 'duty to disclose information' that is material to the examination of the applications to the Patent Office. The failure to disclose may result in an unenforceable patent, or subject the violator to antitrust charges.

CHAPTER 20

# TRADEMARKS, COPYRIGHT AND UNFAIR COMPETITION

## *INTRODUCTION*

Patents, trademarks and copyrights are known collectively as intellectual property. The topic of unfair competition is intertwined with the law of trademarks and copyrights. The United Nations agency charged with the administration of international treaties dealing with patents, trademarks and copyrights is the World Intellectual Property Organization (WIPO).

It is not generally realized, even in the U.S., that registration does not create a trademark or a copyright. Both are created in the U.S. by use. Federal registration of a trademark can only be obtained upon proof of use in interstate or foreign commerce. A trademark that is used, but not federally registered, is a common-law trademark. A copyright arises by the mere creation of the work, and is lost by publication, unless the owner reserves the copyright to himself. Registration may then follow. Although registration is not required, it has certain advantages, which will be stated below; and it may be required if one wishes to assert rights under certain international treaties, likewise discussed below.

The law of unfair competition, as it is known in Central European and other countries, has largely developed in recent decades. Section 5 of the Federal Trade Commission Act, which was enacted in 1914, forbids unfair methods of competition. But the statute was enacted merely in aid of the antitrust laws, and for enforcement by the Federal Trade Commission. Today, it is also used to support private claims. Formerly, uninhibited competition and deception of the public were held to be the mark of an astute businessman. *Caveat emptor* (let the buyer beware) was considered a valid principle of commercial law. But that is a matter of the past. In 1946, the Lanham Act (Federal Trademark Act) gave statutory recognition to the judge-made principles of unfair competition, and to the private enforcement rights that existed then and have been refined since.

The protection of intellectual property rights extends beyond the immediate violator. An advertising agency may be held liable for an infringement or an act of unfair competition of its client. A phonograph record retailer may be held liable for selling records which were produced in violation of a copyright.

## *A. TRADEMARKS*

## 1. NATURE OF TRADEMARK

The primary function of a trademark is to identify the origin of the product to which it is affixed. It also has an advertising function, and a guaranty function, which is to guarantee the origin and the advertised quality of the product.

Trademark protection is designed to protect the goodwill of the trademark owner's business. It extends to the area in which the trademark owner operates, and to the owner's natural expansion areas. When a U.S. citizen registered the trademark of the Bulova Watch Company in Mexico, a U.S. court enjoined him from using the famous trademark in Mexico, which was held to be reasonably within the normal expansion area of Bulova's business. If the defendant had not been a U.S. citizen, the court would not have interfered with the use of the

Mexican trademark. A midwest grocery chain owned the trademark 'Fairway Foods'. The trademark was held not to be infringed when a retail grocer in California used it.

Some trademarks are considered strong, some are considered weak. Sunbeam Corp., a manufacturer of household electrical appliances, owned the registered trademark 'Sunbeam'. It sued the Sunbeam Furniture Corporation. The court enjoined the defendant from using the Sunbeam name for lamps. But the court refused to forbid use of Sunbeam in the name of the defendant, on the ground that 'sunbeam' is a common word and a weak trademark, which will be narrowly protected.

One thinks of a trademark, generally, as a word or a combination of words. However, a trademark can be a unique type of package or bottle (the Haig & Haig pinch bottle), a symbol (the rock of Prudential Insurance Company), a slogan ('Moving air is our business', for fans), or the title of a newspaper (*The New York Times*).

Most trademarks are federally registered pursuant to the Lanham Act. However, registration is not required. A mark that has the essential characteristics may be a valid common-law trademark.

A trademark is distinguished from a trade name. A trade name is the surname or corporate name under which a trader operates. It need not be attached to the product that is traded. If a third party palms off his goods under another's trade name, he may be sued for unfair competition. A trade name may become a trademark. A trademark must be attached to the product that it is intended to identify, or to the container in which the product is packed, or, if the product is exhibited, the trademark may be attached to the point of sale display.

The term *technical trademark* denotes common-law as well as registered trademarks. Sometimes a trademark is referred to as a 'Brand'. Brand names are trademarks. In the business world, no clear difference is perceived in the meaning of the terms trade name, common-law trademark, registered trademark, technical trademark, and brand name. Most businesspeople, when they speak of a trademark, mean a Federally registered trademark. Most states also have trademark statutes that recognize common-law trademarks, but also provide for state registration. However, a businessperson who has a Federal registration sees little need for state registration of his trademark. New York, Illinois, and other states have enacted laws which provide for injunctive relief in the event that a trademark is 'diluted', a remedy not available under the Federal statute. Dilution generally is an act of unfair competition.

## 2. FORBIDDEN MARKS

Certain marks are denied the dignity of a trademark, and therefore cannot be valid trademarks unless they acquire a so-called secondary meaning, which concept will be discussed below (Section 5). The following catalogue of forbidden marks is taken from the Lanham Act (Sec. 2), but it applies to common-law marks as well:

(*a*) Immoral, deceptive and scandalous matter. In determining whether a mark is scandalous, consideration must be given to the goods to which the mark is applied. Thus, the mark 'Madonna' was judged to be scandalous as applied to wine. A liquor exporter furnished Scotch Whisky labels (which were trademarked) to his licensee in Puerto Rico, who applied them to spurious whisky sold in Panama. The registered trademark was cancelled as being deceptive.

(*b*) Any flag or coat of arms.

(*c*) The name or portrait of a living individual, unless with consent.

(*d*) Any mark which is confusingly similar to an existing trademark. It is astonishing how often it is attempted to palm off a product on the public by the use of a confusingly similar name. The confusion, to be sure, is sometimes unintended. A merchant in New York or Amsterdam may adopt a trademark which is similar to one used in a remote place on the West Coast of the U.S., of which the merchant in New York or Amsterdam has no knowledge. It is, therefore, prudent not to adopt a trademark, or a corporate name, before investigating possible conflicts. This sort of investigation can be procured through organizations that examine not only the trademark register, but other lists of names, and telephone books. Upon receipt of the report of the investigation, one must form one's own judgment as to whether the likelihood of confusion exists. The publisher of the magazine *Look* successfully opposed the registration of the trademark 'Look' for face cream and soap because the magazine frequently carried cosmetic advertisements and allowed its advertisers to state that their products were featured in *Look*. This was an extreme case of likelihood of confusion, but it demonstrates the care which is advisable in the selection of a trademark. For more about confusing similarity, see Section 11 below.

(*e*) Descriptive matter. 'Joy' was held not to be a valid trademark for perfume, because it is merely a description of what the user experiences. A word that is descriptive when used on one class of goods may be purely arbitrary and fanciful and, therefore, a valid trademark on another class of goods.

(*f*) A word that is used primarily as a surname or corporate name. This does not apply to names that are unusual or that have an independent connotation, such as Samson, or Atlas.

(*g*) Geographical names. These cannot be protected as trademarks, except that a *certification mark* may identify a regional origin, such as Roquefort cheese.


## 3. TYPES OF TRADEMARKS

There are various types of trademarks, and this applies to registered as well as to common-law trademarks.

(*a*) The ordinary trademark is either a business mark, which identifies the business of the trademark owner (e.g. Xerox), or a merchandise mark, which identifies the product of a particular manufacturer, e.g. Fairway Foods.

(*b*) The Service mark is a trademark of a business that renders services. The trademark is used in the sale or advertising of these services. Examples are the rock emblem of the Prudential Insurance Company and the trademark 'Marriott' for hotel and hotel services.

(c) The Collective mark is a trademark owned by an organized group or association, that is used to identify its members. For example, AAA is the trademark of the American Automobile Association.

(d) A Certification mark is also a trademark owned by an organization for use by its members to certify the origin and quality or mode of manufacture of its product. For example, the producers of genuine Roquefort cheese may use the certification mark owned by the community of Roquefort in France. Another example is the label sewn into certain garments certifying that they have been manufactured by members of the trade union which owns the certification mark. Another example is the 'Good Housekeeping' seal, a trademark owned by *Good Housekeeping* magazine, which, by allowing its use, indicates its approval of the goods sold with the Good Housekeeping seal.

(e) A Related Companies Trademark is a trademark that is owned by one, and is used by others who are related to the owner and whom the owner controls with respect to the nature or quality of the goods or services for which the trademark is used. This need not be a parent-subsidiary relationship. It may be a contractual relationship. That was the case in the classic 'Fruit of the Loom' decision, which antedates the Lanham Act. The trademark was owned by a fabric manufacturer, which allowed garment makers who purchased the fabric to use its trademark on garments made from the fabric, on condition that the garment makers would guarantee the quality, the workmanship and the design of the finished articles. The trademark owner thus controlled the garment makers. A similar contractual situation prevails between the Coca-Cola Company and the many bottlers who are licensed to use the Coca-Cola trademark.


## 4. DISTINCTIVENESS

This is a basic requirement for the validity of any trademark. If it loses its distinctiveness, it is no longer a valid mark and it becomes a free mark. Loss of distinctiveness occurs when the trademark becomes a generic mark, as happened to 'Aspirin', which was originally a trademark owned exclusively by the Bayer Drug Company. A mark becomes generic when it becomes the name of the product itself in the public mind. Another example is 'Cellophane', originally a trademark owned by Dupont. 'Thermos' and 'Linoleum' similarly lost their distinctiveness as the trademarks of particular manufacturers. The risk of becoming a generic name, and therefore a free mark, arises when a trademark becomes too successful, as has 'Sanka', the trademark of a maker of a brand of decaffeinated coffee. The public was beginning to refer to Sanka as synonymous with decaffeinated coffee. Current television advertisements, therefore, emphasize that Sanka is a brand of coffee. The Xerox Corporation is fighting a similar battle to preserve the distinctiveness of its trademark, 'Xerox'. A trademark owner is required to police his trademark. If he allows others to use it or to dilute its distinctiveness, he may lose the trademark. When the owner of the internationally famed game, 'Monopoly', sued the manufacturer of a new game, called 'Anti-Monopoly', for trademark infringement, the court ruled against the plaintiff, holding that 'Monopoly' had lost its distinctiveness as a trademark.

## 5. SECONDARY MEANING

Conversely, an otherwise ineligible word acquires a secondary meaning, and thus becomes a trademark, when the purchasing public connects the word with a particular product or business. A classic example is 'Nu-Enamel', which is a descriptive word, but which was recognized as a trademark because it had acquired a secondary meaning. A secondary meaning may exist in a limited area. 'Bavaria Brewing Co.' had established a secondary meaning for the word Bavaria in the area where it sold its beer. A competing brewer was enjoined from using the word 'Bavarian' in that limited area.

## 6. REGISTRATION

The Federal legislation deals only with registered trademarks. The Lanham Act states what can be registered, how to do it, and what are the remedies for infringement. It deals also with International Conventions. There is no Federal legislation with respect to unregistered common-law trademarks. However, except for the technical rules for registration and for the statutory remedies, the Lanham Act is a fairly comprehensive statement of the common law of trademarks. The principal advantage of registration is that it creates a presumption of validity, so that the owner of a registered trademark (in contradistinction to the owner of a common-law trademark) need not, in case of a contest, prove that the trademark is valid, and that he is the owner. This, however, does not prevent a contestant from proving the opposite, unless the trademark has become incontestable (see Section 8, below).

Registration is made by an appropriate filing in the Patent and Trademark Office in Washington, D.C., in accordance with the provisions of the Lanham Act and the regulations issued thereunder. The Office has established classes that describe the category of the business in which the trademark is registered. For instance, Class 25 covers clothing. A trademark may be registered in more than one class.

The Patent and Trademark Office examines all applications for registration, hears and decides when registration is opposed, cancels a registration when, in appropriate cases, cancellation is applied for, and sometimes becomes involved in litigation over the validity of a trademark. The Office is not required to register a trademark if it concludes that the mark is deceptively similar to an existing trademark. Refusal to register or cancellation of any registered trademark does not, as such, affect the existence of a common-law trademark, although a negative action of the Office may well be grounded on a fact that negates the existence of a common-law trademark.

## 7. DURATION

A common-law trademark is perpetual. The registration of a trademark is good for twenty years, but may be renewed for successive twenty-year periods.

## 8. USE, ABANDONMENT AND CANCELLATION

Commercial use is a required element of every trademark. In an old case, a publisher prepared for publication a magazine called *Quick*. Learning that a competitor had similar plans, the publisher issued an interim newsletter under the name *Quick*. This was of no avail – it was not commercial use, and trademark protection was denied. In order to demonstrate use for the purpose of obtaining trademark protection, merchants frequently ship a product with the trademark attached from one state to another. It may be only from New York to neighboring Jersey City. A shipment from London to Philadelphia may certainly prove use. The circumstances of the single sale must indicate an intent of continued use. An exception prevails when a foreigner seeks to register a foreign trademark in the U.S. He need not show use in the U.S. if he can show previous use in his home country, and if that country is a party to an International Convention to which the U.S. is also a party (see Section 13, below). The foregoing applies also to a common-law trademark.

In the case of a registered trademark, the owner is required after six years to supply an affidavit showing continued use; if that is not done the Commissioner of Patents and Trademarks may cancel the trademark. Quite generally, if a trademark is not actually used, or if it is allowed to degenerate into a generic mark, or if it loses its distinctiveness because the owner tolerates infringement by others, the trademark is considered abandoned. That is why it is necessary for a trademark owner constantly to police the trademark. Many valuable trademarks have been lost because the owners failed to preserve them. The Otis Elevator Company owned the trademark 'escalator'. It published advertisements in which it claimed the safety and other advantages of its elevators and escalators. It did not distinguish between the generic word 'elevator' and the trademarked word 'escalator'. It thus indicated that escalator was just a descriptive word for moving staircase. This led to the cancellation of the trademark 'escalator'.

A registered trademark may be cancelled by the Commissioner or by court order upon the application of one who believes himself to be damaged by the registration or continued registration of an invalid trademark, subject to certain time limits and other provisions set out in section 14 of the Lanham Act. A U.S. manufacturer registered his trademark with the U.S. Customs Service, thus preventing a British manufacturer from importing a competing product (see Section 12 below *re* sec. 526 of the Tariff Act). The British manufacturer alleged and proved that the American manufacturer had procured his trademark registration fraudulently. He therefore succeeded in having the U.S. trademark cancelled.

## 9. INCONTESTABILITY

A registered trademark becomes incontestable after five years of continuous use, subject to various conditions stated in section 15 of the Lanham Act. This is not a shield for a fraudulently obtained registration, nor is an incontestable right acquired in a mark which is the common descriptive name of a product. Otherwise, and unless the other restrictions of the statute apply, incontestability means that the trademark owner is immune to any challenge of his right.

## 10. DISPLAY OF NOTICE

The statute provides for a display of notice of registration. It is sufficient to affix the letter 'R' enclosed within a circle. The notice is not required, but the owner of a registered trademark cannot recover statutory profits and damages unless the notice is affixed. This, of course, is a powerful incentive, apart from the fact that the notice is a warning sign against possible infringement. If registration has been applied for but not yet granted, the owner may affix the notice, 'trademark registration applied for', or 'registration pending', or words to that effect. Affixing a registration notice before registration has been granted may lead to forfeiture of all trademark rights. The owner of a common-law trademark may affix the word 'Trademark', or simply the letters 'TM'.

## 11. INFRINGEMENT AND REMEDIES

A trademark may be infringed by one who uses a confusingly similar mark. Or if may be infringed by one who uses a valid trademark in a manner which tends to destroy the integrity of another valid trademark.

Cases of infringement by use of a confusingly similar mark occur with astonishing frequency. Examples abound, and some have been mentioned in the preceding text of this chapter. The term 'confusingly similar' refers to sound, appearance, or meaning. For instance, the trademark 'Cyclone' for fences is infringed by the use of the mark 'Tornado' on fences. The words are not the same in sound or appearance, but their meaning stimulates similar associations in the minds of the purchasing public. The purchasing public is not, and is not required to be, careful. The infringer generally counts on this carelessness.

If a trademark owner sells the trademarked article, the purchaser has a right to resell it. However, he may not undermine the integrity of the trademark. An old decision held that secondhand sewing machines may not be sold under the trademark of the Singer Sewing Machine Company where the impression was created that the machines were modern models. This infringed the guaranty function of the Singer trademark. On the other hand, a retailer was allowed to advertise that his garments were made from Forstman Woolens (which was true), even though that constituted a use of Forstman's trademark without a license. He had not purchased the material from Forstman.

The principal remedies against infringement are injunction, claim for lost profits, and claim for damages. A court may grant an injunction, but deny, for lack of proof, a claim for lost profits or damages. Where the infringer's business is in a different field, the trademark owner generally has not lost any profits as a result of the infringement, and he may not be able to prove any damages. In an extreme case, a court may order that all goods that bear an infringing mark be destroyed. The court may also order such other remedial action as may seem equitable.

In the infringement action, a plaintiff may assert that the defendant's registered trademark is not valid, and the defendant may assert the same about the plaintiff's registered trademark. Either side may initiate a cancellation proceeding in the Patent and Trademark Office. Such cancellation proceeding does not bar a trademark owner from pursuing his remedies in a court action.

If a trademark owner sits idly by while another uses his trademark, he may be guilty of laches. In that case he has lost the right to recover damages, but, generally, not his right to enjoin the infringing use of his trademark.

## 12. IMPORTED GOODS

A foreign trademark which is attached to imported goods is not protected under U.S. trademark law, except as provided by an International Convention (see below). The domestic distributor of imported goods ordinarily does not acquire any rights in the foreign trademark. An importer is not the owner of the foreign trademark and, therefore, cannot ordinarily invoke the protection of the U.S. trademark laws.

The foreign manufacturer may obtain registration of a U.S. trademark, and he may then assign his U.S. trademark right to the importer. In spite of such an assignment, the importer may not be able to proceed against an infringer. In a number of decisions it has been held that the foreign manufacturer and the domestic importer are to be considered a single international enterprise, and that the goodwill of the enterprise is owned by the foreign manufacturer rather than the domestic distributor. Such holdings have been made in cases involving French perfumes, where the importers stressed the French origin of the goods. The importer is treated as just an extended arm of the foreign manufacturer.

Other decisions teach us how to avoid this, and how the importer can protect the foreign trademark. He must add flesh to the bones of the trademark. He can do so by assuming various contractual obligations, such as promoting sales of the imported goods, and prosecuting trademark infringers. In most instances, the importer will be expected to do these things anyway, but it is helpful to state them in a written agreement between the exporter and the importer. An exclusive license may also help the importer to ward off infringers.

Foreign merchandise bearing a registered U.S. trademark may not be imported into the U.S. without the permission of the U.S. trademark owner. The latter can protect himself against unlawful importation by depositing with the Customs Service a copy of the registered trademark in accordance with Section 526 of the Tariff Act. The consequence of an unlawful importation may be the seizure and forfeiture of the merchandise, an injunction against dealing in such merchandise, or an order to reexport the merchandise, to destroy it or to remove the objectionable trademark. A violator may also be held liable for damages.

The benefits of the statute are available only to owners of a U.S. trademark whose trademark represents an independently created goodwill. This means that an importer whose goodwill consists only of the goodwill of his foreign exporter, as in the case of the French perfume manufacturer, cannot avail himself of the cited Tariff Act provision in order to prevent the importation of a competing product. The foreign exporter may fight back, however, if he finds a flaw in the competition's U.S. trademark. If, for instance, that trademark was fraudulently obtained, the foreign exporter might institute cancellation proceedings in the U.S. Patent Office (see Section 8 above), or he may seek a declaratory judgment for invalidation of the U.S. trademark.

The Tariff Act provision applies only to registered trademarks. This does not prevent the owners of an unregistered trademark from resorting to the conventional remedies against foreign infringers.

## 13. INTERNATIONAL CONVENTIONS

The U.S. is, at present, not a party to the Madrid Convention for the International Registration of Trademarks.

However, it is a party to the Paris International Convention for the Protection of Industrial Property of 1883, as last revised at Lisbon in 1958, and previously revised at Washington in 1911, at The Hague in 1925, and at London in 1934. The U.S. is also a party to the Pan-America Trade Mark Convention of 1929. In addition, many bilateral treaties of friendship, commerce and navigation provide for the protection of intellectual property.

The general principle in all these Conventions is that the foreign trademark owner is entitled to the same protection and is subject to the same restrictions as a U.S. trademark owner. This is the so-called national treatment principle. In addition, the foreigner is entitled to Convention rights, which means he is entitled to such rights and benefits as are provided by the applicable Convention. This may involve a derogation of the U.S. national law.

Under the above Conventions, the foreign trademark owner may register his trademark as a U.S. trademark with the priority of the date of his home country registration, if the U.S. application is filed within six months from the date on which the application was filed in the home country. Unlike a domestic applicant, the foreign applicant need not show use in U.S. commerce. When he applies for U.S. registration he will be required to submit a certified copy of his home registration, and to prove use of the trademark in some country.

Article 6 of the Paris Convention calls this process validation of the trademark registered in the home country.

## 14. THE SUPPLEMENTAL REGISTER

The earlier statements in this chapter concerning registration refer to the so-called Principal Register of trademarks. The Lanham Act also provides for a

Supplemental Register. This is of little practical interest to one doing business in the U.S. Registration in the Supplemental Register lacks the main advantages of registration in the Principal Register, such as the presumption of validity and ownership, and it may not be used to stop the importation of merchandise which bears an infringing trademark. The Supplemental Register is a repository for marks that are not registrable in the Principal Register. Forbidden marks (see Section 5 above), except descriptive marks, cannot even be registered in the Supplemental Register. In order to be registrable in the Supplemental Register, the mark must be distinguishable from other marks and it must be recognized as a trademark by the purchasing public. Thus, registration was denied to a design of two colored bands for socks, because there was no evidence that the public would recognize the two colored stripes as a trademark.

## 15. DILUTION

The erosion of a trademark by dilution is not mentioned in the Lanham Act. It is an act of unfair competition, and provided for in some state laws (e.g., sec. 386-d of the New York General Business Law). A decision of the highest court of New York illustrates this concept. Allied Maintenance Corp. cleans and maintains large office buildings. It sued Allied Mechanical Trade Inc., which repairs and installs heating, ventilating and air-conditioning equipment in large office buildings. The court dismissed the suit, ruling that 'the harm that sec. 386-d was designed to prevent is the gradual whittling away of a firm's distinctive trademark or name. Plaintiff's trade name is neither truly distinctive nor has it acquired a secondary meaning in the mind of the public.'

## B. COPYRIGHT

## 1. NATURE OF COPYRIGHT

Copyright protection is available for all unpublished works, regardless of the nationality or domicile of the author. A copyright is the exclusive right to copy and reproduce an original work of authorship when such work becomes fixed in tangible form or expression. The Copyright Act lists seven main categories: (*a*) literary works; (*b*) musical works, including any accompanying work; (*c*) dramatic works, including any accompanying music; (*d*) pantomimes and choreographic works; (*e*) pictorial, graphic and sculptural works; (*f*) motion pictures and audiovisual works, and (*g*) sound recordings. Computer programs, which are defined as a set of instructions in a computer, are included in the first category.

The copyright does not protect an *idea*, which may be expressed in various ways. It protects only the particular manner in which an idea is expressed. For that reason, the publisher of ex-President Ford's memoirs lost a copyright infringement suit against a magazine which recounted Mr. Ford's version of certain events. The copyright is separate from the physical object in which the idea is expressed, as the soul is distinguished from the body. If one buys a painting, the painter retains the copyright, unless one sells it with the physical canvas. If one buys an old master there may be no copyright left (see Section 2 below). If the picture was painted recently, the copyright may still be owned by the painter or the surviving spouse. In an old case, one purchased an unpublished manuscript by Mark Twain. The testamentary trustee of Mark Twain obtained an injunction against publication of the manuscript because it was doubtful that the purchaser of the manuscript had acquired the copyright. The general rule, though, is that the unrestricted transfer of the physical property, without reservation of copyright, generally carries with it the right to reproduce.

The work must be original. This does not mean it must be novel, as is required of a patent. But the originality must be substantial, not merely trivial, as illustrated by the following case: An importer molded the familiar figure of Uncle Sam into a plastic bank, which he imported from Hong Kong. The design of the bank was copied from an Uncle Sam bank that was in the public domain. The importer claimed a copyright by pointing to the difference in size and other details. The court considered the differences so trivial that it ordered cancellation of the copyright registration. The operations manual for a machine or for an automobile may be copyrighted by the manufacturer. Delivery of the manual to a customer does not entitle him to reproduce it, unless the manufacturer has placed it in the public domain.

The copyright law has always been codified by a Federal statute. The current statute is the Copyright Act of 1976, which became effective on January 1, 1978. It was commonly believed that copyright matters were exclusively in the Federal domain, until California enacted a statute which made non-federally-protected phonograph record piracy a criminal offense, and the Supreme Court in 1973 upheld the validity of that statute.

A title of a musical composition or of a book or motion picture cannot be copyrighted unless it has acquired a secondary meaning (see Part A, Section 6, above). Title infringement may constitute unfair competition.

## 2. DURATION OF COPYRIGHT

A copyright endures during the author's life and for fifty years thereafter. This does not apply to works for hire (see Section 3, below). For such works, the copyright term is seventy-five years from the date of publication or 100 years from the date of creation, whichever is shorter. All of the foregoing applies also to works that were published before the effective date of the present Act, and works that were not registered before that date (i.e., January 1, 1978).

Before 1978, a copyright was secured only when the work was published or registered. The term then was twenty-eight years, with a right to renew for another twenty-eight years. Under present law, the renewal term for copyrights that were registered before 1978 is forty-seven years.

## 3. SOME DEFINITIONS

(*a*) A Work Made For Hire is a work which is created by one or more employees within the scope of their employment. The copyright in such a case is owned by the employer. The copyright of a newspaper advertisement, even if designed by the newspaper, belongs to the advertiser.

(*b*) A Compilation is a work formed by the collection of pre-existing materials, or of data that are arranged in such a way that the resulting work as a whole constitutes an original work of authorship, such as an anthology or a periodical. The compiler owns the copyright.

(*c*) A work is created when it is fixed for the first time in a written copy or a phonorecord.

(*d*) A Derivative Work is the name for an adaptation of a pre-existing work, such as a translation, condensation, musical arrangement or motion picture version. The adaptor obtains a copyright for his original creation.

(*e*) Access is an important concept. If the creator of a work accuses another of plagiarism, it will generally be presumed that the charge is justified if the defendant had access to the work. The accusation of plagiarism may not be justified, because sometimes identical works are created independently of each other. Access is only circumstantial evidence and may be overcome by other evidence.

## 4. INDUSTRIAL DESIGNS

Industrial designs are copyrightable even though they are also patentable (see Chapter 19, Section 1). However, a purely utilitarian design may not be copyrighted. An industrial design qualifies for copyright only if it has some artistic feature, such as a statuette as a lamp base. A copyright is preferable to a design patent because it affords greater protection.

## 5. PUBLICATION, NOTICE AND DEPOSIT

The concept of publication is not simple. The statute states that publication is the distribution of copies or phonorecords of a work of art by sale or other transfer of ownership, or by rental. A distribution of copies or phonorecords to the public for purposes of further distribution, and public performance or public display by the offeror also constitute publication. However, a public performance or display by the copyright owner, in which the material does not change hands, does not constitute publication, even though many persons may be exposed to and become acquainted with the work. An architect's copyright in his drawings is lost when the house is built and exhibited. However, the drawings are not deemed published when they are given to a contractor to enable the latter to bid for the construction.

The importance of publication lies in the fact that it brings the work into the public domain. The copyright may be forfeited thereby, unless a notice of copyright is attached and a copy of the mark is deposited with the Library of Congress, in the manner prescribed by the rules of the Copyright Office. The manner of deposit is prescribed by regulations. Sculptures and other three-dimensional works are deposited by photograph. Errors and omissions in the copyright notice are not fatal if the work is registered within five years and if correction is made at or before that time.

## 6. REGISTRATION

A copyright may be registered at any time with the Copyright Office of the Library of Congress on forms supplied by that Office. As pointed out above, registration is not a condition or requirement of copyright protection. It is a legal formality. Its principal advantages are that it creates *prima facie* evidence of a valid copyright, and that in case of infringement the owner is entitled to statutory damages and royalty payments.

The Register of Copyrights (this is the title of the person who heads the Copyright Office) may refuse to register a copyright, or he may register it wrongfully. This may cause an author to go to court against the Register.

## 7. TRANSFER

A copyright may be transferred like any other property right in accordance with the various state laws which govern assignment, licenses, inheritance and other modes of transfer. Transfers may, but need not, be recorded in the Copyright Register.

Transfers are subject to a rather unique termination feature. Except in case of a work made for hire, a transfer or license granted by the author may be cancelled after thirty-five years, pursuant to the very detailed provisions of section 203 of the Copyright Act.

## 8. INFRINGEMENT AND FAIR USE

Incidents of infringement have multiplied since the invention of the photocopy machine and of videotaping. Theft and piracy abound. Importation of copies or phonorecords of a work that has been acquired abroad, may constitute an infringement, with minor exceptions listed in section 602 of the Act.

In a much debated recent case, the Supreme Court rejected an attempt to impose liability on the seller of a copying machine (a tape recorder) which was used to copy copyrighted television films. The court ruled that this would improperly expand the copyright monopoly. The court also said (four judges dissenting) that the concept of contributory infringement contained in the Patent Code (see supra page 197) is not applicable to copyright. Exhibition of the taped films was held to be fair use.

Some copying is permissible under the Fair Use doctrine. This is an equitable rule of reason, which limits the exclusive right of a copyright owner. It is referred to in section 107 of the Act, but it is much older. Newspaper reviews may quote from a copyrighted work, and excerpts may be used for teaching purposes or research. These are merely examples of fair use. In a celebrated case, the National Institute of Health and the National Library of Medicine copied articles from medical journals. This was held to be fair use despite the substantial amount of copying. On the other hand, when an educational organization videotaped and reproduced commercially manufactured educational films in great quantities and distributed them to schools, it was held not to be fair use but an unlawful infringement. The quotation of three hundred words from the memoirs of former President Ford in the *Nation* magazine was held recently to be fair use.

When the use of copyrighted material constitutes a substantial interference with the copyright owner's business, the defense of fair use is not available.

## 9. INTERNATIONAL ASPECTS

Literary works in the English language that are manufactured abroad (other than in Canada) are barred from importation, with certain exceptions. The so-called 'manufacturing clause' is a protectionist measure for the benefit of the U.S. printing industry.

As stated in Section 1, unpublished works are protected without regard to the nationality of the author.

Published works of aliens are protected as those of U.S. citizens, if the alien's home country is a party to a copyright treaty to which the U.S. is also a party. Stateless persons are always protected. If the author's homeland is not a party to an applicable treaty, the author may nevertheless be granted copyright protection by Presidential proclamation, if the author's homeland grants reciprocity.

The most important of the International treaties is the Universal Copyright Convention, concluded at Geneva in 1952, and revised at Paris in 1971. It became effective in the U.S. on July 10, 1974. The U.S. is also a party to the Buenos Aires Convention of 1911 and the Convention for the Protection of Producers of Phonographs Against Unauthorized Duplication, which was concluded at Geneva in 1971. In addition, the U.S. maintains bilateral copyright relations with a number of countries. Most of the nations which became independent after 1943 have not established copyright relations with the U.S., but are believed to be willing to honour the obligations incurred under their former political status. The Soviet Union is a party to the 1952 Geneva Convention, as are Bulgaria, Czechoslovakia, and East Germany. Czechoslovakia, Romania and Hungary have bilateral treaties with the U.S. Most other states have copyright relations with the U.S.

## C. UNFAIR COMPETITION

## 1. GENERAL REMARKS

The concept of unfair competition is relatively new, because U.S. law has found it difficult to find a satisfactory theoretical basis for the concept. Today, unfair competition is recognized as a tort, which, as earlier noted, is a wrongful act forbidden by law, and an injury to the property right of another, e.g. fraud or theft. The goodwill of the business of another is recognized as a property right and the protection of the purchasing public against deceit is deemed to be an important social objective. One who injures such a property right will be held liable even if he is not in competition with the injured party. It is, therefore, not accurate to treat such cases as hindering unfair competition. Since, however, they are customarily so regarded, the practice is followed here.

Mere puffing is not actionable. Puffing is an obvious exaggeration which nobody takes seriously, such as 'our product is the best in the world', or 'our product is unrivaled'.

There is no precise doctrine of unfair competition. It is not possible to draw up a list of what constitutes unfair competition. It is as impossible as making a catalog of what is fair and what is unfair. An original dress may be copied with impunity in the absence of patent protection, but there is actionable unfair competition if knowledge of the original creation was obtained by stealth or fraud. A French dress designer sued a New York department store for selling dresses which had been copied and sold as copies. The court refused to enjoin the defendant, pointing out that it might have ruled differently if the copies were so poorly made that they reflected unfavorably on the original. Deceptive advertising is another example of unfair competition. As a last illustration, one might refer to an Hungarian nationalization case. The nationalized enterprise had appointed a new U.S. distributor. The former Hungarian owner obtained a court order that directed the new distributor (a) to discontinue business with the nationalized enterprise in Hungary, (b) to discontinue the use of the owner's trademark, and (c) to pay damages.

## 2. PALMING OFF

The gist, in most instances, of unfair competition is that the wrongdoer attempts to palm off his product as that of another by deceiving the purchasing public as to the origin of the product. Section 43 of the Lanham Act forbids the false designation of origin and false description. Section 43 creates Federal unfair competition law, and the Federal courts have jurisdiction without requiring diversity of citizenship and regardless of the amount involved (see Chapter 23). However, an action based on unfair competition is not limited to the Federal statute. The tort of unfair competition is also grounded in the common law of the various states, and may be enforced in the state courts. Deception of the public is generally the principal element of palming off. The deception is usually affected by marketing the tortfeasor's product in a manner that causes it to appear confusingly similar to another's product. The term *confusingly similar* has the same broad meaning as in the trademark infringement cases (see Part A, Section 2(d)). It bears repeating that the test is the likelihood of confusion, not actual confusion. And it must also be remembered that the public is not expected to be sophisticated; that a superficial similarity of words, sound or imagery is sufficient to establish a likelihood of confusion.

The appropriation of another's advertising method is generally not regarded as an act of unfair competition. However, it will be so regarded if the public is led to believe that it is dealing with or obtaining products of the originator, or if there is an attempt to palm off the product of a competitor.

The adoption of a confusingly similar name is a favorite means of competition. The matter becomes more difficult to deal with where a person uses his own name in his business name. However, individuals have been enjoined even from using their names, where they did so in an obvious effort to compete with an established family business. Thus when Mr. Todd, Jr., son of the founder of Todd's Shipyard Corp., after retiring from his father's company, lent his name to Todd Drydock & Repair Corp., a court enjoined the use. David Findlay was an art dealer in New York City who used the business name, Findlay. His brother, Wally, operated a similar business in Chicago and Miami. When Wally opened a shop in New York City next to David's under his own name, the court forbade it. The English owner of the trademark, 'Beefeaters', obtained an injunction against a New York restaurant that used the name. Restaurants often attempt to exploit the fame of far distant other restaurants by use of the latters' names, and this is generally enjoined. The famous tobacco firm, A. Dunhill of London, enjoined a shirtmaker from using the name 'Dunhill'.

Not every unfair trade conduct is actionable. The following cases illustrate situations where trade practices that may well be regarded as unfair were held to be permissible.

The giant mail order house of Sears Roebuck copied the pole lamp design of Stiffel, and sold it at a lower price than Stiffel. The court recognized that there might be confusion of origin, but since Stiffel had no valid design patent, the lamp could be freely copied and the copier could not be held liable for unfair competition. The Supreme Court explained: 'Mere inability of the public to tell two identical articles apart is not enough to support an injunction or an award of damages for copying that which the Federal Patent Laws permit to be copied.' In a companion decision, the Supreme Court held that state law cannot hold a copier accountable in damages for failure to label or otherwise identify his goods, unless his failure to do so violates a state law requiring such labeling or other steps to prevent confusion. These decisions make it clear that state court injunctions against product simulation are unconstitutional if they conflict with Federal policy, and that the public interest in free competition outweighs the doctrine of unfair competition.

The limits of the law of unfair competition are further illustrated by the following case: Schwartz's trademark, 'Syrocol', was held to be confusingly similar to Upjohn's trademark, 'Cheracol' – and Upjohn was granted an injunction. However, Upjohn (a leading pharmaceutical manufacturer) also sued for unfair competition, which suit was dismissed because Upjohn had not shown that 'Cheracol' had a secondary meaning, and there was no proof of actual palming off. Although the court found that the defendant had deliberately copied Upjohn's unpatented pharmaceutical products in order to benefit from the demand that had been created by Upjohn's efforts, the court ruled that the conduct was not illegal.

## 3. TRADE SECRETS

The owner of a trade secret is protected against theft as is the owner of any valuable property, such as an automobile or a watch. However, the matter must be a secret. Often, a vengeful employer sues a former employee for stealing a trade secret, where the former employee is only using information readily available from other sources and, therefore, not a secret, such as the names of potential customers. A trade secret may be a secret process or formula, know-how, laboratory experiments, a scientific idea, a literary idea (for instance, the plot of a story or the theme of a television series), a slogan or an advertising idea, or any other confidential information.

Electronics manufacturers frequently find that employees develop a new device in the employer's laboratory, which device constitutes a trade secret, and then establish their own business to market the device. IBM experienced several instances of this kind, and has pursued such thefts vigorously. The remedy is usually an injunction and damages. The award of damages is satisfied when the thief turns over his profits to the owner of the trade secret. Misappropriation of a trade secret is a continuing wrong. The owner is entitled to sue for the damages suffered during the entire period of misappropriation, except as limited by the statute of limitations. The misapporpriator cannot escape liability by making the secret public. In the language of a court decision, 'A misappropriator cannot baptize his wrongful actions by general publication of the secret'.

The perpetrators of the wrong are generally unfaithful former employees or competitors who appropriate the trade secret to their own use. A third party, to whom an ex-employee discloses his former employer's trade secret, is not liable to the owner for the wrongful use of the trade secret, unless he knows that what has been disclosed, or is about to be disclosed to him, is the trade secret of another. In most instances the ex-employee is employed by the third party because the latter expects disclosure or use of the trade secret. Proof of this expectation may be difficult. It is, therefore, good practice for the owner of a trade secret to send a warning letter to the new employer, and to threaten him with legal action if he should make use of any trade secret that the owner's former employee may disclose or utilize for the benefit of the new employer.

Hiring away (stealing) an employee in order to utilize the former employer's trade secrets is always an actionable act of unfair competition. However, an employer's interest in protecting the fruits of his investment is subordinated to the interest of the employee in the free transferability of his acquired skills. This means that an ex-employer has no right of action against a former employee and his new employer merely because the employee uses in his new job the skills which he acquired in the old – as long as no secrets are involved. This pinpoints the issue that often arises in litigation involving trade secrets.

Employment contracts sometimes contain a clause prohibiting the employee from disclosing trade secrets. Such a clause is superfluous because an employee is never allowed to disclose trade secrets.

It has been argued that the protection of trade secrets is incompatible with the Patent Law, if the owner of the trade secret does not apply for patent protection where available. If the trade secret owner voluntarily forsakes patent protection, or if the secret is not capable of patent protection, so the argument goes, the secret can be used by anybody, just as anybody is permitted to copy an unpatented article. This argument, which has been advanced by lower courts in New York and California, does not represent prevailing opinion. Inventors frequently refrain from applying for a patent because they do not wish to make the disclosure that a patent application requires (see

Chapter 19), for fear that competitors may use the information disclosed. The desire for continued secrecy is legitimate, and deserves the protection of the law.

Misappropriators of trade secrets have sometimes sought to excuse their conduct as being justified by the antitrust laws. The argument is that a competitor must appropriate another's trade secrets in order to survive and to break the industry domination by the owner of trade secrets. A lower court in New York has accepted this argument. The argument is not sound.

## 4. SALE OF IDEAS; SECRECY AGREEMENTS

When an inventor submits his idea to a manufacturer, the manufacturer is free to use it, unless there is an agreement to the contrary. The same is true in other fields. For instance, one may submit to a radio station an idea for a new program, or to an advertising agency a novel advertising concept. An abstract idea is held not to be private property, and no contract is implied by the communication of the idea. However, if A induces B to disclose a trade secret for the purpose of exploiting it as partners, and A thereafter exploits the idea alone, he may be liable for fraud.

An inventor may not be clever enough to demand a contract before he communicates his idea, but most manufacturers know that it is not prudent to accept the submission of a new idea without first making an agreement. It is not prudent because the idea may already be known to the manufacturer, and if he uses it, the inventor may later make a claim for compensation. For that reason, an experienced manufacturer will generally enter into an agreement in which he agrees to compensate the inventor if he utilizes his idea and if the idea (a) is not publicly known or described in the literature, and (b) is not known to the manufacturer. The agreement, generally, also provides that if the idea is not accepted, the manufacturer will return all submitted materials to the inventor, and will not disclose the idea to others. Only after the inventor has signed the agreement, will the manufacturer allow him to disclose his idea. The same applies to parties who are similarly situated, such as the abovementioned radio station and advertising agency. The main purpose of the secrecy agreement is to avoid the inconvenience and hazard of claims. However, even if the party to whom an idea is disclosed does not make such an agreement, it is not obligated to the discloser if at some later time it utilizes the disclosed idea. The submission of a new idea does not generally create a fiduciary relationship.

## 5. DISPARAGEMENT AND COMPARATIVE ADVERTISING

Disparagement of the business or the products of another is generally unfair. It is sometimes called trade libel. The law of libel applies, and the matter is generally not regarded as falling under the unfair competition doctrine.

As to comparative advertising, offending advertisers often argue that they are protected by the constitutional guaranty of free speech. Most advertisers are careful. If they advertise the superior quality of their product, they generally compare it with 'Brand X' and 'Brand Y', without naming the competitor. MacDonald's, the purveyor of hamburgers, sued its competitor, Burger King, for unfair comparative advertising. Burger King paid under a settlement made out of court. U Haul, the giant moving and storage company, sued its competitor, Jartman, as well as Jartman's advertising agency, for $375,000, because of a series of advertisements in which Jartman claimed to render better and cheaper service than U Haul. At this writing, the case has not been decided, and Jartman is in bankruptcy. The well-known company, Honeywell, Inc., published a brochure about the superior quality of its devices for replacing certain worn-out computer parts. Honeywell's only competitor in this specialized field obtained an injunction against Honeywell, on the ground that the brochure was deceptive and obviously directed against the plaintiff.

## 6. NON-COMPETITION CLAUSES

As stated in Chapter 13, a prudent employer will incorporate a non-competition clause in its employment agreements. This offers no problem during the period of employment. However, employers often desire to prevent competition by an employee after termination of the employment. This desire clashes with the public policy of the law, which is opposed to any restriction that hinders an ex-employee from earning a livelihood. For that reason, post-employment non-competition clauses will, generally, only be held valid if they are limited as to territory and in time. For instance, it may be reasonable to forbid competition in the U.S. east of the Mississippi for a period of one year. No precise rules can be stated. An important factor is whether or not the employee was acquainted with the employer's trade before he commenced employment.

A similar problem exists if one sells one's business. Frequently, the purchaser will require a clause that forbids the seller to engage in a competitive business. In California and other states, that is the only instance in which a non-competition clause is permissible; and even in such case, the non-competition generally must be limited to the county in which the business is conducted. In many instances, a business is conducted in several counties and even several states.

Some businesspeople are inclined to disregard what they consider to be legal technicalities. They insist on a broad non-competition clause, on the ground that it will exert moral pressure on an ex-employee. This may be good judgment. But if the judgment proves to be incorrect, the employer runs the risk that a court may rule the agreement contaminated by an invalid clause, as a consequence of which the entire agreement may be held invalid.

In the sale of a business, a non-competition clause has special tax consequences.

## CHAPTER 21

# LICENSE AGREEMENTS

## *1. INTRODUCTION*

Most license agreements pertain to patents. Patent license agreements are often coupled with technical assistance agreements and with know-how licenses. Licensing is a convenient form of hurdling tariff and non-tariff barriers (Chapter 22), and a means of exporting technology to countries that, for a variety of reasons, are unwilling or unable to purchase the finished product of a U.S. manufacturer. Licensing has thus become an important factor in exporting U.S. technology. Conversely, U.S. manufacturers frequently acquire foreign technology through license agreements. Such agreements are, of course, not limited to international trade. They are also made between domestic parties. There are U.S. research organizations whose only business it is to license interested parties.

It must be remembered that a patent license is restricted to the country in which the patent is issued. If a French company wishes to transfer its technology, for which it has only a French patent, to other countries where it owns no patent, it can do so by a know-how license or by a technical aid agreement. A know-how license may embrace know-how and techniques used by the licensor in all parts of the world and incorporated in foreign patents. Trademark licenses are granted when the owner wishes to allow the licensee to use the goodwill associated with the trademark.

A copyright license may be granted as to one or more countries in which copyrights are registered or registration has been applied for.

Franchises are a special form of license agreement. The franchise type of license agreement is present in many fields of commerce, but is used primarily for automobile dealers, hotels, and fast food stores.

There are unwritten license agreements. If A sells or leases a patented article to B, B has an implied license to use the article and to resell it. But he has no license to duplicate it.

License agreements are subject to the general rules of contract law. A notable exception exists with respect to assignments. A licensee may not assign his rights, unless the agreement specifically permits assignment.

License agreements frequently collide with the antitrust laws because licensors tend to misuse their patent monopoly by incorporating in the license agreement clauses or obligations which are not supported by the monopoly, such as an obligation to pay a royalty on non-patented articles. Such patent misuse may destroy the enforceability of the patents themselves. This is discussed in Chapter 17, Section 8.

A notable exception to the application of the antitrust laws is the right of the licensor to fix the resale price of the licensee. The exception does not, however, apply in case of a conspiracy in restraint of trade.

## 2. LIMITATIONS

A license may be exclusive or nonexclusive. If it is exclusive, it does not bar the patent owner from making, using or selling the patented article, unless the agreement says so. The situation is the same as in the case of an exclusive sales agency (see Chapter 13, Section 3). Some courts disagree. It is, therefore, advisable to write the agreement so as to leave no room for argument. An exclusive licensee can sue for infringement; a nonexclusive licensee cannot.

A license may be limited to a particular territory. This often occurs where the licensee is primarily interested in selling the licensed article. The agreement, then, should spell out what happens if the licensee makes a sale into another territory. The license agreement may forbid the licensee to make sales to a buyer in the homeland of the licensor.

There also may be a functional limitation. The license may be limited to a particular machine, to a particular industry, or to a particular class of customers. In a famous decision, the patent owner granted two exclusive licenses, one for sale in the home field, and one for sale in the commercial field. The licensee for the home field sold the licensed products to a commercial user, and was held to be an infringer. CIBA Geigy granted a manufacturing license for a certain drug in specialty form (as distinguished from bulk form). The court rejected the government contention that this was an unlawful restraint, holding that the license limitation was legitimate.

A license may be conditional. U.S. sales representatives for foreign manufacturers are sometimes concerned that, due to political developments, the importation of articles from abroad may be interrupted. If such an emergency arises, they wish to have the right to manufacture the article in the U.S. To this end, sales representatives are sometimes granted a conditional license, and cases are known where a description of the technical know-how needed for the practice of the patented invention was delivered to the U.S. representative in a sealed envelope. The same can, of course, be done with respect to U.S. inventions that are patented abroad.

A licensee does not have the right to sublicense others, unless the license agreement grants such right. If, as a result of an infringement claim by a third party, the licensed patent is invalidated, the license agreement becomes a nullity. The licensee cannot claim a refund for past royalty payments as he has enjoyed patent protection until the patent was nullified. If the licensee is required to pay damages to the plaintiff in the infringement suit, he may or may not be able to claim reimbursement from the licensor, depending on the provisions of the license agreement. In the absence of an indemnity agreement or similar agreement by the licensor, reimbursement cannot be had because, as stated below in Section 5, the licensor is not considered to have warranted the validity of the licensed patent.

## 3. IMPROVEMENTS AND TECHNICAL AID

Patent owners often engage in research that leads to improvements or refinements of the licensed patent. The license agreement generally provides that the licensor will inform the licensee of any such improvements and allow him to use them without additional payment. If additional patents are procured for such improvements, the license generally embraces such improvements.

Conversely, there should be a provision for improvements that are developed by the licensee. The licensee may even develop an improvement that is patentable. It is generally provided that such improvements will be made available to the licensor, and that improvement patents will be either assigned or licensed to the licensor. The licensor generally will be allowed to make such improvements and improvement patents available to his other licensees.

A future invention by the licensor may not be merely an improvement of the licensed patent; but if it is in the same field as the licensed patent, the license agreement may secure the benefit of the future invention to the licensee. This can be done in a variety of ways. Similar provision can be made for future inventions of the licensee.

## 4. DURATION

The number of years during which the license is valid depends on the agreement of the parties. However, the term can never extend beyond the period of validity of the patent. Patent owners sometimes disregard this and try to receive royalty fees after the patent has expired. A common scheme is to obtain improvement patents that have a later expiration date. Another scheme is the package license, in which the licensor licenses a number of patents together, at a fixed royalty fee that the patent owner seeks to collect until the last patent in the package has expired. This may be an illegal patent misuse, as discussed in Chapter 17, Section 3.

## 5. *OBLIGATIONS OF THE LICENSOR*

When a licensee enters into a license agreement, he assumes that the licensed patent is valid. However, in the absence of a clause to that effect, the licensor is not considered to have guaranteed the validity of the patent. Validity is not automatically implied. Both parties to the license agreement should understand this. If the patent is invalidated, as a result of litigation or otherwise, the licensor is not liable for damages, unless he has warranted the validity of the patent. Invalidation terminates the license agreement. The agreement might impose on the licensor the obligation to inform the licensee of any actual or threatened invalidation proceeding.

The patent owner is obliged to maintain the licensed patent. This means that he is responsible for the payment of the required fees and for renewal of the patent, if it is renewable.

## 6. *OBLIGATIONS OF THE LICENSEE*

The licensee must make reasonable efforts to use the licensed patent. Sometimes the licensor reserves the right to terminate the license in case of a change in the licensee's personnel.

The licensee is obligated to protect the reputation of the licensor, and that of the licensed product. This is important not only for the reputation of the licensor, but also for that of other licensees, whose business may suffer if the licensee supplies shoddy products. In trademark license agreements, quality supervision by the licensor must be an integral part.

Frequently, a license agreement requires the licensee to spend a stated amount of money to advertise the licensed product.

License agreements often contain specific provision for servicing of the licensed articles, or of articles manufactured under the license. Generally, licensed equipment is required to bear a name plate, indicating the name of the patent owner, or otherwise comply with the marking requirements of the U.S. patent law (see Chapter 19, Section 7).

It used to be the law that the licensee was required to respect the validity of the patent licensed to him. The licensee was *estopped* from contesting the validity of the patent. The Supreme Court, in 1969, ruled that such estoppel rule violates the integrity of the U.S. patent system. Since that time, a licensee is free to attack the validity of the patent at any time, and thus to destroy the license agreement. A licensee might do this in defense of a claim for unpaid royalties.

Many license agreements contain a clause forbidding the licensee to contest the validity of the licensed patent. Such clauses are invalid and can be disregarded.

## 7. *INFRINGEMENT CLAIMS*

The license agreement should fix the mutual responsibilities of the parties in case of infringement or threatened infringement. Generally, the patent owner is interested in keeping control. He, therefore, might stipulate that the licensee will inform him not only of actual, but also of threatened, infringements of the patent. The owner will also wish to be informed if a third party claims, or threatens to claim, that the licensed patent infringes the third party's patent.

The question then arises, who will defend the infringement suit, if one ensues, and who will be obligated to pay the expenses of the litigation. If the agreement provides that this obligation is to be borne by the licensee, the licensor may, nevertheless, wish to be consulted and kept informed. He may also wish to have a voice in selecting counsel, and to reserve a right of approval of any compromise settlement. Similar questions arise if the patent is infringed or threatened with infringement.

No matter to whom the license agreement allocates the responsibility to litigate, the agreement should also state what happens if a party fails to discharge that responsibility. This would be a breach of contract and lead to a claim for damages. However, action with respect to infringement litigation can generally not be deferred until the damage claim has been settled. Either the licensor or the licensee must take immediate action. This pressure of immediacy exists also when the opportunity for a compromise settlement arises.

There is no fixed rule as to how this problem should be resolved. The point here is that the matter should not be overlooked. In many instances, the licensor has the preponderant interest in the maintenance of the patent, because if it is invalidated in one jurisdiction, attacks in other jurisdictions, by other parties, may follow. In other instances, the licensee has more to lose than the licensor. These considerations will lead to a practial arrangement.

## 8. CROSS-LICENSING, GRANT-BACKS AND POOLING

These terms are sometimes thought of as involving absolute illegality. This is not so. Cross-licensing occurs where licensor and licensee agree to license their patents to each other. Similarly, a grant-back is spoken of when a licensee agrees to grant to the licensor a license for any patent that the licensee may obtain in the field of the principal license. Such grant-backs occur primarily in relation to improvements made by the licensee. The word patent pooling applies to a situation where several patent owners transfer their patents to a common pool, which then issues licenses for the pooled patents. Any such arrangements are legal if they do not violate the antitrust laws. This would be the case if a cross-license agreement, a grant-back, or a pooling arrangement is made in furtherance of a monopoly, or a conspiracy to restrain trade, exclude competition or control prices. Such illegality is generally suspected if more than two parties are involved.

In the leading case supporting interchange of patents, several petroleum producers had developed and patented a cracking process. They sued each other for patent infringement, and finally settled the case by making a cross-licensing agreement. Each of them was given the right to use the various patents. Each retained the right to license its own patents with immunity from infringement claims by the others. Royalties from the licenses were divided among the parties. There were no restrictions as to production, quality or prices. The Supreme Court upheld the arrangement.

The other end of the spectrum is illustrated by another famous Supreme Court decision, the *Hartford-Empire* case. Approximately 900 patents, owned by five major glass manufacturers, were pooled. The pool effectively controlled the industry by agreeing as to who and what should be licensed. Entry into the glass manufacturing industry without the consent of the pool was practically impossible. Clearly, the antitrust laws were violated, and the cross-licensing and pooling arrangement were illegal. In summary, a patent interchange may be essential to feasible patent utilization, as in the case of the petroleum industry; or it may facilitate illegal competitive restraint, as in the case of the glass industry.

Illegal cross-licenses occur in international trade where the illegal purpose is to divide the world markets. In one case, patent licenses were used to keep certain Dupont chemicals out of Great Britain, and to curtail the export to the U.S. of competing chemicals made by Imperial Chemical Industries. Another example is the case in which the Singer Manufacturing Company had agreed with competitors in Switzerland and in Italy to exclude Japanese sewing machines from the U.S.

In the oft-cited case of *Hazeltine Corp.* v. *Zenith Radio Corp.*, the court found that the foreign commerce of the U.S. had been drastically curtailed by patent pools in England, Canada and Australia, and that the combination represented by the pools had the express purpose of preventing the importation into those foreign markets of radios and television equipment made in the U.S. This was illegal.

## 9. ROYALTIES AND LICENSE FEES

These words are generally used interchangeably. 'License Fee' may denote a one-time payment. This may be either a lump-sum compensation for the license or an advance payment. 'Royalties' refers to periodic payments that are stipulated in the license agreement. Royalties are generally computed on a per piece, per ton, per pound, per barrel basis, or as a percentage of the sales or the profits of the licensee. Computation on the basis of sales is preferable to a percentage of profits because it avoids arguments about how profits are arrived at. For similar reasons, gross sales are a more desirable basis than net sales. The license agreement will generally provide for periodic accounting and payment. Sometimes, it is stipulated that the licensee must submit copies of his invoices. The licensor often obtains the right to have the records of the licensee inspected by an independent auditor.

Many license agreements provide for a minimum royalty payment. If that minimum is not reached, the licensor generally has the option to terminate the agreement. If the license is an exclusive one, failure to reach the minimum sometimes converts the license into a nonexclusive one. Of course, the licensee can always avoid this, or other stipulated consequences, by paying the minimum, even if it has not been earned.

Some license agreements contain a 'most favored nation' clause, which provides, in effect, that if the licensor charges any other licensee a lower royalty rate than the one stipulated in the agreement, such lower rate shall also apply to the licensee involved. Absent such a clause, it is legal to charge different royalty rates to different licensees. The prohibition against price discrimination among similarly situated parties applies only to sales (see Chapter 17, Section 3).

In international agreements it may be advisable to fix the currency in which royalty payments are to be made.

## 10. COMPULSORY LICENSE

Sometimes a patent owner is compelled to make a license agreement. The two principal instances of a compulsory license are unrelated. The first occurs in the defense industry and in the field of atomic energy. Because of the critical public interest, the U.S. government can demand of the patent owner that a nonexclusive license be issued to it. The second instance of a compulsory license occurs when a court finds this to be an appropriate remedy in a case of patent misuse. For instance, in the *Hartford Empire* case, which was mentioned in Section 8 above, the court ordered the defendants to grant to anybody who applied for it a license to make, use or sell the patented machines at reasonable royalties.

The Federal Trade Commission also may order compulsory licensing when it finds unfair competition on the part of the owner of a patent or trademark. The Copyright Act provides for compulsory licenses for secondary transmission by cable television.

Compulsory licenses generally are granted at a reasonable royalty rate, but also may be royalty-free.

## 11. TAXES

U.S. licensors used to be able to transfer their patent and similar rights to a foreign subsidiary, preferably in a tax haven country which levied no income tax, and let such subsidiary earn royalty income from foreign sublicensees. This tax avoidance scheme has been eliminated. Royalties are taxable income to a U.S. licensor.

The source of the royalty income is the country where the patent, copyright or trademark is used. Most tax conventions (Chapter 8, Section 25) provide for tax exemption in the source country as long as the licensor has no permanent establishment there. Where no such tax exemption is provided, the applicable withholding tax is generally reduced.

Technical services are generally treated as personal services, and the foregoing does not apply. Generally, such services should be included within the category of industrial and commercial profits, which in most tax conventions are exempt from tax in the country to which the services are rendered, unless the licensor maintains a permanent establishment there.

Frequently, technology is transferred to a foreign manufacturing corporation that is jointly owned by the licensor and foreign interests, in exchange for stock. This is done to avoid exchange control restrictions that would bar payment for the technology. It also allows a U.S. licensor a foreign tax credit for a part of the foreign corporate income taxes. Another reason may be that in some countries the withholding tax on dividends is lower than that on royalties.

Foreign income taxes paid by the licensor qualify for U.S. tax credit.

CHAPTER 22

# INTERNATIONAL TRADE

## 1. INTRODUCTION

This book is written with a view principally to international trade. The present chapter is devoted to the regulatory structure of foreign trade in the U.S. This structure has undergone a fundamental change in recent decades. The nineteenth-century policy of economic isolation has been reversed. Today, U.S. trade policy seeks to foster foreign trade, and particularly to promote exports. Simultaneously, importation is facilitated and tariff as well as non-tariff barriers have been lowered. The U.S. was the leader in bringing about the General Agreement on Tariffs and Trade (GATT), as well as the several rounds of multinational negotiations resulting in lower duties affecting the tariffs of the major trading countries of the world, including the U.S. During the past fifty years most political leaders, regardless of party affiliation, have abjured a protectionist trade policy and have advocated a liberal policy of free trade. Nevertheless, special interests often cause Congress to enact legislation that is designed for their own protection or to still the anguished voices of those who feel hurt by foreign competition. This explains the frequent and sometimes bewildering mass of new trade legislation and tariff changes. At this writing, there is much irritation in the U.S. Congress about what are seen as Japanese non-tariff barriers, and about the subsidized agricultural exports of the European Common Market. In the face of this, President Reagan has warned against protectionist legislation. Stating that the U.S. and its trading partners are in the same boat, the President has said, 'If one partner shoots a hole in the boat, it makes no sense for the other partner to shoot another hole in the boat. That's not getting tough. It's getting wet. And eventually it's sinking the boat.' The deeper cause for irritation in the U.S. seems to be that the postwar recovery of Europe, the formation of the Common Market in Europe, and the outstanding performance of Japan have combined to undermine the competitive advantage which the U.S. used to enjoy as a result of the lowering of the protectionist barriers. U.S. technology, productivity, and management efficiency are no longer regarded as superior, as they were in the first decades after World War II. It has been suggested that the philosophy of the U.S. trade laws is incompatible with the principles of the antitrust laws, to the detriment of the American consumer. The opponents of this view argue that there is no such incompatibility, and that the trade laws merely try to preserve free and fair competition. This is not the place to determine which view is correct.

The international trade regulations of the U.S. are widely dispersed, complex and not neatly packaged. They are subject to shifting trade winds. What follows is a general overview.

## 2. THE TARIFF ACT

Import duties are established by the Tariff Act. Duties are computed either on an *ad valorem* basis, or as a percentage of the value of the imported article. Some articles are exempt from duty. The U.S. still operates under the 1930 Tariff Act, the infamous Smoot-Hawley tariff, which established very high protectionist duties. Fortunately, the Act has been amended more than one hundred times, and its authors would not recognize it today. In 1934, the Reciprocal Trade Agreement Act was adopted, and inaugurated a substantial tariff reduction by presidential action. These were at first negotiated bilaterally, then multilaterally.

The import procedure prescribed by the Tariff Act is complicated. It is customarily handled by customhouse brokers, who are located near the various ports of entry. Freight forwarders are often licensed as customhouse brokers. If the importer is a corporation, the employment of a customhouse broker requires a directors' resolution. The broker will arrange for the entry of the goods through customs, prepare and file the necessary entry papers, attend to inspection by the Food and Drug Administration (where required), settle the appraisal of the merchandise and follow the transaction through to final liquidation.

As will be noted from the discussion below, there may be a considerable time lapse between the arrival of the merchandise in a U.S. port and the final customs liquidation. Importers rarely can wait that long. They generally will post a bond to secure the future payment of the duty.

Mention should be made here of the use of trust receipts in international trade. The trust receipt was discussed in Chapter 15, Section 8. An importer may not have enough money to pay for imported merchandise consigned to a bank under a letter of credit arrangement (see Chapter 14, Section 8) that requires the importer to pay the bank. The bank may release the merchandise to the importer if the latter executes a trust receipt, in which he undertakes to pay the bank with the funds that he expects to collect from the customer to whom he has sold the imported merchandise.

Proper classification of imported merchandise is one of the problems that delay the liquidation of a customs entry. To illustrate: Watch importers must pay duty on three separate components – the watch movement, the casing, and the band. Digital watches have no movements, hence there cannot be any movement duty. Upon accepting this argument, the Customs Service classified digital watches as 'electronic articles not provided for elsewhere'. This saved the importer a considerable amount of duty. Other examples are frog legs, which may or may not be taxed as fish, and doll voices which may be taxed as phonographs or as toy parts. Similar questions arise in connection with the importation of machinery.

A related problem is that of the valuation of the imported article.


## 3. VALUATION OF IMPORTED MERCHANDISE

The valuation by the shipper in the customs invoice required by the Customs Service is not necessarily controlling. Sometimes, the exporter and the importer agree to undervalue merchandise in order to save customs duty. Another motive for such undervaluation may be the desire to enable the importer to earn a higher profit. If the import company is owned by the exporter, the incentive for such arrangement may be the desire to accumulate profits in the U.S. rather than in the homeland. The Customs Service will not disturb such an arrangement, but will insist that duty be paid on the true value. Where the foreign exporter and the importer are related parties, the Customs Service applies special scrutiny in appraising the true value. Section 1401a of the Tariff Act prescribes a six-step method of valuation. The second, third, fourth, fifth and sixth steps are each permissible only if the previous step is not feasible. The six-step system embodied in section 1401a conforms to a recommendation of the Tokyo round of GATT (see Section 9 below). The primary method of valuation is the transaction value as expressed in the commercial invoice. This is generally not applicable to a transaction between related parties. The first three of the five secondary steps, which the Customs Service may employ in descending order, are: the transaction value of identical goods sold for export; the transaction value of similar goods; the resale price of the imported goods. If none of the foregoing yields a basis for valuation, Customs must use the so-called computed value. This is the cost to the exporter of raw materials and labor, plus his expenses and profits. The determination of this computed value is a tedious and time-consuming process. As a last resort, the appraiser is directed to use as basis for valuation such reasonable method as appears appropriate. Section 1401a is the so-called new valuation statute. The old valuation statute, Section 1402 of the Tariff Act, is less important because it applies today to only a few articles that appear in the so-called final list. The noteworthy items on this list are benzenoid chemicals, coal tar products, rubber-soled footwear, automobiles and automobile parts.

One of the troublesome points in connection with valuation is the treatment of commissions. The general rule is that buying commissions are not dutiable, but selling commissions are. It is sometimes difficult to distinguish between a buying agent and a selling agent. An agent may perform both functions, especially in the Far East. Importers should see to it that the relationship and position of a foreign agent is clearly defined.

## 4. MEASURES AGAINST UNFAIR FOREIGN PRACTICES

Business in the U.S. accuses foreign exporters of unfair trade practices. Conversely, U.S. business has been criticized abroad for engaging in unfair practices. Without expressing judgment, the present purpose is merely to explain what measures are provided in the U.S. for combatting what are perceived to be foreign unfair practices.

(a) The most often used weapon is the imposition of *anti-dumping* duties. Dumping occurs when a foreign exporter sells goods to the U.S. at less than fair market value, which means a price which is lower than the price charged in the exporter's home country, if such sale causes or threatens to cause injury to U.S. industry, or prevents the establishment of an industry in the U.S. In such instance, a special dumping duty is assessed in addition to the regular duty. However, this cannot be done unless and until (i) the Customs Service has determined that the price of the imported article is not the fair market value, and (ii) the International Trade Commission in Washington, D.C., has determined that there is injury or threatened injury to U.S. industry. The proceeding for the assessment of the dumping duty starts with a complaint filed by an interested party with the Commissioner of Customs. It entails protracted hearings before the Commissioner and the International Trade Commission.

The anti-dumping provision of the Tariff Act was introduced by the Anti-Dumping Law of 1921. The older Anti-Dumping Act of 1916 (15 USC Sec. 72) has fallen into disuse, although it was resurrected in 1975 by a lower Federal court, in an isolated case involving the Japanese electronics industry. The 1916 Act has the advantage of allowing a treble damages claim by an injured party. On the other hand, it requires proof beyond a reasonable doubt that the dumping by the defendant was committed with the intent of destroying or injuring a U.S. industry.

(b) The second weapon in the U.S. arsenal is the imposition of countervailing duties. Such duties will be assessed if the Customs Service finds that a foreign shipment is subsidized. In such case, the import duty will be increased by the amount of the subsidy. Unlike the case of dumping, the Tariff Act does not require that the subsidy injure or threaten to injure U.S. industry. Although GATT requires that countervailing duties cannot be assessed unless a domestic industry is injured (see Section 10 below), this does not apply to countervailing duty provisions which predate GATT. Consequently, it does not apply to the countervailing duty provisions of the U.S. Tariff Act. There are, however, two exceptions. In 1974, after entering into GATT, the U.S. extended the countervailing duty rules to the importation of merchandise which is otherwise duty-free. No countervailing duty may be assessed against such merchandise unless injury to a U.S. industry is demonstrated. The second exception is more important. In 1979, in the GATT negotiations known as the Tokyo Round, the U.S. agreed to conform to the GATT requirement of a finding of injury. This applies only with respect to subsidies paid in countries that are parties to the multinational trade agreement, or which have enacted substantially similar legislation into their own law. Most trade partners of the U.S. are in this category. However, one should not commence proceedings for the imposition of countervailing duties without first determining whether it is necessary to prove that the foreign subsidy injures U.S. industry.

The subsidy need not be a direct payment to the foreign exporter. In a case involving Italian steel products, the subsidy consisted of an Italian tax credit. Other examples of what constitutes a subsidy are a freight allowance, a special depreciation rate, exemption from real estate taxes, or interest assistance for plant modernization. In a landmark decision in 1973, the Michelin company had been induced to build a tire plant in Nova Scotia by the granting of special benefits, which were held to constitute a subsidy justifying the assessment of countervailing duties. The benefit consisted of the allowance of accelerated depreciation by the Federal Government of Canada, low interest rates, and property tax concessions by the provincial government of Nova Scotia and its municipalities. A significant factor in this case was that the plant capacity exceeded the needs of Canada and was clearly geared to exports to the U.S.

Benefits under a general regional support program and payments from an agricultural development fund have been ruled not to be subsidies.

A petition for the imposition of countervailing duties should be filed simultaneously with the U.S. Department of Commerce and the International Trade Commission. The Department of Commerce determines whether subsidies are being paid, and the ITC determines whether the U.S. industry is being injured by the subsidized imports. The final decision as to whether countervailing duties are to be imposed is made by the Department of Commerce, not by the Customs Service.

(c) A potent weapon in the U.S. arsenal is the *presidential retaliation* power. Responding to the clamor of U.S. industry and labor against what is regarded as unfair practices, Congress enacted the Trade Act of 1974, which conferred upon the President the power to take retaliatory measures against foreign unfair practices. The President acts through the U.S. Trade Representative, whose office was established by the 1974 Trade Act. The Act deals with many other facets of international trade, not only with retaliation. The retaliation power is created in order to respond to any act, policy, or procedure that (i) violates an international trade agreement, or (ii) is unjustifiable, unreasonable or discriminatory, and burdens U.S. commerce. The statute directs the President to take such action as he may deem appropriate in order to eliminate the unfair practice. As a practical matter, this means intergovernmental negotiations. For instance, the retaliation power has been used to induce foreign countries and industries to establish export quotas, which results in limiting imports into the U.S. The President is also authorized to suspend, withdraw, or prevent the application of benefits of trade agreement concessions to the offending country, and to impose duties or other import restrictions on the products of such country.

(d) The Trade Act of 1974 also gave the International Trade Commission a role in combatting foreign unfair competition. It can issue a cease and desist order, or an exclusion order, when it finds that the importation of an article or its sale by the importer tends to destroy, actually destroys, substantially injures a domestic industry that is efficiently and economically operated, or prevents the establishment of such industry. Also the Commission may find that such importation or sale restrains or monopolizes U.S. trade.

While the Commission may proceed on its own initiative, most proceedings under this statute are initiated by a private complaint, which is processed as in ordinary litigation (see Chapter 23). In the past, the majority of the cases were patent infringement cases (see Chapter 19, Section 7).

The requirements for obtaining relief are rather forbidding. A complainant must prove to the satisfaction of the Commission (i) the existence of an unfair method or act in the importation of an article, (ii) that the unfair method or act destroys or substantially injures a U.S. industry or prevents the establishment of such an industry, and (iii) if an existing industry is threatened, that it is efficiently and economically operated.

The injury to an existing industry must be substantial. The word *substantial* does not appear in the anti-dumping law or in the countervailing duty statute. However, if there is not a showing of substantial injury to U.S. industry (not only to the complainant), a complainant is not likely to prevail. This seems to be the major reason why so few petitions for anti-dumping or countervailing duties are successful.

(*e*) Another remedy against unfair conduct abroad is the provision in the Tariff Act that authorizes the President to establish new or additional duties on the products of a country that is found to discriminate against U.S. products. Presidential action will be taken only after an investigation by the International Trade Commission.

(*f*) The restraints of the antitrust laws (see Chapter 17) apply, of course, to international trade. In this connection, the remnants of the old Wilson Tariff Act that are still in force should be mentioned because they specifically condemn restraints in the importation of goods. Section 5 of the Federal Trade Commission Act, which prohibits unfair methods of competition, also applies.

(*g*) To complete this catalog of remedies against unfair actions, Section 526 of the Tariff Act should be mentioned. It bars the importation of goods bearing an unauthorized U.S. trademark. This was discussed in Chapter 20, Part A, Section 12.

## 5. RELIEF FROM IMPORT INJURY

The Trade Act of 1974 provides U.S. domestic industry with relief from foreign competition under certain circumstances. It is an escape from GATT (see Section 9, below) and, therefore, often referred to as the 'escape clause'. The complainant need not show unfair trade practices abroad, but it must be demonstrated that (*a*) imports are increasing, (*b*) domestic industry has suffered serious injury or is threatened with serious injury, and (*c*) the serious injury is caused by the imports. The complaint must be filed with the International Trade Commission, which may recommend import relief or adjustment assistance to the President. If the President accepts the recommendation, he can impose quotas or tariff rate quotas (if imports exceed the quota, the duty goes up), increase import duties, negotiate orderly market agreements (this means foreign quotas) with foreign governments, or order adjustment assistance to businesses or to affected workers. Adjustment assistance means money grants.

Invoking the escape clause, in January 1984, producers of copper, steel and footwear filed petitions with the International Trade Commission, seeking the imposition of import quotas. The copper producers asserted that during the last two years the industry had lost one billion dollars, that production had dropped by 400,000 tons, that imports had more than doubled between 1979 and 1983, and that 18,000 workers had been laid off.

U.S. industry has not had much success with this provision of the Trade Act of 1974. It is very difficult to demonstrate that a particular importation is a 'substantial cause of serious injury'. Thus, the Commission has ruled that the importation of foreign automobiles, which has caused much trouble in Detroit, is not a substantial cause of serious injury.

Another relief provision of the Trade Act of 1974 allows the government to take appropriate action if imports from a communist country cause a market disruption. It is not necessary to demonstrate dumping, or a subsidy, or any unfair action. Nevertheless, this provision has not served any appreciable useful purpose. In 1980, the International Trade commission determined that the importation of hydrous ammonia from Soviet Russia was causing a market disruption. Thereupon, the government imposed an import quota. This restriction soon was lifted, when the International Trade Commission found that there had been no market disruption.

### 6. NON-TARIFF BARRIERS

Non-tariff barriers are the means by which protectionism undermines the free trade policy.

Non-tariff barriers take many forms, among them the following: hidden subsidies, strict standards supposedly to protect health and safety, requirements for testing of products that differ from those used in the exporting country, foreign exchange laws that restrict the purchase of foreign goods, and red tape in processing imports. U.S. exporters have often complained that the import formalities in Japan are so complicated and so drawn out that exportation to Japan is seriously hindered. In November 1982, a U.S. machine tool manufacturer petitioned the President to deprive users of Japanese machine tools of the investment tax credit (Chapter 8, Section 6). This would be a novel U.S. non-tariff barrier; the petition is not likely to succeed. Performance requirements are another form of non-tariff barrier that is not uncommon in developing countries. This means that an exporter must agree, as a condition for entry, to export a certain dollar amount or percentage of the company's production. Developing countries resort to this when they do not allow cash payment for their imports. The performance requirement may compel a cosmetics manufacturer to sell coffee or some other unrelated product. Performance requirements are not limited to developing countries. The U.S., at present, is suing the Canadian government for violating GATT (see below) because of demands made of Canadian subsidiaries of U.S. corporations under Canada's Foreign Investment Review Act. Non-tariff barriers are also found in the field of intellectual property. In some countries, broad areas of invention, such as chemical products, are not subject to patent coverage. Unreasonable compulsory licensing has hampered U.S. exports. Sometimes, there are unreasonably short-term patent rights involving the inability to enjoin infringement, and practically impossible burdens of proof of infringement placed on a patent holder.

Heading the list of non-tariff barriers are the import quotas by which many countries seek to protect their domestic industries. In the U.S. such quotas are constantly sought for such commodities as shoes, textiles, automobiles and steel. The question whether such quotas should be imposed often involves broad policy considerations. For instance, if the importation of steel plate from England is not hindered, the steel processing industry in the U.S. may have to dismiss thousands of workers. The quota system can be circumvented easily, since it is imposed on a country-by-country basis. When sweater quotas were imposed against Hong Kong and Taiwan, the manufacturer shifted to the Maldive Islands, for which no quotas existed. Each category of merchandise from every country requires a separate Department of Commerce investigation before a quota can be set. Another problem with the quota system is that manufacturing rights within the quotas are the object of trading abroad. For instance, in Hong Kong one can buy the right to manufacture sweaters. The U.S. textile industry is the greatest beneficiary of the U.S. quota system, because foreign textile imports have increased tremendously and are threatening to smother the domestic industry. Some U.S. manufacturers resort to manufacture in countries like Korea, or in the Caribbean area, where wages are lower than in the U.S. This embitters U.S. labor leaders. The quotas also involve political problems. The heaviest textile imports come from China. The machinery and electronics industry in the U.S. does not wish to have its exports to China curbed.

The Buy American laws may be viewed as a non-tariff barrier. However, these laws are of limited scope. They apply only to governmental procurement, and are subject to many exceptions. They are no serious threat to international trade.

## 7. EXPORT PROMOTION

This is, of course, the other side of the coin. The Trade Act of 1974, which was referred to above in the enumeration of weapons against perceived unfair acts abroad, was enacted for the purpose of expanding and promoting U.S. foreign trade and exports.

Mention was made in Chapter 8, Section 24, of the income tax incentives designed to promote exports.

The Export Trading Company Act of 1982 is designed to increase U.S. exports, by authorizing banks to invest in export trading companies, and by exempting many joint export activities from the antitrust laws. The Act envisages that many small and medium-sized businesses might alone, or in conjunction with others, especially banks, expand in the export field or form a new Export Trading Company. The statutory definition of the Export Trading Company has been likened to the definition of a camel (a horse designed by a committee). In order to obtain exemption from the antitrust laws, the exporter must obtain a special certification. The practical effect of this legislation is in doubt, but the intent is clear.

Reference must also be made to the Edge Act Corporation (see Chapter 14, Section 12) as a vehicle for export promotion.

## 8. EXPORT RESTRICTIONS

In spite of the general desire to increase exports, the U.S. has found it necessary, or advisable for political reasons, to restrict certain export activities.

Although the export controls, by their language, apply to all countries, the practical effect of the application of the regulations since 1950 has been primarily to limit exports to communist countries. Following the adoption by the Nixon administration of a policy of détente, after the enactment of the Export Administration Act of 1969, the U.S. moved toward the normalization of its economic and trading relations with most of these countries. The restrictions imposed by the Trade Act of 1974, which are discussed above, have slowed that trend. The 1969 Export Control Act states that it is U.S. policy 'to encourage trade with all countries except those countries with which such trade has been determined by the President to be against the national interest' and 'to restrict the export of goods and technology which would make a significant contribution to the military potential of any other nation or nations which would prove detrimental to the national security of the U.S.'.

The foregoing explains the licensing policy of the Department of Commerce. Export licenses for shipment to communist countries are generally granted, unless military equipment or defense-sensitive products are involved. It is sometimes difficult to determine the use to which an exported article can be put. For instance, rock-bit drilling technology, seemingly, is of no conceivable military use, and a license to export such technology to Russia was granted. It has since been learned that the technology has been used by the Russians to develop armor-piercing shells that can penetrate a tank. The Export Administration Act of 1979 requires exporters of sensitive articles to stipulate in their sales contracts that the item will not be re-exported to an Eastern Bloc country. The validity and efficacy of such clauses is dubious, especially since some foreign countries openly disapprove of them. The fact is that the Soviet Union has been hindered but not prevented from acquiring the U.S. high technology in which it is interested.

Export control is a political weapon. President Carter forbade the export of American grain to Russia in protest against the invasion of Afghanistan. President Reagan canceled this measure because it hurt U.S. farmers. President Reagan also forbade the export of U.S. technology and equipment for the Russian pipeline from the Ural mountains to Europe. He canceled this because of political protests from European allies.

The Export Administration Act of 1969 also deals with anti-boycott measures. It forbids participation in boycott measures directed against Israel, South Africa and Rhodesia (Zimbabwe). Proposals for participation in the boycott must be reported to the Export Control Office of the Department of Commerce. There is other anti-boycott legislation in effect in the U.S., which is well policed and with which one doing business in or with the U.S. should be acquainted.

Not all exports are controlled by the Department of Commerce. The export of arms, ammunition and implements of war requires a license from the State Department. Narcotics and marijuana are regulated by the Department of Justice. Specified materials and facilities related to the production of atomic energy are subject to license by the U.S. Energy Research and Development Agency. Watercraft are regulated by the U.S. Maritime Administration. A warship cannot be exported without an additional license from the State Department, but if the vessel is sold to be reduced to scrap, the Office of Export Administration in the Department of Commerce has jurisdiction. The export of natural gas and electric power requires a license from the Federal Power Commission. Agricultural products fall within the jurisdiction of the Department of Agriculture.

Mention must also be made of the Office of Foreign Assets Control of the U.S. Treasury Department, which has issued regulations with respect to assets of China, Cuba, North Korea, Cambodia and Vietnam. Exports to these countries require special licenses. The trade relations between the U.S. and the People's Republic of China are in flux and under constant consideration. The normalization of trade relations between the two countries has been hindered by two principal obstacles: (*a*) U.S. private citizens have substantial claims against China amounting to almost $200 million. Because of the private claims, Chinese ships and aircraft avoid U.S. territory (in order to forestall attachment), and financial arrangements between the U.S. and China must be carried out through third-country banks. Related thereto is the question of the disposition of Chinese assets that are frozen in the U.S.; and (*b*) the U.S. has not granted 'most favored nation' treatment to China. This means that the customs duties on Chinese goods are substantially higher than the duty rates on products of other countries. China is not a party to GATT.

## 9. GENERAL AGREEMENT ON TARIFFS AND TRADE (GATT)

GATT is an agreement between contracting parties, of whom the U.S. is one. It was not conceived as an international organization but it has developed into one. Although not originally so planned, GATT has a secretariat located in Geneva, Switzerland. A U.S. Senator once said, 'Anyone who reads GATT is likely to have his sanity impaired'; and a State Department high official is quoted as saying, 'Only the learned can communicate with it, and then only in code'. The incoherence and legal inconsistencies of GATT are of little interest to the business world. The fact is that GATT is alive, and has functioned since 1955. Originally, only industrialized countries having a free market economy and Czechoslovakia were members. Thereafter, Poland, Hungary and Romania joined. The members meet in negotiation rounds. To date, there have been six such rounds, of which the Kennedy Round of 1967 and the Tokyo Round of 1973/74 are the best known. The Tokyo Round caused significant changes and innovation in U.S. statutory law. The primary purpose of GATT is to arrange for mutual tariff concessions. GATT also imposes on all members the obligation to grant most favored nation treatment to each other. GATT deals also with dumping, export subsidies, export controls, and such international trade problems as are discussed in earlier parts of this chapter. There are many exceptions to the GATT rules, the most important of which is the escape clause (Article XIX).

GATT is not a strong organization, but it has provided an element of stability in international trade. As the U.S. Trade Representative wrote recently, 'Despite the most intense adversity, the trading system has survived these past few troubled years. Without GATT it simply could not have worked.' U.S. courts generally treat the GATT Rules as domestic law of the U.S., which means that GATT Rules can be superseded by subsequent legislation. Lawyers disagree on this point, and this creates substantial legal problems, the discussion of which is not the function of this book.

The complaint by the Common Market countries that the operation of the U.S. Domestic International Trade Corporation (DISC – see Chapter 8) is a violation of GATT has been smoldering for over ten years. The U.S. Government has promised a revision of the DISC system, but it is uncertain what Congress will do.

## 10. FOREIGN TRADE ZONES

These are areas in or adjacent to ports of entry that are treated as outside the customs territory of the U.S. The purpose is to encourage foreign trade. They are enclosed areas with facilities for loading, unloading, handling, storing, manufacturing and exhibiting goods, and for reshipping them. Importers may hold merchandise for display, and pending a sale. They may hold over-quota merchandise until a new quota period begins. They may manufacture parts into a product that carries a lower duty rate. For instance, paper is subject to a high duty. If the paper is printed in the zone, the finished product can be imported at a much lower duty. In a case reaching a Court of Appeals, Armco Steel Corp. tried to prevent the duty-free importation of steel barges by a Japanese steel concern that had brought dutiable steel into the zone and manufactured duty-free barges in the zone. Armco lost the case. Exporters also may derive advantages from the zone. When they move goods into the zone, the goods are considered exported. The exporter is then entitled to any applicable excise tax rebate or drawback. The goods can also be manipulated prior to shipment overseas.

Income derived from any operation within the zone is income from a U.S. source. It may be possible to structure the transaction in a manner that minimizes or eliminates U.S. income tax.

Related to the foreign trade zone program is the trade fair program, which is authorized by the Trade Fair Act. This Act permits the temporary duty-free importation of goods for display at a trade fair or exposition.

## 11. INSTITUTIONS

Among the institutions that are devoted to the promotion of foreign trade, the *Export-Import Bank* (Eximbank), in Washington, D.C., is best known. This is an agency of the U.S. Government. It aids in the financing of exports and imports, by direct financing or by guaranteeing or insuring credits that are extended by private institutions. Insurance is available against political risks or credit risks or both. Insurance is also available to exporters directly. Eximbanks sometimes lend money to the purchasers of U.S. equipment.

Another institution is the *Agency for International Development* (AID). It renders financial assistance to foreign, especially underdeveloped, countries. It is administered by the Department of State.

*The International Bank for Reconstruction and Development*, also known as the World Bank, is a specialized agency of the United Nations, owned by its member governments, of which the U.S. is one. The bank makes loans for projects in the territories of its member governments. The loans are made to the foreign government, or if the foreign government guarantees the payment of principal and interest, to private enterprises. The bank does not make loans that are obtainable in the private market at reasonable rates. It renders technical assistance in the planning of the project for which it lends funds. Affiliated with the World Bank is the *International Finance Corporation*, with headquarters in Washington, D.C., and offices in New York, London and Paris. It is also owned by the various member governments and its primary activity consists of investments in private enterprises. It does not accept any government guaranty. Another distinction from the World Bank is that the IFC subscribes to and purchases shares in private entities, as a means of promoting private enterprise in the member countries. IFC primarily supports industrial enterprises. There are a host of *Development Banks* in all parts of the world. What they have in common is that they provide funds for productive investments, and the technical advice needed to carry out such investments. A development bank may be government owned, privately owned, or mixed. The *InterAmerican Development Bank* was created by nineteen Latin American countries and the U.S. in order to accelerate the economic development of the member countries. All American Republics, except Cuba, are members. The bank makes loans, and is authorized to guarantee loans made by private investors.

*The International Monetary Fund* is sometimes mistaken for the World Bank. It is an international organization, headquartered in Washington, D.C., that is primarily concerned with international monetary problems and exchange rate fluctuations, which at times shake the international commercial community. The Fund also has certain responsibilities in the field of trade practices. By virtue of an agreement with GATT (*supra*), the Fund makes certain findings with respect to balances of payments and monetary reserves, which are binding on the contracting parties of GATT. These findings affect the GATT obligations.

## 12. INTERNATIONAL TRADE COMMISSION AND COURT OF INTERNATIONAL TRADE

The International Trade Commission in Washington, D.C., is the most important institution in U.S. international trade. Its functions have been mentioned throughout this chapter. It used to be called the U.S. Tariff Commission. It is a completely independent body and must be distinguished from the International Trade Administration, which is the name of the administrative arm of the Department of Commerce that administers various export and import programs. As stated above, the principal functions of the International Trade Commissions are: (*a*) to investigate alleged unfair practices, and (*b*) to determine whether a foreign practice complained of causes serious injury to a domestic industry.

The Court of International Trade in Washington, D.C., is an appellate court that reviews decisions of the Department of Commerce and the International Trade Commission. The review is based on the record established in the proceedings before the Department or before the International Trade Commission. A further appeal can be taken to the Federal Court of Appeals for the Federal Circuit.

CHAPTER 23

# LITIGATION

## *1. INTRODUCTION*

Litigation means combat by lawsuit. It is an undesirable, expensive and time-consuming method of settling disputes. But at times it is unavoidable. Some parties simply will not honor an obligation unless they are sued. And, of course, there are genuine disputes that call for a judicial decision.

Litigation in the U.S. is very different from that in many other countries – even England, where the U.S. rules of litigation originated. The U.S. has largely, but not entirely, outgrown the concept that a lawsuit is a sporting event between two adversaries, in which the judge merely acts as an umpire. The worst feature of this concept is that one tries to surprise one's adversary at the trial with unanticipated evidence. The answer to this undesirable tactic is the expanding set of legal procedures known as *discovery*. After a lawsuit has been commenced, each party is entitled to discover what evidence his adversary has or may present at the trial in support of the complaint, the defense, or the counterclaim, as the case may be. For instance, if a commercial complaint seeks the payment of $100,000 as damages, the defendant may wish to discover how the amount of $100,000 is computed. Discovery proceedings may consist of an examination of potential witnesses (which is also referred to as taking the deposition of witnesses) or written interrogatories to be answered by the adversary. Discovery proceedings are also used to elicit documents that will be used to support a claim or defend against it. This is particularly important in patent infringement suits and in antitrust cases. Discovery proceedings are sometimes the principal reasons why it takes a long time for a litigated case to come to trial. The proceedings are generally conducted in the offices of the attorneys for the adversaries, and judges become involved only if one side challenges a discovery request. Defense lawyers have been criticized for abusing discovery for the purpose of delay. There is trend to limit discovery by statutory time limits and by court orders. Finally, when the day of trial arrives, all the admissible evidence, including the pre-trial testimony of witnesses, may be presented again, this time to the judge or a jury.

The jury system generally slows down proceedings considerably, especially because of the strict rules of evidence referred to below. A jury may be used not only in criminal cases, but also in civil litigation. In many commercial cases, especially antitrust cases which extend over a period of months and often years, jurors find it difficult to remember everything they have heard and observed. In some courts, jurors are not permitted to take notes. One of the drawbacks of the jury system is that juries are generally empowered to fix the amount of the damages claimed by the plaintiff, and if they do, the amounts are sometimes enormous. As a limited exception to the sanctity of jury fact-finding, a trial judge may reduce the damages award if the judge finds it grossly excessive.

While most lawsuits are of the conventional kind, there is hardly any field of human endeavor in which disputes are not apt to end up in a court of law. Courts are called upon to decide election disputes or grievances over the actions or inaction of officers of the Federal, state and municipal governments. If an employer closes a plant, he may find himself hauled into court by a trade union. If a property owner feels aggrieved by the valuation of his property for real estate tax purposes, he will sue the municipality. If a nightclub owner feels aggrieved by a city ordinance forbidding topless dancers, he may sue the city. At times, if a citizen is dissatisfied with the administration of justice in the state, he may apply for relief in the Federal court. The possibilities are limitless. De Tocqueville observed some one hundred fifty years ago, in his study of the U.S., that Americans have a penchant for going to law to solve every conceivable kind of political, social and economic problem. This is still true. Foreigners are sometimes astonished that even lower court judges issue decrees of far-reaching political consequence.

Another facet of litigation is the practice of many lawyers of bringing suit against everybody in sight who may possibly be liable. When a real estate developer in Ohio was refused permission by the city council to build homes on his 160 acres of land, he commenced a lawsuit against the city, each individual member of the city council, each member of the city planning commission, the city's law director, the city engineer, the finance director, and the mayor. This is called multidefendant litigation. The expectation of the plaintiff in such a case often is that one of the defendants, or his or its insurance company, will make a settlement in order to avoid the expense of litigation. Another motive may be that one of the defendants has enough money to pay, even if the other defendants do not; or that the statute of limitations may not bar all claims, even if some defendants may use it as a defense.

Federal judges are appointed for life. State judges are generally elected or appointed for limited periods. It is often thought that Federal judges are of higher quality than state judges, but this is an unfair generalization. Both Federal and state judges are generally chosen from among practicing lawyers. Ideally, they are appointed or elected on the basis of professional merit. Actually, the choice depends mostly on their political affiliation or activities, past or present, although there is an increasing effort to minimize that factor. Many years ago, a visiting Lord Chancellor of England told a meeting of the

American Bar Association that he would never appoint as judge a member of his own political party. This astonished the listeners because it was alien to their own thinking.

Lawyers who specialize in litigation work are called *trial lawyers*. Most law firms have one or more trial lawyers in their organization. They carry a heavy burden, because in many instances the judges rely on them not only for an orderly presentation of the facts, but also for legal research. For instance, in New York and elsewhere, judges expect pre-trial legal memoranda, which state (*a*) what the parties expect to prove, and (*b*) what legal principles and precedents apply. After the conclusion of the trial, unless a jury renders a verdict, a post-trial memorandum by the lawyer for each side is expected, to analyze the evidence adduced at the trial and present a legal evaluation. In a non-jury case, judges rarely announce their decision at once. They often do not decide for many months, if not longer.

When a lawyer appears for a litigant, he need not submit a power of attorney. He or she is presumed to be empowered to act for the litigant.

Few litigated cases come to trial. Most are settled by compromise. Indeed, many lawsuits are commenced in the expectation that they will lead to a settlement.

This is also true of the so-called class actions, which merit mention in these introductory remarks. A class action is initiated by one or more individuals for the benefit of all persons who may be in the same position as the plaintiff(s). An important class-action area is securities fraud (see Chapter 18), where class actions are frequently instituted by one or more shareholders who assert that they and others similarly situated have been damaged in connection with the purchase or sale of securities. If the action succeeds, or if a settlement is reached, the other members of the class are entitled to the same benefits as the plaintiff(s). The court must certify class-action status.

## 2. THE COURT SYSTEMS

The U.S. has two court systems, the Federal system and the state system (of fifty-five jurisdictions). Both systems are overloaded, and there have been attempts to remove some litigated matters from the jurisdiction of the courts. The U.S. Supreme Court accepts for review only a small fraction of the appeals brought to it. In many instances people can choose which of the two systems to use.

However, if a case involves a matter that is exclusively regulated by Federal law, such as patent matters (Chapter 19) or bankruptcy matters (Chapter 25), the Federal courts have exclusive jurisdiction. In all other matters, resort to the Federal courts is optional. The Federal courts have jurisdiction if the litigants are resident (domiciled) in different states or countries (diversity of citizenship), and if the subject matter in dispute has a value of more than $10,000. The Federal system consists of District Courts, in which one of a complement of District Judges acts as sole judge. The Bankruptcy Judges are attached to the District Courts. Federal magistrates are subordinates of the District Court. Appeals from the District Court go to one of the twelve regional Circuit Courts of Appeals, where decisions are generally made by a panel of three judges. There is also the U.S. Court of Appeals for the Federal Circuit, discussed in Chapter 19. Its jurisdiction is nationwide, but it is limited to patent appeals, appeals from decisions of the Court of Claims and decisions of the Court of International Trade. Above the Circuit Courts of Appeals is the Supreme Court of the U.S., whose nine judges always sit together as one panel. The Federal Court of Claims in Washington, D.C., is on the level of the Federal District Courts, and adjudicates claims against the Federal Government, including tax claims. The District Courts have concurrent jurisdiction of such claims. Other examples of claims against the Federal Governments are damages claims by inmates of a Federal prison (e.g. for wage payments), and damages claims by the former Iranian hostages. The Court of International Trade is also a Federal court (see Chapter 22). The U.S. Tax Court in Washington, D.C., renders decisions as a collegial body, but its judges hear cases in all parts of the country. It is a court of limited jurisdiction. Its decisions are appealable to the appropriate Circuit Court of Appeals.

The lowest courts in most states are the justice courts, presided over by a justice of the peace. Generally, a justice of the peace has no legal training, and handles little more serious than local traffic violations. Above the justices of the peace are lower courts of limited jurisdiction, called municipal courts, county courts, district courts, or, in New York City, Civil Court. The jurisdiction of these courts is limited because a statutory ceiling is set on the amounts they may handle and certain types of litigation are excluded from their jurisdiction. The New York Civil Court also handles disputes between landlords and tenants.

Above the courts of limited jurisdiction are the courts of general jurisdiction. They bear different names. In California and New Jersey, for instance, they are called Superior Court. In New York, the court of general jurisdiction is called Supreme Court. In Pennsylvania, the name is Court of Common Pleas. Most states have a special court for the administration of decedent's estates and related matters. These courts are most often called Probate Court. In New York, the name is Surrogate's Court. In Pennsylvania, it is Orphans Court. There are also Family Courts, which have a circumscribed jurisdiction in family matters and proceedings involving juveniles. All these state courts are courts of first instance. Most states have intermediate appellate courts. The highest court of appeal in the state is generally called the Supreme Court. In New York, though, the highest court is named Court of Appeals. Appeals from the highest state court go to the U.S. Supreme Court, when, for example, a federal constitutional issue is involved, but only if the Supreme Court allows it, which is rare.

Almost always, appellate courts will not review the fact finding of lower courts. They will review only questions of law. If a lower court errs in excluding proffered evidence, a question of law is presented which may be the basis of an appeal.

## 3. JURISDICTION

If a court does not have jurisdiction, it has no power to adjudicate a dispute brought before it, and whatever the court does or decides is a legal nullity.

There is subject matter jurisdiction and there is personal jurisdiction. As was stated above, a state court does not have subject matter jurisdiction in a patent infringement suit. A Federal court has no subject matter jurisdiction where a New Jersey creditor sues his New York debtor in New York for less than $10,000.

The matter of personal jurisdiction is more complicated. Personal jurisdiction must be distinguished from *venue*. The term *venue* denotes the proper geographical location of the court, which is determined by statute and which may be the residence of the plaintiff or the residence of the defendant, or the place where the defendant is engaged in business. Thus, if A of New York sues B of Chicago in a California court regarding a matter having nothing to do with California, the California court would not be the proper venue for the suit, although it would have personal jurisdiction of the defendant if the defendant was personally served in that state.

Personal jurisdiction generally requires personal service of a summons upon the defendant.

An important exception to the requirement of personal service is the so-called long-arm statute, which in one form or another has been enacted in most states. The theory of such a statute is that personal jurisdiction exists if one or one's agent comes into the state to transact some business (or if one commits a tort in the state). In product liability cases (Chapter 10) a foreign manufacturer may be sued in a state where his product was sold by a distributor. A sustained activity, which would constitute doing business, is not required. In practice, this often gives the plaintiff a choice of the forum in which to litigate. A prominent judge wrote, 'Doing business is to transacting business what a full-length mink coat is to tennis shorts. A single transaction in New York may satisfy the requirement of purposeful activity necessary for a finding of transacting business.' Some courts have held that the existence of a subsidiary corporation in the state can confer jurisdiction over the parent, which might be located in a foreign country. In an Iowa case, long-arm service on the German manufacturer of three drop forging hammers sold to the plaintiff in Iowa by an intermediary was upheld on the basis of warranties made by the manufacturer. This was an extreme and probably erroneous decision, but it illustrates a risk of doing business in the U.S.

Germany and other countries allow the parties to stipulate the forum for adjudicating future disputes, i.e., exclusive jurisdiction of a particular court. An exporter of Dutch herring could stipulate in his conditions of sale to a customer in Germany that all claims must be submitted to the courts in Düsseldorf. Such a provision violates the general rule in the U.S. that a forum must have substantial contacts with the transaction in suit. Seemingly, this principle was changed by a U.S. Supreme Court decision which upheld the parties' stipulation of the courts of England as the forum for litigating any future dispute under a maritime contract between a German company and a South American company. It would be risky, however, to consider that decision as abrogating the U.S. principle, because the decision involved a possible maritime dispute, regarding which English judges have superior expertise and apparently were considered being like arbitrators.

It is a fundamental principle that a defendant must be served, which means that he must receive a summons (usually accompanied by a complaint). This notice provision is not unique. In the Federal District Courts, the complaint is filed with the clerk of the court, and must be served on the defendant within 120 days thereafter. The summons usually is served directly on the defendant by a professional process server engaged by the plaintiff's attorney. When it is impossible to make personal service on the defendant, alternate service may be resorted to as authorized by statute or court order. One alternate method of service is service by publication, which is favored in situations where the whereabouts of the defendant is unknown. It is a rather ludicrous method, because the court ordering publication in one or two newspapers generally selects a favored newspaper that needs the advertising revenue but does not have a wide circulation. The defendant is quite unlikely to see the advertisement. If the defendant resides in a foreign country, service may be made by an official foreign process server, by a foreign lawyer, or by mail. Since 1967, the U.S. has been a party to the Hague Convention of 1954 on the Service Abroad of Judicial and Extrajudicial Documents in Civil and Commercial Matters. This is discussed in Section 8 below.

When the defendant resides outside the U.S., the need for personal service and *in personam* jurisdiction may be avoided by attaching property of the defendant within the U.S. If the plaintiff finds such property in the U.S. and is able to obtain a court order of attachment, he obtains *quasi in rem* jurisdiction, i.e. jurisdiction over the attached property. Attachment is one of the provisional remedies discussed in Section 7, below. If the plaintiff wins the lawsuit, he can seek satisfaction out of the attached property. This remedy may be worthwhile, especially if the attached property consists of a bank account. However, the procedure is complicated and expensive (see Section 7, below). Sometimes, however, it is the only effective remedy available.

The appearance in the action by a defendant or his lawyer makes personal service unnecessary. Parties in the U.S. who contract with parties abroad will often demand that the party abroad appoint somebody in the local jurisdiction on whom process can be served.

## 4. THE PLEADINGS

Strictly speaking, the pleadings consist only of the complaint and the answer thereto, and a reply to any counter-claim in the answer.

A lawsuit is commenced by the service of the summons on the defendant. The summons is not a pleading. It merely summons the defendant to appear before the court. In some jurisdictions, the summons may be served on the defendant without a complaint, because it is expected that the firing of an opening salvo will suffice to bring the defendant to terms. Occasionally, the summons is served without a complaint because the plaintiff does not have enough time to prepare the complaint before the statute of limitations will outlaw the claim. When the defendant is served with a bare summons, he can demand that he be furnished with a complaint. The complaint is a detailed statement of claim. The complaint may state several claims or causes of action. They need not be consistent with each other.

The complaint is limited to a statement of ultimate material facts. Legal arguments have no place in it. They belong in a separate memorandum of law.

Within a prescribed period of time after service of the complaint, the defendant must serve an answer, in which the allegations of the complaint are either admitted or denied. The answer may also plead so-called affirmative defenses, such as the statute of limitations (prescription). The answer will also allege any counterclaim that the defendant may have, again limited to an averment of the material facts.

When the complaint and the answer have been served, issue is said to be joined. There usually follow discovery proceedings, as discussed in Section 1, above, and various motions. Then comes the trial, which may take place several years after the summons and complaint are served. After the jury verdict, or, in case of a non-jury trial, after the decision of the court, an appeal may follow. As stated above, the appeals court accepts the fact finding of the lower court, and rules only on errors of law. To enable it to do so, a transcript of what transpired at the trial must be furnished to the appellate court. The transcript contains not only the testimony of the witnesses, but also every word that the judge and the lawyers spoke at the trial. Generally, the transcript also contains copies of the motion papers that bear on the appeal, but not any memorandum of law. The appeals court requires fresh memoranda of law.

## 5. MOTION PRACTICE

This section lists some significant motions that may be made in the litigation. Motions are addressed to the court and must be decided by the judge. A motion is generally supported by an affidavit of facts and a memorandum of law. Motions are usually contested, and result in an answering affidavit and an answering memorandum of law. Motions consume a considerable amount of time, and delay readiness for trial.

The following list of motions is illustrative, not exhaustive.

(a) The defendant may make a motion to dismiss the complaint, if he believes that the complaint does not state an actionable claim or if the alleged claim is outlawed by the statute of limitations.

(b) The defendant may move to make the complaint more specific.

(c) The request for an examination of witnesses, or the production of documents, or the reply to written interrogatories, referred to under the collective name of Discovery, may be contested and be the subject matter of motions by both sides.

(d) A frequently made motion of great importance is the motion for summary judgment. The basis of such a motion is that there is no real dispute about the facts with respect to one or several of the pleaded causes of action, or the counterclaim. The theory is that the contest between the parties is purely legal, and that a judge is in a position to decide the legal question or questions involved without a trial. If the judge finds that this is so, he will decide the case, or a part of the case, summarily. If he denies the motion, the case will proceed to trial and the party who lost the motion for summary judgment might still win the case after trial.

There are other possible motions too numerous to mention.

## 6. EVIDENCE

Before one starts a lawsuit or decides to defend one, it is important to evaluate what evidence is admissible in support of one's position. Unlike the legal tradition in other countries, the Anglo-American legal system does not allow the free evaluation of all evidence that a litigant may wish to submit. Strict rules of evidence exclude certain types of proffered proof. The principal justification for these rules is the need to prevent jurors from being led astray, but the rules of evidence apply also in non-jury trials.

One of the most characteristic principles is that no testimony is admissible at a trial unless the witness giving such testimony can be cross-examined. This explains why a trial court in the U.S. will not accept the written opinion of an expert who is not present at the trial. Hearsay evidence (Jones says he heard Smith complain of the defendant) is not admissible because (Smith) the person who is reported to have said something out of court is not present and cannot be cross-examined. The hearsay rule is rather complicated and subject to a number of exceptions.

The statements of a deceased person are usually not admissible as evidence, and generally, a witness may not testify about conversations with a deceased, in connection with claims by or against the estate of the deceased. There are many exceptions and qualifications to this rule (the so-called 'Dead Man's Statute'). There are many more rules of evidence which must be observed, but the foregoing suffices to illustrate what trial lawyers have to contend with. If a litigant relies on foreign law to support a claim or a defense, it is necessary to prove the foreign law, like any other fact. Documentary proof may be available, but may not be persuasive. It is best to prove foreign law by the testimony of an expert. Although fact finding in a jury trial is ordinarily the province of the jury, the determination of foreign law is made by the judge. The law of a sister state is foreign law, like the law of Brazil or China. However, the procedural statutes of most states provide that a court may take judicial notice of the law of a sister state. In some states, this is mandatory.

In international cases, the rule of *forum non conveniens* may be important, especially when a foreign plaintiff seeks adjudication in the U.S. because U.S. law is more favorable to him than the law of another available forum. The rule allows a court in the U.S. to decline jurisdiction if the preponderant proof is located outside its jurisdiction. The doctrine was successfully invoked by Piper Aircraft Corp. and Hartzell Propellers Inc. These two U.S. manufacturers were sued in the United States by the survivors of six Scottish residents who died in a plane accident in Scotland, where the wreckage and the witnesses were located.

The suit was based on a claim of product liability (see Chapter 10), as to which a manufacturer is held to a stricter standard in the U.S. than in Scotland. In its decision rejecting the lawsuit, the Supreme Court recognized that a plaintiff's choice of forum should be given deference but 'a foreign plaintiff's choice deserves less deference'.

## 7. PROVISIONAL REMEDIES

The principal provisional remedies are the temporary injunction and the attachment. Both are available upon a unilateral application to a judge, by a so-called *ex parte* motion, which means a motion made without notice to the adversary (but notice must be given promptly thereafter). An application for an *ex parte* order must be supported by a sworn affidavit and such other proof as the applicant considers pertinent. The application will not be granted unless the applicant supplies a bond as security for the damage that may be inflicted on the adversary if the latter should prevail either in opposing the *ex parte* order or on the trial of the merits of the case.

A temporary injunction may be granted where an applicant can convince the judge that the applicant is threatened with irreparable injury by the conduct of his adversary, if the conduct is not enjoined at once, pending the issuance of a permanent injunction after trial. Judges are reluctant to grant a temporary injunction. They prefer to order a speedy trial at which it will be determined whether the applicant is entitled to a permanent injunction.

The provisional remedy of attachment is important in international business, especially when it is difficult to obtain personal jurisdiction over the defendant. As stated above (Section 2), the attachment establishes a quasi *in rem* jurisdiction over the property of the defendant.

## 8. INTERNATIONAL LEGAL ASSISTANCE

International legal assistance is necessary when it is desired to effect service on a person who resides in another country, or to obtain evidence in another country.

Service of process in countries which are parties to it is regulated by the Hague Convention on the Service Abroad of Judicial or Extrajudicial Documents in Civil and Commercial Matters. The Convention was ratified by the U.S. in 1956. It requires service through consular channels. A court recently ruled that substituted service by mail on the defendant in Germany made pursuant to a court order was invalid, and that U.S. courts are bound to use the channels prescribed by the Convention. In other cases the Inter-American Convention and Protocol on Letters Rogatory must be followed. This applies alike to U.S. plaintiffs and to plaintiffs abroad who wish to institute a lawsuit in the U.S. Plaintiffs and their lawyers in the U.S. are sometimes unwilling to make the extra effort required to observe the Convention.

Americans who contract with a party abroad can sometimes avoid the problem of obtaining jurisdiction over the foreign party by demanding that the latter appoint a local agent for the service of process (usually his lawyer). In some instances, an out of state resident is deemed to have appointed a local agent to accept process. For instance, in New York and other states the Commissioner of Motor Vehicles is considered as having been appointed as such agent by any motorist who drives his or her automobile in the state. The articles of incorporation of a corporation in New York and other states must contain an appointment of the Secretary of State for service of process against the corporation.

Foreigners whose home countries are not a party to an international convention can arrange for service in the U.S. through diplomatic channels. Upon receipt of such a request from abroad, the Department of State will transmit the request to the Department of Justice, which will arrange for service by a U.S. marshall. Unlike the practice in some other countries, the U.S. has no objection if the service is made by a consular officer of the foreign country requesting the service.

The same route may be followed if evidence is sought in the U.S. The request for such evidence must emanate from a foreign judicial authority, which usually means a foreign court. If a witness in the U.S. declines to comply with the foreign request, the Department of Justice will petition the competent Federal District Court to apply appropriate measures of compulsion, requiring the witness to produce the evidence. If the petition is granted, the court will issue a subpoena to the witness and appoint a commissioner to secure the evidence. The commissioner is usually a local lawyer. The request for judicial assistance need not be made through diplomatic channels. The foreigner may also petition the appropriate Federal court directly, through a local lawyer. An even simpler method is to arrange for the taking of testimony by a foreign consul in the U.S. Some countries consider the taking of evidence by foreign consular officers, in the absence of a treaty, as an impermissible infringement of the nation's own sovereign judicial powers. In the U.S. no such restrictions exist.

When Americans sought to obtain evidence in a foreign country, foreign judicial assistance used to be obtained through *letters rogatory*, which is a translation of the civil law concept of *commission rogatoire*. Letters rogatory are issued by a U.S. court and addressed to a foreign court. In what manner they are transmitted depends on the law of the foreign country. Letters rogatory must still be used for any country that is not a party to the Hague Convention on the Taking of Evidence Abroad in Civil or Commercial Cases. As stated above, the U.S. is a party to this Convention and so are the major nations of the Western World. The Convention calls for a letter of request by a U.S. court. This is obtained on motion, accompanied by draft letter of request. It is advisable to prepare the draft with the assistance of a lawyer of the foreign country, because when received abroad, the letter of request is subject to objections based on the law of the receiving country. For instance, parties abroad may argue that discovery is not a judicial proceeding within the meaning of the Convention. The seeker of foreign evidence must be prepared to overcome formidable obstacles that stem from the different practices and customs abroad. The procedure is expensive and time-consuming. The problem of foreign resistance to attempts at extending U.S. jurisdiction beyond its borders has been touched upon above. (Chapter 1, Section 13.)

## 9. FOREIGN JUDGMENTS

The valid final judgment of a sister state of the U.S. enjoys full faith and credit in all other states by command of the U.S. Constitution. Foreign judgments are usually recognized as a matter of international comity. This means that a U.S. court will accept the judgment of a foreign court without requiring that the issues decided by the foreign judgment be relitigated. It must be understood, however, that recognition is not the same as enforcement. There is a Uniform Foreign Judgment Enforcement Act, but so far only a few states have adopted this Uniform Act. The principal commercial states, such as New York, Illinois and California, have not.

One enforces a foreign judgment by using it as a basis for a domestic judgment. The plaintiff in the domestic enforcement action must produce a properly authenticated foreign judgment that, on its face, appears to be valid and final, and ask the U.S. court for the relief granted in the foreign judgment. As the foreign judgment may be expressed in a foreign currency, the plaintiff must translate the foreign currency and ask for a U.S. dollar judgment. The usual rule for currency translation is the judgment day rule, which means that the plaintiff is awarded the U.S. dollar value as of the date the U.S. court enters its judgment.

Some courts refuse recognition of a foreign judgment, if there is no reciprocity. This point is rarely raised. In any event, it is a matter of defense that must be pleaded and proved by the defendant. Other possible defenses are that the foreign court had no jurisdiction, or that it has disregarded the due process of law, as that concept is understood in the U.S. Foreign default judgments will be recognized if the defaulting defendant was given notice of the foreign lawsuit and was given an opportunity to defend against it.

The defendant may also plead *res adjudicata* or *collateral estoppel*, which are legal shorthand expressions for asserting that the identical claim has already been adjudicated in another litigation between the parties, or that the disputed issue has been adjudicated in a litigation between the plaintiff and another party.

As is true of all other branches of the law, the enforcement of foreign judgments follows no uniform guidelines and is subject to qualifications and exceptions.

## 10. EXPENSES

The expense of litigation is a cause of concern. When a judgment directs that the losing party must pay the costs of the proceedings, it means generally the court costs, which are low. It does not mean the cost of the lawyers, which may be high. Generally, each party must pay its own lawyers. There are exceptions to this rule. Certain statutes in the fields of civil rights, environmental law and consumer law allow the courts to assess all lawyers fees to the losing party. In other instances, the court has the power to direct the loser to pay all fees if the action has been brought frivolously. This judicial power is seldom exercised. It seems, though, that it is being done in a growing number of cases. Mac-

Donald's, the fast food chain, was able to collect nearly two million dollars from a French franchisee which had brought a frivolous suit against it. The Shell Oil Company had similar success after it won a suit brought by a Brooklyn gasoline station which had been closed down by Shell.

The fees of most lawyers are computed on an hourly basis. The charges range generally between $50 and $250 per hour, although 'big time' lawyers often charge considerably more. Sometimes lawyers will agree on a contingent fee, which means the lawyer gets a percentage of any monies recovered if he wins the case, and nothing if the case is lost. While contingent fees are illegal in most countries, they are legal in the U.S.

It is advisable to make an explicit fee arrangement, preferably in writing, when one employs a lawyer.

Out-of-pocket disbursements are not part of the lawyer's fee.

CHAPTER 24

# ARBITRATION

## 1. INTRODUCTION

Until the early part of this century, many practicing lawyers and judges disliked and distrusted arbitration as a method of resolving disputes. For a variety of reasons, this antagonism persists in some quarters. The laws of a few states are inhospitable to arbitration, and arbitration agreements made in those states are not binding.

Arbitration has become very popular in the U.S., not only in the commercial community but also as a means of resolving industrial disputes. This chapter is, of course, concerned only with commercial disputes. Most states have enacted arbitration statutes. They include all commercially important states. There is also a Federal Arbitration Act. The Federal Act governs arbitration submissions involving maritime transactions and interstate and foreign commerce. The Act's recognition of arbitration as a valid means of resolving disputes is considered Federal substantive law, which prevails even in states that do not recognize arbitration. The significance of this is illustrated by a case in which the contract between a Missouri corporation and a Delaware corporation provided for arbitration. Missouri does not recognize arbitration, and the Missouri corporation revoked its agreement to arbitrate. This was sound under the law of Missouri, where the contract was made. but since the contract involved interstate commerce, Federal law applied. As Federal law recognizes the validity of an arbitration agreement, the revocation was held inoperative.

Except for certain non-arbitrable matters (see Section 2, below) all commercial disputes may be decided by arbitration. An award may direct specific performance. The principal advantages of arbitration are that it consumes less time than court proceedings, it is free of many legal strictures, such as the rules of evidence (Chapter 23, Section 6), one can choose the locale

255

of the proceedings, and in many instances the arbitrators are experts on the subject matter of the dispute. Privacy and informality are also prized as advantages of arbitration. A disadvantage is that, except in the case of misconduct of the arbitrator(s), the arbitration award is final and not appealable. Whether arbitration proceedings are less or more expensive than court proceedings cannot be stated with any degree of assurance. Lawyer's fees aside, court costs in the U.S. are low, and generally lower than the expenses of institutional arbitration proceedings. Arbitrators sometimes serve without fee; but, if not, their fees are generally modest. Lawyers' fees are not much different from those in court proceedings, but as arbitration proceedings are usually of shorter duration than court litigations, the legal fees for arbitration will aggregate less. They will be higher if the lawyer is required to travel to a foreign forum for the arbitration. In some arbitration proceedings, savings are sought to be effected by dispensing with the services of a lawyer. This may turn out to be an expensive saving!

A public policy advantage of arbitration is that it relieves the workload of the courts. Indeed, some state laws prescribe compulsory arbitration for issues of minor importance.

The arbitration clause in an agreement may be waived. It is held to be waived if a party to an arbitration agreement commences court proceedings. The other party to the agreement need not accept this result, and may bring on a court motion to compel arbitration; but if such other party appears and participates in the court action, it is considered as having likewise waived the arbitration clause.

## 2.  NON-ARBITRABLE MATTERS

The former bias against arbitration caused the exclusion from arbitration of all matters involving family relations, the administration of decedents' estates, and issues concerning corporate management. These exclusions no longer prevail. However, disputes involving the public interest are still reserved to the judiciary, and are not arbitrable. They include divorces, antitrust claims, securities law violations, and claims alleging violation of the usury laws. Punitive damages claims are likewise excluded from arbitration.

Any issue of public policy is outside the scope of arbitration. An employee asserted the invalidity of a clause in his employment contract, which stipulated forfeiture of profit-sharing rights in case he resigned and took employment elsewhere. The court denied enforcement of the arbitration clause, because the forfeiture provision involved a matter of public policy in California. Disputes about restrictive covenants in employment contracts, although often involving public policy considerations, have generally been allowed to proceed to arbitration.

The rule of non-arbitrability of disputes concerning the Federal securities laws, is subject to exceptions. The rule is based not only on public policy considerations, but also on statutory prohibitions and on a seminal Supreme Court decision. The Supreme Court has allowed an exception in international disputes involving a disagreement between a U.S. manufacturer and a German citizen. Another exception exists for disputes between members of a stock exchange, who unlike the public at large, are supposedly able to fend for themselves. Finally, no bar to arbitration exists if the arbitration agreement is made after a securities law violation is claimed to have occurred. The rationale for this exception is that since the parties may settle such claims out of court, they must also be free to settle the claims by arbitration.

The same rationale has been suggested with respect to existing claims (as distinguished from future claims) for violation of the antitrust laws. This is doubtful, because any antitrust claim involves the continuing interest of the public.

With respect to antitrust disputes, it should be noted that the exclusion applies also to state statutes. Thus, it has been ruled that the Consumer Protection Act of the state of Washingon is an antitrust law, and that claims thereunder may not be settled by arbitration.

To prevent frivolous securities or antitrust claims from delaying arbitration, a court may, in appropriate cases, allow arbitration to proceed prior to the resolution of the non-arbitrable claims, or it may decide the non-arbitrable issues prior to arbitration.

## 3. THE ARBITRATION AGREEMENT

The arbitration agreement is in the nature of a contract, subject to the general rules of contract law (see Chapter 9). The agreement must be in writing but it need not be signed. There must be consent to the arbitration by both parties; e.g., reference in a sale agreement to the 'cotton yarn rules' has no effect unless it is shown that both parties clearly understood that those rules include an arbitration agreement. If an arbitration clause is not part of a purchase order, and appears for the first time in the seller's confirmation, it constitutes a material alteration of the proposed contract and is not binding unless agreed to by the purchaser. If the printed acknowledgement of a purchase order contains, in small print, an inconspicuous arbitration clause, the buyer can claim that he did not consent to arbitration, even though he accepted the merchandise.

If a party claims that an entire agreement, which contains an arbitration clause, is invalid because it was induced by fraud or for some other reason, the question frequently arises whether the arbitrator(s) have any authority to act. If the agreement is invalid, so the argument goes, the arbitration clause is necessarily invalid. The courts have almost unanimously overruled this argument, and held that the arbitrator(s) must decide whether the agreement was induced by fraud or is invalid for any other reason. The rationale for this holding is that the agreement as a whole and the arbitration clause are separable. Consequently, the situation is different when the validity of the arbitration clause alone is in dispute. In that case, resort must be had to the courts. Illegality of a part of the contract does not vitiate the arbitration clause. When an Italian company resisted arbitration on the ground that the contract as well as the arbitration clause had been obtained by fraud on the part of the U.S. contracting party, the court ruled that there was no fraud, and ordered arbitration. This was a practical way of avoiding theoretical arguments.

If the potential defendant resists the institution of arbitration proceedings, the aggrieved party may apply for a court order to compel arbitration. This is not necessary where the applicable rules of arbitration allow the arbitration to proceed if the defendant, after due notice, defaults.

A party who disregards an existing arbitration clause may do so as a matter of oversight, or because there is a question of arbitrability. If a party disregards the arbitration agreement and commences a legal action in court, the defendant may apply to the court for a stay of court proceedings, or for an injunction.

Conversely, when arbitration is improper, the court may order a stay of arbitration. This applies, generally, where an issue is not arbitrable (see Section 2, above). It is illustrated by a case involving an agreement that purported to bind a corporate director to a specific course of conduct rather than allowing him to exercise his best judgment (see Chapter 11, Section 10).

## 4. THE ARBITRATOR(S)

Some consider it inadvisable to depend on the decision of one person and, therefore, recommend the use of three arbitrators. The International Chamber of Commerce, the American Arbitration Association, and similar institutional organizations will generally honor such agreements, even if they might ordinarily appoint only one arbitrator.

The conventional method is to stipulate that each party will appoint one arbitrator, and the two persons so appointed will select an umpire. The two appointed persons are generally partisans, and not arbitrators in the true sense. The method followed by the American Arbitration Association seems preferable. In the absence of an agreement to the contrary, the Association will submit to each party a list of potential arbitrators. Each party may strike out the names of unwanted candidates, and the Association will then pick one or three of the remaining names. The procedure under the auspices of the American Arbitration Association is less expensive than the procedure of the International Chamber of Commerce in Paris. If other methods fail, a competent court in the U.S. will appoint one or more arbitrators.

If an arbitrator has any connection with any of the parties or any of the witnesses who are to be produced, the fact should be disclosed promptly. Arbitrators must avoid the appearance of partiality. In a case which reached the Supreme Court, the third arbitrator (chosen by the two party nominees) failed to reveal to the plaintiff that he had performed occasional consulting work for the defendant. There was no proof that the arbitrator was guilty of fraud or bias. The Court ruled, nevertheless, that the award was void. This was an extreme decision and courts are generally not so severe. Nevertheless, an arbitrator should adhere to a high standard. If a party to an arbitration proceeding is aware that an arbitrator has a business connection with the adversary, a failure to object constitutes a waiver.

An active American judge is not permitted to serve as an arbitrator.

## 5. THE ARBITRATION PROCEEDING

Arbitration is usually conducted in a manner similar to that of a court hearing, although with less formality and without strict adherence to the legal rules of evidence (Chapter 23, Section 6). The arbitrator is in complete control. He need not follow customary procedure, even though he may thereby upset the lawyers who represent the parties. Arbitrators generally tend to receive all evidence that is offered, because refusal to hear material evidence after objection to such refusal may constitute grounds for *vacatur* of the eventual award. A conscientious arbitrator will require the parties to clarify their positions prior to the hearing, so as to determine the material issues in dispute. This may enable the arbitrator(s) to limit the presentation of evidence and to shorten the hearing. Disclosure and discovery are as important as in ordinary litigation (see Chapter 23, Section 1). The Federal Arbitration Act, and many state statutes, give the arbitrator broad discretionary powers to require the production of documents and to compel the testimony of witnesses. In New York, for instance, the arbitrator(s), and even the lawyers for the parties, have the power to issue a subpoena, which compels the attendance of witnesses or the production of documents. If the subpoena is not obeyed, a court order must be obtained. Courts are reluctant to grant relief on a direct application, preferring to have the arbitrator(s) act first; but they may do so in exceptional circumstances. Parties who wish to pursue this course, are advised to first investigate the practice of the particular court which they seek to approach.

In any event, applicants for court aid must make sure, and may have to go on record to confirm, that they are not thereby waiving the right to arbitration. This applies also if a party seeks a provisional remedy (see Chapter 23, Section 11), which only a court can grant. Courts are not inclined to, but occasionally may, grant a termporary injunction in an arbitrable matter. The Federal Arbitration Act makes provision for the libel and seizure of a vessel or other property in aid of an ensuing arbitration proceeding. Outside the field of maritime law, it is not possible to make a general statement about the availability of attachments prior to arbitration. The highest court in New York recently ruled that attachment in aid of a future arbitration award is impermissible. It is likely that the legislature will change this.

At the beginning of the arbitration hearing, it is customary for each side to make an opening statement, in which they outline their respective positions. The arbitrator(s) may or may not wish to hear this. The same is true of the closing statement. Often, after the closing of the hearing, the lawyers for the contestants may offer to submit to the arbitrator(s) memoranda or briefs. The arbitrator(s) are free to decide whether they will hear opening or closing arguments or receive briefs.

## 6. THE AWARD

The award must be rendered within the time period fixed by the agreement or the rules of the organization under whose auspices the hearing has taken place. An award rendered after the expiration of that time is a nullity.

The award need not, and as a rule does not, state the grounds of the decision of the arbitrator(s). This rule differs from the arbitration law of many countries. Most arbitrators adhere to this practice. It eases their workload and may avoid attacks on the award. On the other hand, it is often disappointing to the unsuccessful party, which would like to know why it lost. Mistakes of law or fact are permissible, but irrationality is not. The following New York case is an example of irrationality. A contract for the sale of textiles limited the seller's liability to the purchase price. In the arbitration award, the buyer was awarded a sum in excess of the purchase price. The court voided this award. It recognized that the arbitrator might have considered the clause that limited the seller's liability as unconscionable and hence unenforceable. But it was not apparent that the arbitrator had this in mind. His award was, therefore, deemed to be irrational. The *vacatur* of the award might have been avoided if the arbitrator had deviated from the usual practice and had given an explanation of his reasoning.

## 7. MODIFICATION OF THE AWARD

Arbitrators may generally modify an award after it has been rendered, if a minor unintentional mistake has occurred, such as an error in a computation.

The competent court will modify an award, upon application of a party, if it is shown to the satisfaction of the court that the arbitrator(s) made a miscalculation of figures, or a mistake in the description of any person, thing or property. The court may also modify an award if it was rendered on a matter not submitted to the arbitrator(s). However, the court will not make any decision that affects the merits of an award on the matter submitted to arbitration. In New York, the court may order a rehearing before the arbitrator(s) if it finds that there was an unintended mistake. If the court finds corruption or misconduct, it may order a new hearing before new arbitrators.

## 8. CONFIRMING OR VACATING THE AWARD

In most instances, the unsuccessful party will abide by the award, and make it unnecessary for the successful party to take steps toward the enforcement of the award. However, the successful party has the right to apply to the court for confirmation of the award. A confirmed award is enforced like any other court judgment.

The unsuccessful party may challenge the award. He can do so by opposing the motion to confirm the award. Or he can make a motion to vacate the award. The motion will succeed if it can be shown that there was fraud, corruption or misconduct, or that the arbitrator(s) exceeded their power; or that the award failed to decide all questions submitted to arbitration; or if the award contains non-arbitrable matter.

Misconduct of one of three arbitrators is sufficient ground for *vacatur*, even if the award was made unanimously and the other two arbitrators were innocent.

A favorite reason for alleging misconduct is that the arbitrator(s) refused to adjourn the hearing in order to allow an absent witness to appear. Courts are rarely impressed by such allegation.

## 9. *INTERNATIONAL ARBITRATION*

The complexities of international commerce and the universal distrust of foreign courts have fostered a growing resort to arbitration in agreements between parties who are domiciled in different countries.

The preparer of an international arbitration agreement must consider, and should cover in the agreement, (*a*) the legal system under which the arbitration will operate, (*b*) the arbitration system that is to be used, and (*c*) the law that will govern.

The last point is the easiest. The general preference is that no law shall govern the decision of the arbitrator(s). This does not mean that, if an agreement made in country X is not valid there unless in writing, the arbitrator(s) can disregard this. If the arbitrator(s) are free to apply such principles as they deem fair and just, the likelihood exists that they will be guided by their national notions of justice, which may be different from the notions of the contestants. This consideration may, or may not, lead to an agreement on the applicability of some national law.

As to the arbitration system, the preference seems to be arbitration under the rules of the International Chamber of Commerce (ICC). The system of the American Arbitration Association (AAA) is less well known abroad, although it has very attractive features (see Section 3, above). Then there are the Uncitral rules, adopted by the UN Commission on International Trade Law in 1976. Unlike the ICC and the AAA, Uncitral is not an institution and performs no administrative services. Another choice is the rules of the Arbitration Institute of the Stockholm Chamber of Commerce (SCC). SCC is often used in arbitration agreements with parties in Soviet Russia and other Eastern countries.* There are other institutions and a number of trade associations that provide arbitration rules and services. An alternative to all of the foregoing is *ad hoc* arbitration. This choice has the advantage of avoiding the payment of administration fees to any of the institutions. But precautions must still be taken to insure that the death or unavailability of an appointed arbitrator, or the refusal of one party to comply with the agreement, does not make the arbitration agreement ineffective. One method of dealing with this problem is to stipulate the application of an existing national code. Another method is to let some mutually acceptable judge or institution fill the vacancy.

The legal system is the one that prevails at the agreed upon location for the arbitration. The procedural laws of that country govern, regardless of where the agreement was made. When parties agree to conduct arbitration in a named jurisdiction, they undertake to submit themselves to the procedures of that jurisdiction to bring the arbitration to an effective conclusion.

---

* See optional arbitration clause for use in contracts in USSR–USA trade, reprinted 27 Am. J. of Comp. Law 478 (1929).

The U.S. procedural system has been outlined in the preceding sections of this chapter. Preferred locations abroad are London (England), Paris (France), Zurich (Switzerland) and Stockholm (Sweden). Before agreeing on arbitration in any of these or other places, it is advisable to inquire into the applicable local procedures.

The decisions of arbitrator(s) everywhere are subject to a minimum degree of judicial scrutiny. In civil law nations, as in the U.S., arbitral awards can only be set aside by the courts when elementary procedural guaranties have been abridged, as when there has been a denial of due process or misconduct by an arbitrator. In England the courts used to supervise the arbitrators to a degree that made London an undesirable place for arbitration. This was drastically changed by the 1979 Arbitration Act. This English legislation abolished, at least for international arbitration, the 'case stated' doctrine, which allowed a party and any arbitrator to request, at any stage of the proceeding, a court ruling on a question of law. This rule often had caused substantial delay and expense. The 1979 Act also curtailed judicial review of awards, but not entirely. It is advisable to include, in any agreement that calls for arbitration in England, a so-called exclusion agreement. Next to London, Zurich is a favorite locale for international arbitration. There have been complaints that, under the practice in Zurich, a clerk of the court, or an outside lawyer acting as clerk, is present at all arbitration hearings and at all meetings of the arbitrators. This may or may not be desirable, but in any event, should be investigated.

One of the features of arbitration in Stockholm is that under the rules of the Stockholm Chamber of Commerce, the chairman of the arbitration tribunal, or the sole arbitrator, is always appointed by the SCC, and the parties do not participate in the selection of the arbitrator(s). Another feature is that Swedish law gives the arbitrator(s) the authority to appoint experts on their own initiative.

The foregoing is in no way intended as an exhaustive statement of the points to be guarded against before stipulating a particular foreign location for arbitration.

The parties and their advisers must not forget to agree on the language in which the arbitration is to be conducted.

A U.S. party to an international arbitration agreement must also determine how to handle questions that are not arbitrable under U.S. law (see Section 2, above).

It is often advisable to provide for pre-hearing proceedings and the depositions of witnesses, as this may shorten the arbitration hearing and save expenses. Not all arbitration tribunals permit such procedures and others leave the matter to the discretion of the arbitrator(s).

The enforcement of the eventual award in the country of the losing party is, of course, of paramount importance. This is practically guaranteed by the Convention on the Recognition and Enforcement of Foreign Arbitration Awards of 1958, which was developed under the aegis of the United Nations and which is generally known as either the UN or the New York Convention of 1976.* At this writing, eighty countries have adhered to the Convention,

* See article by Pieter Sanders in 27 Am. J. of Comp. Law 433 (1976), with appended text of the Convention.

including the U.S. It applies to the enforcement of arbitration awards, not to the enforcement of judgments that confirm the awards. If enforcement is sought against a party in a country that has not accepted the Convention, it is necessary to have the award judicially confirmed and then to sue abroad on the basis of the confirming judgment.

Enforcement under the Convention may be refused if that would violate 'the public order'. However, this is usually understood to mean the international public order, not the national public order. To illustrate: the public policy of some countries is violated by an arbitration award rendered without attaching thereto a statement of the reasons for the award. but such an omission is not regarded as violating the international public order, and the countries adhering to the Convention will enforce arbitral awards which have statements of reasons attached.

When the U.S. Supreme Court, in the decision mentioned above in Section 2, stated that the principle of non-arbitrability of an agreement concerning the securities laws of the U.S. did not apply to international contracts, it cited the adoption and ratification of the New York Convention as demonstrating that national public policy is different from international public policy. Shortly thereafter, the Circuit Court of Appeals in New York wrote: 'The public policy limitation of the Convention is to be construed narrowly, and to be applied only where the enforcement would violate the forum state's most basic notions of morality and justice.'

Apart from the public order ground, enforcement of a foreign arbitral award can be refused under the New York Convention only on five enumerated grounds, which concern procedural irregularities.

The countries of Latin America have been slow to subscribe to the Convention. They have concluded their own Convention on International Commercial Arbitration in Panama in 1975, known as the Panama Convention. The U.S. has not yet ratified that Convention.

CHAPTER 25

# INSOLVENCY

## 1. INTRODUCTION

A debtor is insolvent when he or she cannot pay his debts as they become due. Such a debtor then frequently resorts to bankruptcy proceedings. The bankruptcy proceedings have two purposes: (*a*) to provide for the equitable distribution of the debtor's non-exempt assets, and (*b*) to allow the debtor a fresh start, financially speaking. The objective of the proceedings is either liquidation or rehabilitation. The latter is more frequent than liquidation. It is discussed in Sections 10 and 11, below. The term *bankrupt estate* refers to the assets of the debtor, less his or her exempt property, plus the property that is restored to the estate because the debtor has disposed of it by a voidable preference (see Section 3, below). Exempt property applies only to individuals. Every state has exemption laws that shield individuals from complete destitution by keeping certain property out of the reach of creditors. A number of Federal non-bankruptcy laws are to the same effect, e.g., the Social Security Act. The Bankruptcy Code gives the debtor the choice between claiming state exemption or Federal exemption. The Federal exemptions are generally more generous than the state exemptions. Some state laws prohibit the choice. The constitutionality of such prohibition is doubtful, because bankruptcy is the exclusive domain of Federal law.

265

The Bankruptcy Code (hereafter referred to as the Code) was promulgated in 1978, and has superseded the Bankruptcy Act of 1898. It is applicable to all proceedings initiated after September 30, 1979. The former law, which is not discussed here, is still applicable to proceedings that were pending on that date. Some of the judicial interpretations of the former Act are still of value. The original source of bankruptcy law is the U.S. Constitution, which vests in Congress the exclusive power to establish uniform laws on the subject of bankruptcy. The states have no authority to pass bankruptcy laws. They may, however, regulate other insolvency devices, which are discussed in Sections 14 and 15, below. The principal distinction between state laws and the Federal law is that a state may not provide for the discharge of a debtor's obligations without the creditor's consent, which is one of the main features of the Federal bankruptcy law (see Section 2, below). The Code also provides that certain institutions, such as banks, insurance companies, railroads, and municipalities may not be declared bankrupt. Banks and insurance companies may be liquidated under state law. Railroads and municipalities may be reorganized under special provisions of the Code.

In 1973 and 1975, prior to the enactment of the Code, the Supreme Court promulgated rules and forms to govern the procedural aspects of bankruptcy cases. They are not dealt with in this chapter. Suffice it to say that the old rules and forms are still valid, unless inconsistent with the Code. New rules and forms are in the making. This is not the only uncertainty. The position of the bankruptcy judges under the Code, and indeed the validity of the entire Code, has been put into doubt by a decision of the Supreme Court in 1981. Pending the resolution of this difficulty, the nation operates under the Code. This chapter is written without regard to this infirmity of the Code, considering it to be remediable. Bankruptcy judges used to be subordinate to the Federal District Judges; under the Code they are on an equal level with District Judges within the scope of their jurisdiction.

## 2. DISCHARGE – NON-DISCHARGEABLE DEBTS

The primary purpose of bankruptcy, from the debtor's standpoint is to obtain relief from indebtedness. Discharge from debts is the ultimate goal. It is available to individuals who seek liquidation of their affairs. It is not available to partnerships and corporations that seek liquidation. Partnerships and corporations may obtain discharge as part of a reorganization plan under Chapter 11 of the Code. It is also available to individuals who seek reorganization of their affairs, rather than liquidation, as provided in Chapter 13 of the Code, entitled Debt Adjustment for Individuals with Regular Income (see Section 11, below). A debtor may wish to pay his debt rather than be relieved of it. This calls for reaffirmation of the debt. It is allowed only upon notice to all creditors, and requires a court order.

In all instances, the discharge requires a court order. The discharge may be denied if the debtor is shown to have committed a dishonest or improper act. What this means is spelled out in section 727 of the Code, which is incorporated in the Code Chapter 11 provisions for reorganization. There is no such incorporation in Code Chapter 13, relating to personal reorganization; but since Chapter 11 and Chapter 13 proceedings both require that there be a reorganization plan between debtor and creditors, it may be assumed that dishonest or improper acts of the debtor will not be countenanced if not remedied.

All of the foregoing refers to *objections* that may be made to a discharge. This must be distinguished from the so-called *exceptions* to discharge. These exceptions refer to the fact that certain debts are not dischargeable in any bankruptcy proceedings (Code, section 523). The most frequently arising exception is taxes. In order to soften the blow of omitting taxes from a discharge, the Code gives the taxing authorities a priority in distribution (Section 5, below), which often reduces the amount that remains payable. Unscheduled debts are not dischargeable, i.e. debts that were not listed in the bankruptcy application. Debts incurred by fraud or other illegal acts of the debtor are not dischargeable. Also in this category are family obligations, such as alimony, and support payment. Fines and penalties are not dischargeable, nor are student loans.

It is not unusual for a debtor to dispute non-dischargeability, in which case a court hearing may ensue.

## 3. PREFERENCES

Before a debtor's insolvency becomes public, a favored creditor may obtain payment or security for the debt owing to him. This violates the principle of equal treatment of all similarly situated creditors, and the Code discourages such preferential treatment. It gives the trustee in bankruptcy the power to avoid such preferences, and to force repayment of preferential payments and annulment of a preferentially granted security. A preference is any transfer of the debtor's property to or for the benefit of a creditor, on account of a previously existing debt, while the debtor is insolvent and within ninety days (one year in the case of an insider who had reasonable cause to believe that the debtor was insolvent) before the filing of the bankruptcy petition. To constitute a preference, the creditor must have received more than he would obtain in the bankruptcy proceedings.

It is obvious that this provision is a cause for concern for creditors, and gives rise to much litigation.

The trustee who seeks to avoid a preferential transfer within ninety days prior to bankruptcy, need not show that the transferee knew of the debtor's precarious financial situation. However, if avoidance is sought of a transfer to an insider made within one year prior to bankruptcy, it must be proved that the insider had reason to believe that the debtor was insolvent. If at the time of the transfer the debtor had sufficient assets to pay all obligations, creditors have no cause to complain when the debtor makes a payment. However, the Code establishes a presumption that the debtor was insolvent during the ninety-day period prior to bankruptcy. The debtor may rebut this presumption.

Even exempt property may be reclaimed from a creditor if the other conditions of a voidable preference are present. Although a transfer of exempt property does not deprive other creditors, the protection of the debtor's assets and the policy of equality among creditors are held to be facilitated by applying the trustee's avoiding power to transfers of exempt assets. An important exception to the preference rule exists with respect to payments made in the ordinary course of business. A payment made within ninety days prior to bankruptcy is not regarded as a preference if it is made in accordance with prevailing business practice, provided it is made within forty-five days after the debt was incurred.

It must be borne in mind that a preference exists only if the transfer is made in payment of a pre-existing (so-called antecedent) debt. If during the ninety-day period the debtor pays $100,000 for equipment worth that much, there is no preference because new value is received for cash. Preferences are the cause of much litigation. For instance, it is arguable whether payment under a letter of credit constitutes a preference.

## 4. SECURED CREDITORS

The creditors most in need of protection in a bankruptcy proceeding are the unsecured creditors. But, secured creditors, who have a lien on some of the debtor's property, do well to register their claims and participate in the proceeding. The property on which the secured creditor has a lien is part of the bankrupt estate, and the lien is subject to attack. The automatic stay (Section 7, below) inhibits the secured creditor in many respects, except as provided in Sec. 362 of the Code. This applies to all three categories of liens mentioned in Chapter 15, Section 1 (Statutory Liens, Consensual Liens and Judicial Liens against Real Property).

Another category of secured creditors is created by the Code. The Code regards as secured a creditor who has a right of *set off*. For instance if a bank has made a $10,000 loan to a debtor, and the debtor has a bank deposit of $6,000, the bank is secured in that it can set off the $6,000 against its claim for repayment of the loan. With respect to the remaining $4,000, the bank is an unsecured creditor.

In structuring a security agreement, the secured creditor should try to avoid becoming an insider within the meaning of the Code, which could result in depriving him of some creditor's rights.

## 5. PRIORITIES

Certain types of unsecured claims and expenses are entitled to priority in the distribution of the bankrupt estate over other unsecured claims, but only after satisfaction of the secured claims. There are six priority claims, which must be satisfied in the order stated in Section 507 of the Code, meaning that one priority must be satisfied in full before payment may be made on the claims in the next ranking category. The priorities are as follows: (*a*) Administrative expenses, which include salaries earned after the commencement of bankruptcy proceedings, and professional fees; (*b*) claims arising in the ordinary course of the debtor's business, after an involuntary petition for bankruptcy has been filed, but before the court has acted on it; (*c*) wage claims up to $2,000 (wage claims above that amount remain valid, but have no priority); (*d*) contributions to employee benefit plans, up to $2,000 per employee; (*e*) consumer deposits paid to a retailer for merchandise or services to be delivered in the future, up to $900 (this includes advance payments for dance lessons or a health club membership; and (*f*) tax claims. This last priority is limited to tax claims enumerated in the Code. Tax claims have a preferred status in other ways. In most cases, the government also has a tax lien, and is thus a secured creditor. Most tax claims are also in the non-dischargeable category (see Section 2, above), and it is to the debtor's advantage if a tax claim is paid as a priority claim.

## 6. *UNPERFORMED CONTRACTS*

The technical term is *executory contracts*. It refers to contracts which, at the beginning of the bankruptcy proceedings, are not, or are only partly, performed. Examples are an unexpired lease, a license agreement, contracts for the delivery of goods in the future, options to purchase land, and contracts to build and operate a shopping center. Another example is the collective bargaining agreement between a trade union and an employer. At this writing, Continental Airlines has filed for reorganization in bankruptcy, in the expectation that it will be relieved of its obligations under a collective bargaining agreement that it considers burdensome. The union calls this a union-busting tactic and asserts that the Airline is misusing the Bankruptcy Code in derogation of applicable labor law. The Code gives the trustee the power either to reject the executory contract or to assume it. If he assumes it, it becomes an obligation of the bankrupt estate, and full payment must be made. If the trustee assumes a lease, he must pay all arrears that may be due to the landlord. He may not assume a contract that requires a third party to render financing or certain other contracts of a personal nature.

The power of the trustee to assume or reject an executory contract is not absolute. Court approval of the trustee's decision is required. The court will generally approve rejection if assumption of the contract would be burdensome to the bankrupt estate. Whether it is burdensome is a matter of business judgment.

Some contracts contain a clause that makes the contract automatically terminable if one of the parties becomes insolvent, and especially if bankruptcy proceedings are instituted. Such claims are often called *ipso facto* clauses. They violate the policy of the Code which allows the trustee to reject or assume. The clauses are, therefore, invalid, unless the contract requires the extension of new credit to the bankrupt estate.

What happens if the contract is made subject to the laws of a country where an *ipso facto* clause is valid? This happens, for instance, in a license agreement where the licensor resides in country X, and is loathe to continue the license with a U.S. bankrupt. If the U.S. trustee wishes to assume the contract, he would probably be upheld because the center of gravity of the license contract is situated in the U.S.

If an executory contract is rejected by the trustee, the other party has a breach of contract claim for damages, which is treated as an unsecured creditor's claim.

Any contract, other than a personal service contract, which can be assumed may also be assigned. Clauses that prohibit such assignment are invalid. However, the non-bankrupt party is entitled to demand adequate assurance of future performance by the assignee.

## 7. AUTOMATIC STAY

This is an outstanding and most important feature of bankruptcy proceedings. Upon the filing of the petition, all actions against the debtor are automatically stayed. This means that all collection efforts are stayed, and that no new actions may be commenced. This was why the Johns Manville Corporation filed bankruptcy proceedings under Chapter 11, although it was solvent and remained so. However, it was threatened with numerous product liability suits by asbestosis victims, which, it said, would drive it into insolvency. As a result of the bankruptcy petition, nobody can commence or prosecute a lawsuit against Johns Manville, and the company continues to be solvent and prosperous. The case has raised many as yet unresolved questions about the fairness of the Code.

The automatic stay applies to the enforcement of any pre-bankruptcy judgment, any act to obtain possession of property, any act to create, perfect or enforce a lien, and any set off. However, there are certain exceptions, which are listed in Section 362(b) of the Code. The most important exceptions are that criminal proceedings against the debtor are not stayed, that governments may continue to enforce their police and regulatory powers, and that alimony, support and maintenance claims are not affected. Water and telephone service may not be discontinued because of unpaid bills. The supplier may demand assurance of future payments, which is usually furnished by a cash deposit.

An interested party may apply to the court for relief from the stay. The bankruptcy judge will grant such relief if shown good reason. A secured creditor is entitled to relief if he is not adequately protected. If a secured creditor shows that the collateral held by the bankrupt estate is depreciating in value, and that the trustee has made no provision for adequate protection of the secured party against such depreciation, he may grant relief by either allowing a foreclosure sale or effecting some other equitable arrangement. The problem of granting relief to secured creditors has proved particularly troublesome in Chapter 11 situations, where the aim is to rehabilitate the debtor and to continue the business. While the trustee has the power to sell assets of the bankrupt estate, he may not sell a secured creditor's collateral without court approval, which will not be granted unless the trustee has provided adequate protection for the secured creditor.

## 8. *VOLUNTARY PETITION*

Most bankruptcy proceedings are commenced by the voluntary petition of an individual debtor who is overwhelmed by his or her debts. A voluntary petition may look toward reorganization (Section 10, below) or toward liquidation under Chapter 7 of the Code.

A voluntary petition looking toward liquidation is available only to individuals, not to partnerships or corporations. While a partnership is not eligible, individual partners are. Partnerships and corporations can, of course, be dissolved in accordance with applicable state law. But they then do not enjoy the advantages of the automatic stay and of the discharge of unpaid past debts. Stockbrokers and commodity brokers are eligible, but subject to special rules. Nonresident aliens who have a bank account or accounts receivable in the U.S. are eligible, but only, of course, with respect to property located in the U.S.

The proceedings are commenced by the filing of a petition in the proper district, together with a list of creditors and a schedule of assets and liabilities. There are prescribed official forms. The filing operates as an automatic stay (see Section 7, above).

After the petition is filed, the court will appoint an interim trustee, who has all the powers of a regular trustee, and who will take charge of the bankrupt estate. At the creditors' meeting that follows, the creditors will elect a regular trustee, and they may elect a creditors' committee.

## 9. *INVOLUNTARY PETITION*

The involuntary petition is filed against the debtor by one or more creditors. One creditor is sufficient if the debtor has fewer than twelve creditors. In determining the number of creditors, the following are not counted: (*a*) employees of the debtor, (*b*) insiders, and (*c*) creditors who have received a preference (see Section 3, above), or a fraudulent conveyance, or who have a statutory lien or any other lien. While the foregoing classes of creditors are not counted in order to determine whether there are fewer than twelve creditors, they are not precluded from filing a petition for involuntary bankruptcy. The petitioning creditor must have unsecured non-contingent claims of not less than $5,000.

In all other cases, the petition requires three creditors who together have unsecured non-contingent claims of at least $5,000.

The fact that a creditor's claim is entitled to a priority (Section 5, above) does not disqualify the creditor. Priority creditors often file an involuntary petition when the debtor makes an assignment for the benefit of creditors (Section 14, below), or otherwise proceeds under state laws that would deprive the creditor of a priority position.

An involuntary petition is a pleading (see Chapter 23, Section 4) that commences a legal action. The allegations of the pleading will state the financial difficulties of the debtor. The prayer for relief will be either liquidation or reorganization under Chapter 11. The debtor may, of course, file an answer to the petition. The answer will usually challenge the standing of the petitioning creditors, or the alleged grounds of involuntary bankruptcy. The case will then proceed like any other litigation. While the case is pending, the debtor may continue to operate the business, but creditors may seek court appointment of an interim trustee to remove the debtor from possession and to proceed with liquidation. If the creditors have petitioned for liquidation under Chapter 7, the debtor has the right to convert the case into one for reorganization under Chapter 11 or Chapter 13. Conversely, if the original petition was for reorganization, the debtor does not have the right to demand liquidation; but the court may order such conversion if it considers it in the best interest of the creditors and the bankrupt estate.

If a debtor's estate is the subject of a bankruptcy proceeding abroad, the representative of the foreign bankrupt estate may file an involuntary petition against the debtor in the U.S., to permit the administration of the debtor's U.S. assets. The foreign representative may also apply for ancillary administration in accordance with Sec. 304 of the Code.

A creditors' meeting will be held, as in the case of the voluntary bankruptcy petition described above.

## 10. REORGANIZATION (CODE, CHAPTER 11)

This is the most constructive part of the Code because it looks to a rehabilitation of the debtor's business. Chapter 11 provides a method by which a financially distressed business may restructure its finances with a view to continued operation. Chapter 11 attempts to balance the competing rights of the debtor, the secured creditors, the unsecured creditors, and the shareholders of the debtor. Chapter 11 is not self-contained. There are many references to other parts of the Code that are applicable.

At this point it seems appropriate to introduce the U.S. Trustee, who has been appointed in eighteen Federal judicial districts pursuant to a pilot program established by Chapter 15 of the Code. The program has been established in one of the four districts of New York, in one of three districts of California, in the District of Columbia, the districts of Massachusetts, New Jersey and Delaware, and twelve other districts. The general task of a U.S. Trustee is to relieve the bankruptcy judge of administrative functions. In non-pilot districts, the court performs the functions otherwise delegated to the U.S. Trustee. In a reorganization case, the U.S. Trustee will appoint a committee of unsecured creditors. He may also appoint additional committees of secured creditors and of shareholders, if that becomes desirable. He will also appoint a trustee in bankruptcy, but that is, generally, only necessary if there has been misconduct on the part of the debtor. Generally, the debtor in a reorganization case is left in possession of the bankrupt estate and is allowed to operate the business that is sought to be rehabilitated.

The gist of the Chapter 11 proceedings is that a plan shall be worked out that will allow the debtor to resume unfettered operations. This requires coopera-tion among all interested parties. Generally, it involves a rearrangement of the positions of the various classes of claimants, and of the owner or owners of the debtor, who may be an individual, or partners, or shareholders. When a reorganization plan has been worked out among the various parties, a disclosure statement must be prepared and submitted to the court for approval.

The objective is a confirmation of the reorganization plan by the court. Any creditor, shareholder, committee, debtor, or, in appropriate case, the Securities and Exchange Commission, may object to the confirmation. It is not necessary, although desirable, to obtain approval of every class of creditors that is, in the technical language of the Code, *impaired*. The court may confirm the plan if at least one class of claimants approves. This is called the 'cram down' method because the plan is figuratively crammed down the throats of the non-assenting classes. However, the court may only approve the plan if it meets certain statutory requirements, which are stated in Section 1122 of the Code. Above all, the plan must be fair and equitable. A plan is not considered fair and equitable if it permits shareholders to retain their shares while proposing to pay a dissenting class of unsecured creditors less than 100% of their claims.

## 11. DEBT ADJUSTMENTS FOR INDIVIDUALS (CODE, CHAPTER 13)

The full title of Chapter 13 is, 'Adjustments of Debts of an Individual with Regular Income'. Its purpose is the same as that of Chapter 11, namely to effect the financial rehabilitation of an insolvent individual who wishes to satisfy his or her creditors rather than go into liquidation and obtain a discharge. The individual debtor, while under the protection of the court and the automatic stay, will work out a plan that will allow him or her to apply a portion of future earnings to the repayment of the debts over an extended period of time.

## 12. INTERNATIONAL BANKRUPTCY

The Code deals with several aspects of International Bankruptcy. The following merit mention.

The bankrupt estate includes all property of the debtor, wherever located. This includes property abroad. However, the U.S. has no means to force a foreign creditor to accept the automatic stay provisions of the Code or the discharge rules with respect to property abroad.

The Code applies only to persons that reside in the U.S. or have a domicile or a place of business or property in the U.S.

Where a foreign proceeding is pending, and assets of the debtor are located in the U.S., the foreign representative (defined in Section 101(20) of the Code) may commence an ancillary proceeding under Section 304, if he does not wish to commence a full bankruptcy case. Such an ancillary proceeding can be used to administer the U.S. assets, and prevent dismemberment thereof by local creditors.

If a foreign proceeding is pending, the U.S. court may dismiss or suspend a case that may have been commenced here.

A foreign bank or insurance company not doing business in the U.S. but having property in the U.S., may be the subject of a petition for liquidation under Chapter 7, or for reorganization under Chapter 11; but an involuntary proceeding against such a bank may only be commenced under Chapter 7, and only if a foreign proceeding concerning such a bank is pending (Section 303(k) of the Code).

## 13. ASSIGNMENT FOR THE BENEFIT OF CREDITORS

This is the most common of the state (as distinguished from Federal) devices for handling insolvency proceedings. It is an ancient method, by which a financially embarrassed debtor would assign all his property to a person who would undertake to pay the debtor's creditors out of that property. The assignee had the position of a trustee. However, the debtor could fix the terms of the trust. He could prefer one creditor over another and, generally, write his own bankruptcy law. Creditors had no control, nor could they be forced to consent to the proceeding. This led, gradually, to the abolition of the common-law method. Today, the assignment for the benefit of creditors is regulated by statute in all U.S. jurisdictions. But there is no uniformity, the lack of which at times creates difficulties in administration. When an assignment is made in one jurisdiction and the property is located in another, the question arises whether the assignee's title is superior to the claim of local creditors. A creditor who is dissatisfied with a debtor's choice of a state insolvency procedure will usually be able to file an involuntary bankruptcy petition under the Code.

## 14. OTHER STATE INSOLVENCY PROCEDURES

A debtor may make a composition with creditors, which is, in essence, an agreement as to how the debts will be paid. There would seem to be little objection to such voluntary agreement, if all creditors agree.

Sometimes, a receiver is appointed by a state court. If this is done, it is usually upon the application of a party who has lost confidence in the manner in which the owner of a particular property manages it. This is not a true insolvency measure, as it does not concern all creditors. The administration by the receiver is generally limited to a particular property.

If a corporation is insolvent, dissolution will often serve as the answer to the problem of equal distribution to all creditors.

## 15. TAXATION

In 1980, Congress amended the Internal Revenue Act to provide for the tax treatment of bankruptcy and insolvency proceedings. The statute is called the Bankruptcy Tax Act of 1980. It is an amendment to the Internal Revenue Code.

While forgiving a debt generally creates taxable income to the debtor, the Rule does not apply if the debt is discharged in connection with insolvency proceedings. The amount of the discharged debt is excluded from taxable income. This advantage is offset by the statutory provision that certain loss carryovers and credit carryovers from previous years must be reduced by the amount of the tax-free debt discharge. The statute provides for a sequential order in which these tax attributes are to be reduced. The law permits the debtor an alternative. Instead of reducing the above mentioned tax attributes, the debtor may choose to apply the amount of the debt discharged to a reduction of the basis of any depreciable property that the debtor may own. This would deprive the debtor of the tax benefit of depreciation. To illustrate: assume that an insolvent corporation in a Chapter 11 reorganization proceeding is discharged from a debt of $1,000,000. Assume also that the corporation has a debt carryover of $1,000,000 and a $1,000,000 basis for depreciable property. By electing to reduce the depreciation basis, the corporation preserves the net operating loss. It then can use the net operating loss to reduce future taxable income, and thus ease its cash flow problem.

CHAPTER 26[1]

# ACCOUNTING

## 1. INTRODUCTION

Virtually every business in the U.S. is expected to have its accounting records examined or reviewed by a public, i.e., independent, accountant. A certified public accountant (hereafter referred to as CPA) is a rigorously trained public accountant, who is certified as having established a thorough knowledge of accounting principles and applicable tax laws. Most businesses engage a certified public accountant or a firm of certified public accountants.

The present chapter deals only with some important highlights of accounting that are believed to be of particular interest to foreigners.

The functions of accountant and lawyer sometimes overlap. Some accountants try to be lawyers, some lawyers want to be accountants. Indeed, there are professionals who hold academic degrees in both fields, and are legally qualified as accountants and lawyers. At times, people wish to save professional fees by employing one person or firm to perform both functions. Most businesspeople in the U.S., however, recognize that the special skills of accountants and lawyers complement each other, and that both are needed.

One distinguishes between internal and external users of accounting information. Internal accounting, sometimes called management accounting, provides information for planning or controlling current operations. The directors of a corporation are responsible for the establishment of a proper internal accounting system. They are generally guided by the advice of the CPA.

The principal external users are investors, potential investors, creditors, potential creditors, the tax authorities and, sometimes, the Securities and Exchange Commission.

The independent auditor's primary function is to express an informed

---

1. This chapter was contributed by Lewis A. Helphand, CPA and Roy W. Hoffman, CPA of Lewis Helphand & Co., Certified Public Accountants.

professional opinion on the financial statements of the business enterprise he is examining. This attest function, as it is known, is highly valued by most external users.

The preparation of financial statements, and the audit, requires the exercise of professional judgment in a wide variety of situations and circumstances. Thus, the auditor's opinion is based on his examination of the financial statements and reflects his judgment of the fairness of the financial statements' presentation, in accordance with generally accepted accounting principles.

The auditor is responsible for his work and, accordingly, the issuance of an opinion imposes serious obligations on him. While the auditor has the sole responsibility for his opinion, as expressed in his report, the primary responsibility for a company's financial statements, including any accompanying footnotes, rests with the management of the enterprise under examination. This responsibility cannot be relieved by the engagement of an independent auditor.

There are three major types of audit reports which a CPA issues, depending on the instructions of the client. These are an audit opinion, a review, and a compilation. Each indicates the degree of work performed by the certified public accountant, and the extent of his responsibility. The distinction is best illustrated by quoting a typical auditor's letter. A certification letter reads as follows:

'We have examined the balance sheets of ABC Company as of (at) December 31, 19X2 and 19X1, and the related statements of income, retained earnings, and changes in financial position for the years then ended. Our examinations were made in accordance with generally accepted auditing standards and, accordingly, included such tests of the accounting records and such other auditing procedures as we considered necessary in the circumstances.

In our opinion, the financial statements referred to above present fairly the financial position of ABC Company as of (at) December 31, 19X2 and 19X1, and the results of its operations and the changes in its financial position for the years then ended, in conformity with generally accepted accounting principles applied on a consistent basis.'

A review letter's principal paragraph briefly explains the difference between a full examination and a review:

'A review consists principally of inquiries of company personnel and analytical procedures applied to financial data. It is substantially less in scope than an examination in accordance with generally accepted auditing standards, the objective of which is the expression of an opinion regarding the financial statements taken as a whole. Accordingly, we do not express such an opinion.

Based on our review, we are not aware of any material modifications that should be made to the accompanying financial statements in order for them to be in conformity with generally accepted accounting principles.'

A compilation letter's principal paragraph disclaims all responsibility:

'A compilation is limited to presenting in the form of financial statements information that is the representation of management (owners). We have not audited or reviewed the accompanying financial statements and, accordingly, do not express an opinion or any other form of assurance on them.'

The most comprehensive report is the certified statement, in which the CPA certifies that he has examined the inventory and the records of the company, and expresses the opinion that the statement accurately reflects the financial position of the company. In the second category, the CPA expresses no such opinion, because the review of the company records was more cursory and was based primarily on information supplied by the client. However, the CPA still confirms that the statement conforms to generally accepted accounting practices. The third category of the CPA statement is a mere compilation of the client's financial records, without independent audit.

## 2. RESERVES AND WRITEDOWNS

Foreigners must be cautioned that, in the U.S. the use of reserves and writedowns is not as permissible as in other countries. There is a strong trend to avoiding the use of the word reserve altogether. Generally accepted accounting principles recognize expensing an item when a liability has been incurred and/or an asset has been impaired. Reserves that represent liabilities that have not been incurred with reasonable certainty do not represent generally accepted accounting principles. The auditors of financial statements must analyze the nature of these reserves, and determine whether a liability has been incurred, or an asset impaired, or whether the reserves improperly relieve future accounting periods of expenses and losses.

The existence of hidden or secret reserves in a corporation's balance sheet means that the shareholders' equity is understated. This understatement may result from using higher than normal depreciation rates, by excessive provision for doubtful accounts (there are limited provisions in both accounting and the income tax law for allowances for bad debts and doubtful accounts), by debiting capital expenditures to expense, or by any other action that understates assets or overstates liabilities. The deliberate creation of hidden or secret reserves is inconsistent with generally accepted accounting principles.

The amount of a corporation's retained earnings available for distribution to its shareholders may be restricted by the action of the board of directors. The amount restricted, which is called an appropriation of retained earnings, remains a part of the retained earnings and should be so classified in the financial statements. Examples of appropriations of retained earnings are: appropriation for expansion of plant, appropriation for retirement of bonds, appropriation for redemption of preferred stock, and appropriation for contingencies. Generally accepted accounting standards usually preclude the use of the word reserve. Because its principal purpose is to indicate a restriction of retained earnings, the nature of the restriction can be set forth more clearly in a note to the financial statements than by an appropriation of retained earnings.

Slow moving inventory must be maintained at cost or the lower market value (see Section 5). Unlike the practice in some other countries, slow moving inventory cannot be written down arbitrarily, unless it is offered at a lower price to the customers. It can, of course, be destroyed, in which case it does not appear at all and for tax purposes it will be considered a total loss.

## 3. CAPITALIZATION v. EXPENSE

A common question is whether an expenditure for repairs or improvements should be regarded as an addition to the cost of acquiring the capital asset, or as a business expense. One speaks of *capitalizing* or *expensing* the cost of repairs or improvements. The dividing line between capitalizing the costs and recognizing expenses is often difficult to determine. Generally, capital expenditures are expenditures that add to the utility of the asset for more than one accounting period. Expenses are those costs that are chargeable to current operations and affect one accounting period. Generally the term *current* stands for one accounting period, defined as one year.

Capitalized items are charged against income through depreciation or amortization, as discussed in the following Section.

## 4. DEPRECIATION, AMORTIZATION AND DEPLETION

Depreciation is a system of accounting which aims to distribute the cost, or other basic value, of tangible capital assets, less the salvage value (if any), over the estimated useful life of the unit (which may be a group of assets), in a systematic and rational manner. It is a process of allocation, not valuation.

The meaning of the term *depreciation*, as used in accounting, is frequently misunderstood, because the same term is also commonly used in business to connote a decline in the market value of an asset.

*Depreciation* is the term generally used when discussing tangible capital assets.

*Amortization* is the term used to distribute the cost of intangible capital assets over the estimated useful life of that asset.

*Depletion* is the term used to describe the periodic charges against revenue made as 'wasting assets' are exhausted. The principal types of wasting assets are mineral deposits, oil and gas deposits, and standing timber.

The first factor to be considered in computing the periodic depreciation of a long-term asset is its cost. The other two factors to be considered are the length of life of the asset, and its market value at the time it is permanently retired from service. It is evident that neither of these last two factors can be accurately determined until the asset is retired. Therefore, they must be estimated at the time the asset is placed in service.

There are no hard and fast rules for estimating the period of usefulness of an asset. For example, the length of the estimated useful life of a building may vary from twenty to fifty years. While the trend seems to be to use twenty-five to thirty-five years of depreciable life for buildings, for financial statement purposes, it is not uncommon to see a fifty-year life used.

As stated in Chapter 8, Section 6, the Internal Revenue Service uses the Accelerated Cost Recovery System (ACRS) instead of depreciation. ACRS is a substitute for depreciation only with regard to the length of lives of depreciable assets. In order to encourage capital spending, the Congress allowed capital assets to be depreciated or 'recovered' much faster than under previous laws. ACRS is primarily used for income tax purposes, but it also may be used in financial statements, provided that there is no material distortion to the financial statements in which they are reported. The only exception seems to be with regard to buildings. Under the ACRS method, a building may be depreciated in as short a period as fifteen years. For financial statement purposes, this shorter period does not seem to be an acceptable period of time over which to depreciate a building.

It should be noted that there is provision made on the income tax forms to reconcile differences between financial statement accounting and tax accounting.

## 5. INVENTORY

The term *inventory* is used to designate merchandise held for sale in the normal course of business, and materials to be used in the process of production for sale. Excluded from this category are supplies that will be consumed in nonproducing operations. By definition, inventories are current assets because normally they will be converted into cash or other assets within one operating cycle. As mentioned previously, the term *current* denotes the operating cycle, which generally is assumed to be one year. There are two major concerns when examining inventories. The quantity of materials used and left over at the end of the operating cycle must be accounted for. Secondly, a value must be assigned to the material used and left over at the end of the accounting period.

The periodic system and the perpetual system are the two general methods employed to ascertain the quantity of material on hand at a specific time. The periodic system relies on a periodical physical count of the goods on hand as the basis for control. The perpetual system requires a continuous record of all receipts and withdrawals of each item of inventory. Many companies rely on both systems. The perpetual inventory system is used during the year and periodically test-checked.

The common objective of inventory measurement is the attempt to match costs with related revenues, in order to compute net income. The generally accepted accounting principles that govern inventory are consistency and disclosure. If the method used to value inventory from period to period is consistent, then the reader of the financial statements will have a basis for comparison. The reader of the financial statements must be made aware of the methods used to value inventory.

There are several methods of accounting for the cost of inventories. The two most widely-used methods are FIFO and LIFO. The first-in, first-out method (FIFO) assumes a flow of costs based on the assumption that the oldest goods on hand are sold first. The last-in, first-out method (LIFO) assumes a flow of inventory costs on the assumption that the most recently acquired goods on hand are sold first, because current costs are incurred to make current sales and to maintain an adequate inventory on hand. Under this view, the latest costs are most closely associated with current revenue and, thus, the matching principle of income determination is carried out. Both FIFO and LIFO are acceptable for accounting and tax purposes.

Determining the cost of inventory is only the first step in establishing the value to be placed on the balance sheet. Once the cost is known, the market value of the goods must be determined, in order to arrive at proper valuation for balance sheet purposes. The key to inventory valuation is the phrase *lower of cost or market*. The word *market*, as used in this phrase, means the cost of replacing the merchandise at current market value on the inventory date. Generally accepted accounting principles employ a conservative approach. Inventories are to be stated at the lower of *cost or market* for financial statement purposes. The resulting writedown, when the market is below cost, is a permanent charge to income. There is no generally accepted accounting principle that recognizes a writeup of inventory. It must be stressed that, for tax purposes, no reserves are permitted against inventory. The only adjustment allowed is the writedown to market.

When using the lower of cost or market approach, tax implications must be considered.


## 6. FOREIGN CURRENCY

All financial statements are expressed in U.S. dollars, and income taxes are computed in U.S. dollars. Foreign currency transactions must be translated into U.S. dollars. Such translation is also required if a U.S. corporation has foreign branches or subsidiaries that report their operating results in other than U.S. dollars. Because of currency fluctuations, it may occur that a foreign currency translation results in a gain or loss where, in terms of the foreign currency, the opposite result was reached.

Realized gains and losses due to foreign currency exchange rate differences should be segregated from unrealized gains and losses. Unrealized gains and losses due to foreign currency exchange differences are contingencies that are booked on the financial statements. These gains and losses are contingent upon the payment or receipt of cash, thus converting them into realized gains and losses. A turnaround in foreign exchange rates may cause, for example, an unrealized loss to turn into a realized gain. The unrealized gain or loss account acts as a warning to management with respect to the realization of future gains and losses.

It is important to note that realized gains and losses due to foreign currency exchange differences are includable on U.S. income tax returns. Unrealized gains and losses due to foreign currency exchange differences are not includable on U.S.income tax returns.

Another area of concern is the accounting problem associated with translation of foreign currency fianancial statements, by foreign branches or subsidiaries, into dollars. There are several ways to translate foreign currency balance sheets. However, one method has been adopted as a generally accepted accounting principle in the U.S., namely translating all assets, liabilities, and contributed capital accounts at the current exchange rate as of the balance sheet date. Foreign currency revenues and expenses are also translated at the current rate, under this method. At first glance, it seems that the current rate method would eliminate exchange translation gains and losses. Unfortunately, such is not the case. A translation gain or loss arises when one attempts to reconcile retained earnings. Translation of beginning-period retained earnings at the end of the period exchange rate produces a translation gain or loss. The resulting gain or loss is accounted for in retained earnings as a residual, consisting of current rates of previous periods.

## 7. BUSINESS START-UP COSTS

It is recognized that the expense of starting a new business is generally substantial. The Internal Revenue Code defines as start-up expenditures the cost of investigating the creation or acquisition of an active trade or business, as well as the cost of creating such a business. These costs are not currently deductible as ordinary and necessary business expenses. The cost must be capitalized (see Section 3, above), but, as an alternative, the taxpayer is granted the option to treat such expenditures as deferred expenses that may be amortized over a period of not less than sixty months.

Expenses of creating a business are start-up costs that are incurred after the time a decision to acquire or establish a particular business is made, and before the business actually begins. Such expenses include: advertising costs, salaries and wages paid to employees who are being trained, and to instructors; travel and other expenses incurred in lining up prospective distributors, suppliers or customers; salaries or fees paid or incurred for executives, consultants, and professional services.

For accounting purposes, the determination of whether a particular cost should be charged to expense when incurred, or should be capitalized or deferred, should be based on the same accounting standards, regardless of whether the enterprise incurring the cost is already operating or is in the developmental stage.

# BIBLIOGRAPHY

*Chapter 2    Methods of Doing Business*

H. Henn, *Handbook of The Law of Corporations and Other Business Enterprises* (2nd ed., 1970). St. Paul, Minn.: West Publishing Co.

*Chapter 4    Constitutional Law Affecting Business*

J. Nowak, R. Rotunda, J. Young, *Constitutional Law* (2nd ed., 1983). St. Paul, Minn.: West Publishing Co.

*Chapter 5    Citizenship And Immigration Laws Affecting Business*

C. Gordon and H. Rosenfield, *Immigration Law and Procedure* (rev. ed., 1982). New York, N.Y.: Matthew Bender.

*Chapter 6    Investments and Acquisitions in the U.S.*

Fox and Fox, *Corporate Acquisitions* (1983) (four volumes, loose leaf). New York, N.Y.: Matthew Bender.
Kirk and Guillerm, *Direct Investment Techniques for the USA* (1983). Deventer, The Netherlands: Kluwer.
Starchild and Brundage, *Tax Planning for Foreign Investors in the United States* (1983). Deventer, The Netherlands: Kluwer.

*Chapter 7    Real Property Investments*

R. S. Barak, *Foreign Investments in U.S. Real Estate* (1981). New York: Harcourt Brace Jovanovich.
G. Osborne, G. Nelson and D. Whitman, *Real Estate Financing Law* (1979). St. Paul, Minn.: West Publishing Co.
Knight, *Structuring Foreign Investments in U.S. Real Estate* (1983). Deventer, The Netherlands: Kluwer.

*Chapter 8    Taxation*

B. Bittker and J. Eustice, *Federal Income Taxation of Corporations and Shareholders* (4th ed., 1979). Boston, Mass.: Warren, Gorham & Lamont, Inc.
B. Bittker and J. Eustice, *United States Taxation of Foreign Income and Foreign Persons* (2nd ed., 1968). Branford, Conn.: Federal Tax Press, Inc.
Mertens, *The Law of Federal Income Taxation* (1977) (21 volumes). Chicago, Ill.: Callaghan & Co.

*Chapter 9   Contracts*

S. Williston and W.H.E. Jaeger, *Williston on Contracts* (3rd ed., 1957). New York, N.Y.: Baker Voorhis & Co., Inc.

*Chapter 10   Sales*

J. White and R. Summers, *Uniform Commercial Code* (2nd ed., 1980). St. Paul, Minn.: West Publishing Co.
J. Honnold, *Uniform Law for International Sales* (1982). Deventer, The Netherlands: Kluwer.
Van Boeschoten and Den Drijver, 'Report on the Convention Governing the International Sale of Goods', *New York Law Journal*, August 31, 1981.

*Chapter 11   Corporations*

C. Rohrlich, *Organizing Corporate and Other Business Enterprises* (2nd ed., 1970). St. Paul, Minn.: West Publishing Co.
Wm. Fletcher, *Fletcher's Encyclopedia of the Law of Corporations* (1982) (rev. ed., 1983) (20 volumes). Wilmette, Ill.: Callaghan & Co.
F. Hodge O'Neal, *Opposition of Minority Shareholders*. Wilmette, Ill.: Callaghan & Co.

*Chapter 12   Partnership and Joint Ventures*

H. Reuschlein and W. Gregory, *Handbook on the Law of Agency and Partnership* (1979). St. Paul, Minn.: West Publishing Co.
H. Henn, *Handbook of the Law of Corporations and Other Business Enterprises* (2nd ed., 1970). St. Paul, Minn.: West Publishing Co.
W. Friedman and G. Kalmanoff, *Joint International Business Ventures* (1961). New York, N.Y.: Columbia University Press.

*Chapter 13   Agency and Employment Relations*

H. Reuschlein and W. Gregory, *Handbook on the Law of Agency and Partnership* (1979). St. Paul, Minn.: West Publishing Co.
H. Henn, *Handbook of the Law of Corporations and Other Business Enterprises* (2nd ed., 1970). St. Paul, Minn.: West Publishing Co.

*Chapter 14   Banking and Finance*

*Federal Banking Laws* (rev. ed., 1979). Boston, Mass.: Warren, Gorham and Lamont.
J. Cochran, *Money, Banking and the Economy* (4th ed., 1979). New York, N.Y.: Macmillan Publishing Co., Inc.
D. Fisher, *Money, Banking and Monetary Policy* (1980). Homewood, Ill.: Richard B. Irwin, Inc.

*Chapter 15   Secured Transactions*

J. White and R. Summers, *Uniform Commercial Code* (2nd ed., 1980). St. Paul, Minn.: West Publishing Co.

R. Henson, *Handbook on Secured Transactions Under the Uniform Commercial Code* (2nd ed., 1979). St. Paul, Minn.: West Publishing Co.

*Chapter 16   Insurance*

R. Keeton, *Basic Text on Insurance Law* (1971). St. Paul, Minn.: West Publishing Co.

*Chapter 17   Antitrust Laws*

Julian O. von Kalinowski, *Antitrust Laws and Trade Regulation* (1983). New York, N.Y.: Matthew Bender.

*Chapter 18   Federal Regulations Affecting Business*

L. Loss, *Securities Regulation* (2nd ed., 1961) (3 volumes plus 1969 2-volume supplement). Boston, Mass.: Little Brown and Co.

*Chapter 19   Patents*

Ridsdale Ellis, *Patent Assignments* (3rd ed., 1955). New York, N.Y.: Baker, Voorhis & Co., Inc.

*Chapter 20   Trademarks, Copyright and Unfair Competition*

R. Callmann, *Callmann, Unfair Competition, Trademarks & Monopolies* (4th ed., 1981). Chicago, Ill.: Callaghan & Co.
Melville B. Nimmer, *Nimmer on Copyright, A Treatise on the Law of Literary, Musical and Artistic Property, and the Protection of Ideas* (1983). New York, N.Y.: Matthew Bender.

*Chapter 21   License Agreements*

R. Callmann, *Callmann, Unfair Competition, Trademarks & Monopolies* (4th ed., 1981). Chicago, Ill.: Callaghan & Co.
R. Ellis, A. Deller, *Patent Licenses* (3rd ed., 1958). New York, N.Y.: Baker Voorhis & Co., Inc.
G.M. Pollzien, G. Bronfen, *International Licensing Agreements* (1965). Indianapolis, In.: Bobbs-Merrill Co., Inc.

*Chapter 22   International Trade*

E. Rossides, *U.S. Customs, Tariffs and Trade* (1977). Washington, D.C.: Bureau of National Affairs, Inc.
*International Business Transactions*, edited by Walter Sterling & Don Wallace (2nd ed., 1977). Philadelphia, Pa.: American Law Institute.

*Chapter 23   Arbitration*

M. Domke, *Law and Practice of Commercial Arbitration* (1968). Chicago, Ill.: Callaghan & Co.

F. and E. Elkouri, *How Arbitration Works* (1973). Washington, D.C.: BNA Incorporated.

*Chapter 24    Litigation*

Charles Alan Wright, *The Law of the Federal Courts* (4th ed., 1983). St. Paul, Minn.: West Publishing Co.

J. Moore, A. Vestal and P. Kurland, *Moore's Manual; Federal Practice and Procedure* (1982). New York, N.Y.: Matthew Bender.

Weinstein-Korn-Miller, *New York Civil Practice* (1983) (10 volumes, loose leaf). New York, N.Y.: Matthew Bender.

*Chapter 25    Insolvency*

L. King, *Collier on Bankruptcy* (15th ed., 1983). New York, N.Y.: Matthew Bender.

Weintraub and Resnick, *Bankruptcy Law Manual* and *1983 Cumulative Supplement*. Boston, Mass.: Warren, Gorham & Lamont.

# INDEX

Page references in **bold type** indicate *sedes materiae*